COOK ONCE
eat ALL WEEK

26 weeks of gluten-free, affordable meal prep to preserve your time & sanity

Cassy Joy Garcia, NC

VICTORY BELT PUBLISHING INC.

Las Vegas

Food photography by Cassy Joy Garcia

Cover photo and additional photography by Jessica Rockowitz

Cover and Interior design by Yordan Terziev and Boryana Yordanova

Printed in Canada

TC 0621

Contents

PART 1: WEEKLY MEALS

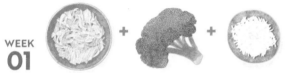

PART 2: SUPPLEMENTAL RECIPES

INTRODUCTION

It all started with shredded chicken.

Once upon a time, back in 2014, I was preparing for a spot on a local TV show. The producer wanted to feature "easy meal prep for busy parents." I love a good riddle, so I strapped my thinking cap on tight and started brainstorming. Despite my several years in the professional food blogging world, I really hadn't seen a meal prep method that MADE COMPLETE SENSE to me. Most suggested that you choose five to ten recipes for the week, rack and stack the ingredient lists (turned grocery list), unload your impressive haul from the grocery store, and then spend a FULL DAY cooking all of the food. At the end of your long, arduous day in the kitchen, usually a Sunday, you're left with a refrigerator full to the brim of prepared dishes.

Then you spend all week eating and (usually) microwaving leftovers.

This method works for some people, but does it work for all? Heck no. It's too complicated, too expensive, and takes too long, and I know fewer than five people who would happily eat leftovers every day.

I went back to the drawing board, determined to think up a simplified meal prep solution…and that's when I thought of shredded chicken. Shredded chicken is one of those basic components that can be used in *many* different dishes. You can use shredded chicken on nachos (mmm…nachos), in a casserole, in soup, in a stuffed potato, in enchiladas, and so on.

I posed the question: what if we prepared components in advance and then *assembled* dishes the day of?

I took a crack at it. I cooked and shredded chicken, riced cauliflower, and baked some sweet potatoes. Then I assembled those components into a chicken taco casserole, twice-baked Buffalo chicken sweet potatoes, and chicken teriyaki bowls. The meals were varied, delicious, easy, and inexpensive, and by golly they were fresh.

With the preliminary meal prep done, making each meal the day of took just about as much time as tossing a frozen skillet dinner on the stove, putting a prepared lasagna in the oven, or even ordering in Chinese takeout…but the meals were healthier and tastier.

Three years went by after this first stab at a Cook Once, Eat All Week prototype. I recommended the mini-series (which lived on my blog) to *countless* people who asked for meal prep advice before I realized that I could (and should) create more.

So I did! In January 2018, I launched the Cook Once, Eat All Week series on the *Fed + Fit* blog, with five weeks' worth of recipes (more on what this entails later). Our team was *floored* by the positive response. You thought what I thought: finally, a meal prep method that MAKES COMPLETE SENSE! You loved the simplicity, the variety, the affordability, the time saved, and the wholesome dishes. And then you asked for more.

So here you have it, dear reader! Our team has been *hard* at work to bring you 26 weeks (that's six months!) worth of Cook Once, Eat All Week recipes. With our best and most practical meal-prep-strategy foot forward, this book offers a quality solution to your meal prep needs.

My hope is that this book helps you breathe a little easier when you plan for the week ahead. I hope it offers up recipes that your family will love and grocery lists that fit your budget. I hope that this book gives you just a bit more freedom so that you can chase your kids, goals, and passions, all the while knowing that a fresh, nutritious dinner will be ready whenever you are.

We're in this together!

In friendship,
Cassy Joy Garcia and the Fed + Fit Team

Our Nutritional Approach

If you own a copy of my previous book, *Fed + Fit*, you may notice that the recipes in this book call for a wider range of ingredients than you've seen before! While my first book was written to support a stricter Paleo-type plan, this book calls for ingredients such as peanut butter, honey, maple syrup, quinoa, grits, and cheese. While the goal of *Fed + Fit* is to support your journey to health with the most benign ingredients possible, this book is filled with ingredients that I still consider to be *real* foods—just through a less restrictive lens. If you've worked through *Fed + Fit*, you've likely arrived at your own "Perfect You Plan." It's probable that you found foods such as dairy, corn, and peanuts aren't as disruptive to your health as maybe you once thought. The recipes in this book are healthy, real food–based dishes that can support your expanded list of healthy-for-you foods.

All this being said, if you prefer to follow a low-carbohydrate, Paleo, grain-free, dairy-free, or egg-free plan, I have marked the weeks that are suitable for these eating styles with icons and have included any needed recipe modifications.

Here's a brief overview of this book's nutritional principles so that you know what kind of thinking went into the development of the recipes:

Choose **REAL, NUTRIENT-DENSE FOODS** over processed, refined foods.

Replace highly processed oils with **NOURISHING FATS**; for example, swap out canola oil for olive oil.

Whenever possible, buy **ORGANIC** fruits and vegetables and **GRASS-FED, PASTURE-RAISED** proteins.

Eat **BALANCED MEALS** that incorporate protein, vegetables, and healthy starches.

Eat what works **BEST FOR YOUR BODY**: If eating grains works for you, great! If lower-carb eating works better for you, also great!

How It Works

PROTEIN

+

VEGGIE

+

STARCH

=

x3

In a nutshell: The recipes in this book are organized into what I call "weeks" of dinners. Each week consists of three main recipes plus two bonus dinners. If you're cooking for a family of four and need five dinners in a week (I'm looking at you, school nights), know that the three main recipes and two bonus dinners included will help you get a hot dinner on the dang table in a flash all five nights. What to do on the other two nights? I know that most families enjoy a night or two out each week, so I've accounted for that by covering the majority of your dining-in needs.

Every dinner in this book revolves around three components: a protein, a veggie, and a starch (sometimes this starch is a second veggie). Using strategic directions that minimize work time, you will cook or prep each of these components on your kitchen prep day. Then, when you're ready to make dinner, you use those already prepared components to assemble and heat your meal with minimal or zero cooking required. You can think of yourself on prep day as your own personal sous chef, and on the day you make one of the recipes as the chef, speedily executing a fantastic meal with components that have been prepped for you! The concept is similar to the meal kit services, like Blue Apron, that have become wildly popular, except our version is much less expensive and easily modifiable to suit your dietary needs. (Note that the prep work required to make the bonus dinner options is not included in the weekly list of prep day tasks; however, the bonus recipes are simple and easy to incorporate into your weekly meal prep without much additional time and effort.)

How many people does each weekly meal plan feed?

Though you will find a handful of recipes in the weekly plans that yield five or six servings, most of the recipes are designed to serve four. But you can easily utilize the weekly plans to fit your needs, whether you're a family of two or four, or whether you care for leftovers or not.

For example, if you're a family of two, the three main recipes in a week will provide you with leftovers that can be enjoyed every other night, making a total of six meals for the week. If you prefer to serve your family of two a fresh dinner six days a week and reserve the leftovers for lunches, choose two "weeks" to make.

If you're a family of four, I have several flexible scenarios to offer you. If you would like to use this book to feed your family of four five fresh dinners each week, then all you need to do is to make the two bonus recipes suggested for that week. (Look for the "Need More Dinners?" sidebar.)

If your goal is to feed your family of four six dinners each week, you have two options: you can either double the recipes in a given week to double the yield and eat the leftovers for dinner the next day or, if you prefer a fresh dinner each day, choose two "weeks" to make!

If you opt to prepare two weeks of recipes in the same week, I recommend preparing one week at a time. For example, you can do the prep day work for the first "week" of recipes on Sunday (to enjoy easy preparation of the recipes Monday through Wednesday) and then do the prep day work for the second "week" of recipes on Wednesday (to enjoy easy recipe preparation Thursday through Saturday).

Here's a chart to help you navigate exactly how much to make depending on your family size and weekly meal needs:

FAMILY SIZE	MEALS NEEDED	MAKE
	3 fresh dinners + 3 lunches or 3 frozen meals	1 week's worth of recipes (excluding the 2 bonus dinners). Enjoy half of the recipe for dinner and half as leftovers for lunch the next day OR store for later as a freezer meal.
	6 dinners	1 week's worth of recipes (excluding the 2 bonus dinners). Enjoy half of the recipe for dinner one night and the other half as leftovers for dinner the next day. You will assemble and cook fresh dinners and serve leftovers on alternating days.
	6 fresh dinners + 6 lunches or 6 frozen meals	2 weeks' worth of recipes (excluding the 2 bonus dinners). Enjoy half of the recipe for dinner and half as leftovers for lunch the next day OR store for later as a freezer meal. On day 3 of your week, prep the additional 3 recipes from your second chosen group of meals.
	3 fresh dinners + 3 leftover servings for 1 additional dinner (for the whole family), lunches, or the freezer	1 week's worth of recipes (excluding the 2 bonus dinners). Enjoy 3 servings' worth of each recipe for dinner, reserving the last serving as leftovers for a lunch, an off-dinner, or store later as a freezer meal.
	6 fresh dinners + 6 leftover servings for 2 additional dinners (for the whole family), lunches, or the freezer	2 weeks' worth of recipes (excluding the 2 bonus dinners). Enjoy 3 servings' worth of each recipe for dinner, reserving the last serving as leftovers for a lunch or an off-dinner, or store later as a freezer meal. On day 3 of your week, prep the additional 3 recipes from your second chosen group of meals.
	3 fresh dinners	1 week's worth of recipes (excluding the 2 bonus dinners).
	5 fresh dinners	1 week's worth of recipes including the 2 bonus dinners.
	6 fresh dinners	2 weeks' worth of recipes (excluding the 2 bonus dinners). On day 3 of your week, prep the additional 3 recipes from your second chosen group of meals.
	3 fresh dinners + 9 leftover servings for additional dinners, lunches, or the freezer	1 week's worth of recipes (excluding the 2 bonus dinners)— DOUBLE THE RECIPES.
	5 fresh dinners + 15 leftover servings for 3 additional dinners (for the whole family), lunches, or the freezer	1 week's worth of recipes including the 2 bonus dinners— DOUBLE THE RECIPES.
	3 fresh dinners + 6 leftover servings for 1 additional dinner (for the whole family), lunches, or the freezer	1 week's worth of recipes (excluding the 2 bonus dinners)— DOUBLE THE RECIPES.
	5 fresh dinners + 10 leftover servings for additional dinners, lunches, or the freezer	1 week's worth of recipes including the 2 bonus dinners— DOUBLE THE RECIPES.

How does this approach save money?

Cook Once, Eat All Week saves you money because it allows you to purchase ingredients in bulk while drastically reducing food waste. For example, you will not see a recipe that calls for half of a bell pepper—or, if it does, the other half of that pepper will be used in another recipe that same week. Additionally, the weeks are written with seasonality in mind! For example, you will not find a week that calls for both acorn squash and fresh tomatoes. Instead, you will find recipes with ingredient lists that can be easily sourced at the same time of the year.

BULK + **NO WASTE** + **IN SEASON** = **SAVE $$$**

How does this approach save time?

This concept comes from the heart and mind of a true-blue maximizer (it's my number-one strength). Though I do love to cook, both for the health benefits and for the pure joy of creating in the kitchen, I don't like to spend unnecessary time slaving over the stove. As such, each week is designed with minimal active kitchen time in mind! Preparing your basic components—protein, veggie, starch—in advance means that you will spend much less time making your finished dishes.

How do I have variety if I'm using the same ingredients?

You'll find that with a little creativity, the same ingredients, when assembled differently, result in a *lot* of variety. In any given week, you will find only one soup, one casserole, and one sheet pan dinner. You will see Thai, Mexican, and Creole dishes. I want to make sure you do not experience food boredom!

 + + =

 Italian Wedding Soup + Texas Beef Chili + Asian Beef Lettuce Cups

What about low-carb and other dietary requirements?

I've got your back. This book has icons for people who follow low-carb, Paleo, grain-free, dairy-free, egg-free, and nut-free diets. Additionally, if a recipe isn't written explicitly for your dietary requirements, I have included notes on how to modify it when modifications are possible. If a recipe in a weekly meal plan doesn't fit your dietary needs and can't be modified, simply skip that week and choose another that works for you. I've included a table at the back of the book (see pages 386 to 389) so that you can see, at a glance, which weeks are low-carb, Paleo, grain-free, dairy-free, egg-free, and/or nut-free (or can easily be modified). For those of you with children who tend to be suspicious of new foods, I've also noted which weeks are particularly kid-friendly.

LOW-CARB   **PALEO**   **GRAIN-FREE**   **DAIRY-FREE**   **EGG-FREE**   **NUT-FREE**   **KID-FRIENDLY**

What are the two weekly bonus dinners all about?

I have included two simple supplemental recipes for each week so that a family of four can enjoy a fresh dinner five nights a week with minimal additional effort. You'll find these five-ingredient-or-less "mini recipes" easy to prepare and incorporate into your weekly meal planning; I've included notes about how to account for the extra ingredients you'll need in the weekly shopping list. For variety, these two recipes are not made with the same key protein used in the week's three main recipes. I decided that the typical family would probably enjoy a change in the meal components for dinners four and five. (I realize that although you may enjoy shredded chicken, for example, transformed into three meals, I might be pushing my luck to stretch it to five.) The bonus dinner recipes are completely optional, however; if you have no need for them, pass them by.

Using This Book

Let's break up this book into steps! By following these steps, you can customize your own Cook Once, Eat All Week approach.

STEP 1:
Choose a Week

When picking a week of recipes, consider the following:

- Will your family love these dishes? If you have young children who tend to be picky eaters, keep an eye out for the kid-friendly icons.

- Do these dishes meet your nutrition requirements, either as written or with modifications?

Once you've chosen your week, determine the number of servings you will need based on the size of your family and your weekly meal needs. For additional guidance, see the meal guide chart on page 11.

STEP 2:
Go Shopping

Use the Weekly Ingredients list, which is downloadable over at fedandfit.com, to gather what you'll need! The Weekly Ingredients list, found at the start of each week, tallies the exact amounts of all of the ingredients you'll need for the week. By checking to see what you have on hand first—you may already have enough!—and purchasing just what you need, you'll avoid waste. (I haven't included salt and pepper in the weekly shopping lists because they are basic to every kitchen; I assume you have plenty of each.)

Look to the right of the Weekly Ingredients list to discover if ingredient substitutions are possible for grain, dairy, egg, or nut allergens or to make a recipe low-carb or Paleo. Look for the "Ingredient Subs" heading.

Note that while I have included recipes for homemade sauces, condiments, and spice blends in this book, you can absolutely substitute store-bought equivalents. In fact, because this book is all about how to save your time (and sanity), the store-bought options are given precedence in the weekly shopping lists! Note that if you're following a stricter Paleo (or other nutritionally restrictive) plan, I have included excellent homemade equivalents. For a list of my favorite store-bought sauces, condiments, and the like, see page 381.

If you wish to make any of the bonus dinner recipes on pages 345 to 369, take a moment to jot down the ingredients you'll need to make them; you'll find them listed under "Bonus Dinner Shopping Lists."

STEP 3:
Prep the Components

Follow the prep day instructions for the week you've chosen! These tasks might include searing meats, roasting vegetables, and washing and chopping produce.

When possible, I provide different cooking methods to suit your needs. For the protein components, you can use the oven or stovetop, an Instant Pot (or other brand of electric pressure cooker or multicooker), or a slow cooker.

For baked dishes, you can use casserole dishes, pie pans, ovenproof skillets, or even rimmed baking sheets. For blended components, you can use either a blender or an immersion blender for easier cleanup.

> **tip:** *To streamline organization even further, I occasionally suggest that you label the prepped components with the name of the recipe for which they're destined. On page 19, you'll find storage tips for prepped components.*

STEP 4:
Make the Recipes

When you're ready to make a meal, pull out one of the recipes for the week from the Recipes section. Following the recipe instructions, make the dish with the already prepped and cooked components, which are marked with check marks. *Note:* You could easily make all three weekly recipes in one day if you prefer. But because the recipes come together so quickly with the major components already prepared, I find it just as easy, and a whole lot less work-intensive, to assemble the recipes throughout the week as I need them. The same principle applies to the bonus dinners, should you choose to add them. I find that these meals are easy to assemble and heat through on the day I serve them.

STEP 5:
Store the Leftovers

For guidance on storing and reheating leftovers so that you can enjoy the same dish later in the week, see the section "Meal Storage and Reheating" on pages 17 to 20.

STEP 6:
Rinse & Repeat

As you need more meals, repeat the process!

Meal Storage and Reheating

Of all the questions I get on the *Fed + Fit* blog, this one is the most-asked of the most-asked: *How do I store/reheat this?* Though the recipes in this book are designed so that you can enjoy the meals fresh, I want to address how to handle leftovers that need to be stored in the refrigerator or freezer. So, once and for all, let's get you some good answers. In order to properly address storing and reheating meals, I need to acknowledge that there are different strategies for different types of meals: uncooked, stovetop, and oven-baked (food cooked in a slow cooker or pressure cooker falls into this latter category, too).

But before I dive into the specifics of storing and reheating each type of meal or component, let's begin with some universal storage safety tips that apply to all foods.

I hope you find this section empowering!

Food Storage Best Practices

Here are a handful of food storage best practices to keep in mind as you prep and cook your way through this book! I've broken them up into four easy tips:

- Let cooked foods cool to the point that you can handle them barehanded before transferring them to the refrigerator or freezer for storage. This will help keep your refrigerator and freezer at a constant temperature. *Note:* Don't let dishes sit out on the counter too long! You ideally want to serve or store them within one hour of being finished.

- Mark your stored meals and prepped components with the dates on which you made them! This will help you tremendously as you prioritize leftovers or what to cook throughout the week/month (if frozen).

- Use airtight containers for storing foods. If you're storing something in a plastic freezer bag, be sure to remove as much air as possible before sealing the bag.

- Enjoy your frozen foods within the time ranges recommended on the next page for ideal texture and flavor.

Storing Various Types of Meals

The following are my best storage tips organized by basic type of meal.

	FOR THE REFRIGERATOR	FOR THE FREEZER
Salads, Slaws, and Quick Pickles	Place in a glass bowl and cover with a lid. Slaws and quick pickles will keep for an average of 5 days, while dressed salads will keep for just one day. To extend the life of a salad, leave it undressed until just before serving so that you have the option to enjoy it a few days later.	Not freezer-friendly.
Casseroles	Store in the refrigerator covered with a tight-fitting lid or aluminum foil for up to 5 days. You can also store casseroles in individual serving–sized containers with lids for preportioned meals. To reheat individual servings, either microwave on high for 1 minute 30 seconds or place in a preheated 350°F oven for 5 to 10 minutes, until warmed through. To reheat multiple servings in a larger casserole dish, place in a preheated 350°F oven for 5 to 10 minutes, until warmed through. *Note: When reheating casseroles, avoid putting a chilled glass or ceramic casserole dish in a preheated oven; the heat could cause a cold dish to shatter.*	Casseroles can either be frozen whole or divided into individual portions and frozen in smaller containers. They will keep for up to 5 months in the freezer. To reheat from frozen, place on a rimmed baking sheet in a preheated 350°F oven until warmed through (10 to 15 minutes) or microwave on high for 2 to 4 minutes.
Sheet Pan Dinners and Pizza	Sheet pan dinners and pizza can be stored in the refrigerator directly on the original sheet pan or baking sheet, covered with aluminum foil, for up to 5 days. You can also store them in single-serving containers with lids for preportioned meals. To reheat individual servings, either microwave on high for 1 minute 30 seconds or place in a preheated 350°F oven for 5 to 10 minutes, until warmed through. To reheat multiple servings on a sheet pan or baking sheet, place in a preheated 350°F oven for 5 to 10 minutes, until warmed through.	Sheet pan dinners and pizza can be placed in plastic freezer bags or in single-serving containers and stored in the freezer for up to 5 months. To reheat from frozen, place on a rimmed baking sheet in a preheated 350°F oven until warmed through (10 to 15 minutes) or microwave on high for 2 to 4 minutes.
Soups, Stews, Chili, Stir-Fries, Bowls, and Tacos	Soups, stews, chili, stir-fries, bowls, and tacos can be stored in sealed containers in the refrigerator for up to 5 days. For anything with components, such as a slaw, garnish, or tortillas, I recommend storing each component separately. To reheat, you can microwave individual servings in microwave-safe bowls or plates for 1 to 2 minutes, until warmed through. You can also reheat components in a skillet or saucepan on the stovetop over medium heat for about 5 minutes, until simmering. Once the soup, taco meat, or bowl is heated through, plate with the rest of the components.	Soups, stews, chili, stir-fries, bowls, and tacos (protein fillings only) can be stored in single-serving containers in the freezer for up to 5 months. To reheat from frozen, place in a saucepan, cover, and heat on medium-low for 10 to 15 minutes, until simmering. Alternatively, you can microwave on high for 2 to 4 minutes.
Stuffed Peppers, Potatoes, and Meatloaf	Stuffed peppers, potatoes, and meatloaf can be stored in the refrigerator in sealed containers for up to 5 days. To reheat, either microwave for 1 to 2 minutes, or until heated through, or place in a preheated 350°F oven for 5 to 10 minutes, until warmed through.	Stuffed peppers, potatoes, and meatloaf can be stored either in freezer bags or in single-serving containers in the freezer for up to 5 months. To reheat from frozen, place on a rimmed baking sheet in a preheated 350°F oven until warmed through (10 to 15 minutes) or microwave on high for 2 to 4 minutes.

Prepped Meal Components

One of my primary goals with this Cook Once, Eat All Week approach is to eliminate as much of the prep day headache as possible. As such, it's important to apply some strategy when storing prepared meal components. The following chart walks you through the different kinds of meal components, noting how long they'll keep in the refrigerator and how long they'll keep in the freezer. Though prepared components are intended to be assembled into dinners later that same week, I understand that life sometimes gets in the way! If you ever need to freeze the components, preserving your work for another day, I've got some guidance for you.

	REFRIGERATOR (40°F or below)	FREEZER (0°F or below)
Cooked meats (beef, chicken, pork, etc.)	3 to 4 days	2 to 3 months
Cooked rice (white rice, cauliflower rice)	3 to 4 days	2 to 3 months
Cooked vegetables (boiled, mashed, roasted, etc.)	3 to 4 days	2 to 3 months
Toasted nuts (pine nuts, etc.)	2 weeks	9 months
Assembled meals with raw meats (burgers, meatloaf, etc.)	1 to 2 days	3 to 4 months
Assembled meals with cooked meats (casseroles, taco fillings, stuffed peppers, etc.)	3 to 4 days	2 to 3 months
Raw meats in marinade (marinating beef, chicken, pork, etc.)	1 to 2 days	9 months
Raw produce (onions, garlic, ginger, broccoli, carrots, etc.)	3 to 5 days	Does not freeze well.
Fresh herbs (chives, cilantro, parsley, etc.)	1 week	Do not freeze well.
Homemade dressings and condiments (salad dressings, mayonnaise, etc.)	1 to 2 weeks	Do not freeze well.
Homemade sauces (BBQ, pesto, teriyaki, etc.)	1 to 2 weeks	9 months*

*freezer tip: *If you can't enjoy the entire batch of a homemade sauce within one to two weeks, spoon the remainder into an ice cube tray and freeze until solid. Then transfer the sauce "ice cubes" to a sealed container and keep in the freezer. Reheat as many cubes as you need in a saucepan over medium heat or in the microwave.*

Storage Containers

While I'm a big fan of using what works for you, the following are the containers I've found to work best for storing meal components and prepared dishes, whether destined for the refrigerator or the freezer. Don't forget to have masking tape and a permanent marker to label and date your containers!

Prepped components in the refrigerator: After your prep day, you will have a good number of components needing storage! I store my components in covered glass containers in the refrigerator.

Prepped or finished dishes in the refrigerator: Maybe you prepared a casserole in advance (minus the final baking step) and you want to store it in the fridge. Just cover the top of your almost-finished dish and refrigerate it until you're ready to heat and serve it.

If you have leftovers that you want to store in the refrigerator, I recommend portioning them into either single-serving glass containers (with fitted lids) for lunches or into larger glass containers for family-friendly servings.

Prepped components in the freezer: Every once in a while, I have an excess of washed and chopped fresh produce or cooked protein (like shredded chicken). I let the component cool completely (if cooked) and then transfer it to a freezer-safe plastic bag. If you're concerned about your food touching plastic, you can line the freezer bag with wax paper first. Be sure to label and date the item.

Finished dishes in the freezer: Dishes can be frozen either whole or portioned into individual servings (my personal preference). If freezing a meal whole, make sure you have an airtight seal on the top (think: a well-sealed casserole dish). A whole casserole can be frozen either in the glass/ceramic dish in which you baked it or in a disposable aluminum container. If using a disposable container, be sure to tightly cover the top of the food with aluminum foil before placing the fitted lid on top. This will help preserve freshness.

For individual servings, I like to use 24-ounce BPA-free plastic containers. Spoon a serving into each container, label the container with the name of the dish and the date, and place in the freezer.

Stocking Your Kitchen

While you can absolutely shop for each week of meals as you go, the following lists contain what I consider essential ingredients. These are items that are worth having on hand at all times.

PANTRY ITEMS

Avocado oil

Avocado oil mayonnaise

Chicken and beef broth

Coconut aminos or tamari
(Use tamari only if you tolerate soy; note that tamari is MUCH saltier than coconut aminos. See the sidebar on page 29.)

Diced tomatoes

Extra-virgin olive oil

Fish sauce

Ghee

Tomato paste

Tomato sauce

Vinegars (apple cider, balsamic, red wine, unseasoned rice wine, white wine)

SEASONINGS

Chili powder

Curry powder

Dried oregano leaves

Garlic powder

Ginger powder

Ground black pepper

Ground cumin

Onion powder

Sea salt, coarse and finely ground

BAKING INGREDIENTS

Arrowroot powder

Baking powder

Baking soda

Chocolate chips, semi-sweet

Gluten-free flour blend

Pure vanilla extract

SWEETENERS

Coconut sugar

Honey

Pure maple syrup

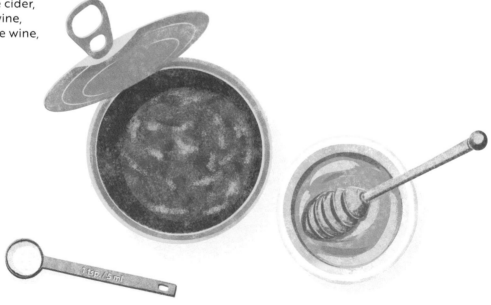

Customizing Meals (Ingredient Swaps)

I understand that every person and every family has its own unique mix of dietary requirements! Some families need nightshade-free meals, some need egg-free recipes, and some, dairy-free recipes. Some folks prefer to eat grain-free and others low-carb. As such, I have a quick list of ways to modify the recipes in this book.

Note: Possible modifications are also listed on the individual recipe pages.

Dairy-Free Swaps

- If a recipe calls for heavy cream, you can substitute an equal amount of full-fat coconut milk (canned is best).
- If a recipe calls for cream cheese, you can substitute an equal amount of Kite Hill brand dairy-free cream cheese–style spread.
- If a recipe calls for dairy cheese, you can omit it altogether or substitute an equal amount of dairy-free cheese.
- If a recipe calls for Parmesan or another grated hard cheese, you can substitute nutritional yeast! It has a wonderful cheesy flavor.

Grain-Free Swaps

- If a recipe calls for white rice, you can substitute an equal amount of riced cauliflower.
- If a recipe calls for gluten-free pasta, you can substitute an equal amount of zucchini noodles.
- If a recipe calls for corn tortillas, you can substitute either lettuce (Bibb lettuce is ideal) or thinly sliced jicama as veggie-based tortillas. You can also purchase grain-free tortillas.
- If a recipe calls for fresh or frozen corn, you can omit it entirely without sacrificing the integrity of the dish.
- If a recipe calls for cornmeal (like polenta), you can substitute mashed potatoes (white or sweet, your choice).

Low-Carb Swaps

- If a recipe calls for white rice, you can substitute an equal amount of riced cauliflower.

- If a recipe calls for gluten-free pasta, you can substitute an equal amount of zucchini noodles.

- If a recipe calls for mashed potatoes, you can substitute an equal amount of mashed cauliflower.

Protein Swaps

- If a recipe calls for a ground protein that you do not have or do not want to use, you can exchange it for any other ground protein of your choice.

- If a recipe calls for a shredded protein that you do not have or do not want to use, you can exchange it for any other shredded protein of your choice.

Veggie Swaps

Substitute your preferred green for any leafy green veggie (for example, collard greens for kale or Swiss chard for spinach). Adjust cooking time if needed, as some greens require longer cooking than others.

part

1

WEEKLY MEALS

Weekly Meals and Bonus Dinners by Protein

If you're hungry for a particular type of protein, either for a whole week of meal prep or for a bonus dinner to supplement another weekly plan, use this list to find the weekly meal plans and bonus dinners that feature that protein.

 CHICKEN

Week 01: Shredded Chicken, Broccoli, and Rice (page 28)

Week 03: Roasted Chicken and Cauliflower (page 52)

Week 05: Baked Chicken Breast, Tomatoes, and Rice (page 76)

Week 06: Ground Chicken, Bell Peppers, and Rice (page 88)

Week 09: Baked Chicken Breast, Kale, and Corn (page 124)

Week 11: Roasted Chicken, Green Beans, and Yukon Gold Potatoes (page 148)

Week 13: Baked Chicken Breast, Bell Peppers, and Spaghetti Squash (page 172)

Week 17: Roasted Chicken, Brussels Sprouts, and Parsnips (page 222)

Week 20: Baked Chicken Breast, Collard Greens, and Sweet Potatoes (page 258)

Week 24: Roasted Chicken, Mushrooms, and Spaghetti Squash (page 306)

Seared Chicken Breasts (page 346)

Lemon Pepper Chicken Breasts (page 347)

Paprika-Lime Chicken Breasts (page 347)

Crispy Curried Chicken Thighs (page 348)

Balsamic Chicken Thighs (page 348)

Ranch Chicken Thighs (page 349)

 TURKEY

Week 07: Turkey Breast Tenderloins, Cherry Tomatoes, and Yukon Gold Potatoes (page 100)

Week 18: Baked Turkey Breast, Kale, and Butternut Squash (page 234)

BEEF

PORK

FISH AND SEAFOOD

SHREDDED CHICKEN, BROCCOLI, and RICE

This week brings together three healthy cooking mainstays—chicken breast, fresh broccoli, and rice—in three totally different recipes! You're going to mix and match so that you're never bored. First up is a BBQ Chicken and Rice Casserole that hides broccoli in a brand-new way. Then we dive into a tangy and creamy White Chicken Chili. Last up is a classic Chicken and Broccoli Fried Rice that's even better than takeout. If you'd like to supplement this week's three main dinner recipes with two additional meals, see the suggested "Bonus Dinner Options" on the next page.

Weekly Ingredients

FRESH PRODUCE

Avocado, 1

Broccoli, 3 medium heads (about 2 pounds), or 1½ pounds precut florets

Carrots, 2 medium

Cilantro, 12 sprigs

Garlic, 5 cloves

Ginger, 1 (1½-inch) piece

Green onions, 1 bunch

Limes, 1½

Onion, yellow, 1

FROZEN FOODS

Yellow corn, 8 ounces (1 cup)

MEAT

Bacon, 10 strips (about 12 ounces)

Chicken breasts, boneless, skinless, 5 pounds

DAIRY/EGGS

Butter, salted, 1 tablespoon

Eggs, 2 large

Sour cream, 4 ounces (½ cup)

PANTRY

Avocado oil or ghee, 2 tablespoons plus 2 teaspoons

BBQ sauce, store-bought or homemade (page 373), 12 fluid ounces (1½ cups)

Chicken broth, 40 fluid ounces (5 cups)

Coconut aminos, Coconut Secret brand, 2⅔ fluid ounces (⅓ cup) (see sidebar below)

Diced green chilis, hot or mild, 1 (4-ounce) can

Extra-virgin olive oil, 2 teaspoons

Toasted sesame oil, 2 teaspoons

White beans, 1 (15-ounce) can

White rice, 20 ounces (3 cups)

SEASONINGS

Garlic powder, 1 teaspoon

Ground cumin, ½ teaspoon

Dried oregano leaves, 1 teaspoon

Red pepper flakes, ½ teaspoon

Ingredient Subs

To make this week LOW-CARB:

· *Omit the corn and white beans.*

· *Use a low-carb BBQ sauce.*

· *Replace the white rice with 3 medium heads cauliflower (5 to 6 pounds total) or 3 (12-ounce) bags frozen riced cauliflower.*

To make this week PALEO:

· *Use the substitutions listed below for making the week grain-free and dairy-free and omit the beans.*

To make this week GRAIN-FREE:

· *Omit the corn.*

· *Replace the white rice with 3 medium heads cauliflower (5 to 6 pounds total) or 3 (12-ounce) bags frozen riced cauliflower.*

To make this week DAIRY-FREE:

· *Replace the butter with avocado oil.*

· *Replace the sour cream with 1 (13½-ounce) can full-fat coconut milk.*

About Coconut Aminos
When it comes to coconut aminos, I'm a big fan of the brand Coconut Secret. I've tried a few different coconut aminos on the market and keep coming back to this brand. Others tend to be saltier, which can really impact the final flavor of a dish or sauce, especially when a large quantity of coconut aminos is used and/or reduced (as when making the Teriyaki Sauce on page 373). For this reason, I specify the Coconut Secret brand of coconut aminos in the Weekly Ingredients lists to ensure the best results when making the recipes in this book.

Bonus Dinner Options

Dinner 1

Pan-Seared Steak

(page 352)

Wilted Spinach

(page 358)

Baked Sweet Potatoes

(page 365)

Bonus Dinner Ingredients

Butter, salted, 3 tablespoons

Lemon, ½

Sirloin or rib-eye steaks, boneless, 1 inch thick, 4 (4 to 6 ounces each)

Spinach, fresh, 1 pound

Sweet potatoes, 4 small to medium (about 1 pound)

Texas Grill Rub, 2 tablespoons (see page 374 for ingredients)

Dinner 2

Pan-Seared Salmon

(page 355)

Steamed Green Beans

(page 361)

Roasted Carrots

(page 364)

Bonus Dinner Ingredients

Butter, salted, 1 tablespoon

Carrots, slender, 2 bunches (about 1 pound)

Extra-virgin olive oil, 4 teaspoons

Green beans, fresh, 1 pound

Lemon, ½

Salmon fillet, 1 (1½ pounds)

Prep Day

Today you will be cooking and shredding chicken, cooking rice and bacon, and prepping broccoli florets, onions, cilantro, garlic, and carrots. I find it most efficient to get the chicken going first since it takes the longest to cook, and then get the rice and bacon going. While those two are cooking, I do the raw vegetable prep.

note: *If you're planning to make homemade BBQ sauce rather than use store-bought, I recommend that you add it to your prep day tasks so that it's ready for use later in the week.*

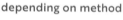

Cook and shred the chicken

Yield: about 10 cups

Prep Time: 10 minutes

Cook Time: 20 minutes or 8 hours, depending on method

1. Season 5 pounds of boneless, skinless chicken breasts with 1 teaspoon of coarse sea salt and ½ teaspoon of ground black pepper.

2. Cook the chicken using one of these three methods:

   • **Stovetop Method** (Cook Time: 20 minutes)
   Put the chicken in a large saucepan with a lid over medium-high heat and cover with 5 cups of water. Place the lid on the pan and simmer for 15 to 20 minutes, until the chicken easily falls apart when poked with a fork, then remove the chicken from the pan.

   • **Instant Pot Method** (Cook Time: 20 minutes)
   Place the chicken in a 6-quart Instant Pot along with 1 cup of water. Seal the lid onto the Instant Pot, set the cooker to Poultry mode, and set the timer for 20 minutes. When the timer goes off, quickly release the pressure manually by turning the pressure valve to "venting." Once the pressure has been fully released, open the pot and remove the chicken.

   • **Slow Cooker Method** (Cook Time: 6 to 8 hours)
   Place the chicken in a 6-quart slow cooker and cover with 5 cups of water. Cook on low for 6 to 8 hours, until the chicken easily falls apart when poked with a fork, then remove the chicken from the slow cooker.

3. Shred the cooked chicken with two forks. Put 4 cups of the shredded chicken in a container labeled "Casserole," 3 cups in a separate container labeled "Chili," and the remainder, about 3 cups, in a third container labeled "Fried Rice." Store in the refrigerator for use later in the week.

Cook the rice

Yield: 9 cups

Prep Time: 2 minutes

Cook Time: about 20 minutes

Cook 3 cups of white rice according to the package instructions, then let cool. Scoop 4½ cups of the cooked rice into a container, then scoop another 4½ cups of the rice into a separate container. Label one container "Casserole" and the other "Fried Rice." Store in the refrigerator for use later in the week.

LOW CARB **P** ❇ **LOW-CARB/PALEO/GRAIN-FREE RICE SUBSTITUTE**
Make a double batch of Basic Cauliflower Rice (page 363), then follow the storage instructions for the white rice above.

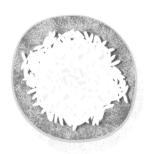

Cook and chop or crumble the bacon

Prep Time: 3 minutes

Cook Time: 18 minutes

1. Preheat the oven to 400°F.

2. Lay ten strips of bacon on a rimmed baking sheet and bake until crisp, 12 to 18 minutes. The total cooking time will depend on the thickness of your bacon.

3. Transfer the bacon to a paper towel–lined plate and let cool. When the bacon is cool enough to handle, coarsely chop or crumble six strips. (If you used thick-cut bacon, chopping it will be easier; if you used regular bacon, crumbling it will be easier.) Put the chopped or crumbled bacon in a container and label it "6 Strips Bacon." Repeat with the remaining four strips and put in a separate container labeled "4 Strips Bacon." Store in the refrigerator for use later in the week.

Prep the broccoli

Yield: 3 cups small florets and
4 cups broccoli "rice"

1. Cut a head of broccoli into small florets; discard the stem. (If you purchased precut florets, cut one-third of them into small florets.)

2. Cut the florets off of the remaining two heads of broccoli. Put the broccoli florets (or the remaining two-thirds of the packaged florets) in a food processor. (You may need to work in two or three batches, depending on the size of your food processor.) Pulse until the broccoli has a coarse, ricelike texture.

3. Store the broccoli "rice" and florets in separate containers in the refrigerator for use later in the week. Label the rice "Casserole" and the florets "Fried Rice."

Dice the onion

Dice a yellow onion, then store in the refrigerator for use later in the week.

Slice the green onions

Thinly slice one bunch of green onions, or until you have ¾ cup of sliced green onions. (You may not need the entire bunch.) Store in the refrigerator for use later in the week.

Shred the carrots

Shred two medium-sized carrots either with a box grater or with the shredder attachment of your food processor. Store in the refrigerator for use later in the week.

Mince the garlic

Mince five cloves of garlic, or until you have 1 tablespoon plus 2 teaspoons of minced garlic. Store in the refrigerator for use later in the week.

Grate the ginger

Grate a 1½-inch piece of ginger until you have 2 teaspoons, then store in the refrigerator for use later in the week.

BBQ Chicken and Rice Casserole

Yield: 6 servings   Prep Time: 5 minutes   Cook Time: 35 minutes

1 tablespoon salted butter or other cooking fat of choice

4 cups raw broccoli "rice" ✓

2 teaspoons coarse sea salt, divided

4½ cups cooked white rice or cauli-rice ✓

1 teaspoon garlic powder

½ teaspoon ground black pepper

4 cups shredded chicken ✓

1½ cups BBQ sauce

6 strips bacon, cooked and chopped or crumbled ✓

2 tablespoons thinly sliced green onions, for garnish ✓

1. Preheat the oven to 350°F.

2. Melt the butter in a large sauté pan over medium heat, then add the broccoli "rice." Season with 1 teaspoon of the salt and cook for 3 to 4 minutes, until softened. Remove from the heat.

3. Add the cooked white rice, garlic powder, pepper, and remaining teaspoon of salt to the pan with the broccoli. Toss to combine, then transfer to an 8-inch square casserole dish.

4. In a medium-sized bowl, toss the shredded chicken with the BBQ sauce, then spread the chicken on top of the broccoli-rice mixture. Top with the bacon.

5. Bake for 30 minutes, or until the top is just starting to brown.

6. Remove from the oven, garnish with the green onions, and serve!

White Chicken Chili

Yield: 4 servings   Prep Time: 5 minutes   Cook Time: 15 minutes

2 teaspoons extra-virgin olive oil

1 yellow onion, diced ✓

2 teaspoons minced garlic ✓

1 (4-ounce) can diced hot or mild green chilis, drained

3 cups shredded chicken ✓

1 teaspoon dried oregano leaves

1 teaspoon coarse sea salt

½ teaspoon ground cumin

½ teaspoon ground black pepper

5 cups chicken broth

1 (15-ounce) can white beans, rinsed and drained (omit for low-carb and Paleo)

1 cup frozen yellow corn (omit for low-carb, Paleo, and grain-free)

½ cup sour cream or coconut cream

Juice of 1 lime

4 strips bacon, cooked and chopped or crumbled ✓

1 avocado, sliced, for garnish

2 tablespoons fresh cilantro leaves, for garnish

4 lime wedges (from ½ lime), for garnish

1. Heat the olive oil in a large saucepan over medium heat. Once hot, add the onion and garlic and sauté for 3 to 4 minutes, until the onion is translucent.

2. Add the green chilis and cook for 1 minute, until fragrant, then add the shredded chicken and seasonings and stir to combine.

3. Pour in the broth and increase the heat to medium-high. Stir in the beans and corn. Cover and simmer for 10 minutes, then turn off the heat and stir in the sour cream, lime juice, and bacon.

4. Garnish each serving with avocado slices, cilantro, and a lime wedge and enjoy!

Chicken and Broccoli Fried Rice

Yield: 4 servings   Prep Time: 5 minutes   Cook Time: 15 minutes

2 tablespoons plus 2 teaspoons avocado oil or ghee, divided

2 large eggs, whisked (omit for egg-free)

2 teaspoons grated ginger ✓

1 tablespoon minced garlic ✓

3 cups small broccoli florets ✓

½ cup shredded carrots ✓

3 cups shredded chicken ✓

½ cup plus 2 tablespoons sliced green onions, divided ✓

4½ cups cooked white rice or cauli-rice ✓

⅓ cup coconut aminos

2 teaspoons toasted sesame oil

½ teaspoon coarse sea salt

½ teaspoon red pepper flakes

Leaves from 2 sprigs fresh cilantro, finely chopped, for garnish

1. Heat 2 teaspoons of the oil in a large sauté pan or wok over medium-high heat. Once hot, add the whisked eggs and scramble until cooked through. Remove from the pan and set aside.

2. Add 1 tablespoon of the oil to the pan, then add the ginger and garlic. Cook for 30 seconds, until fragrant.

3. Add the broccoli and carrots to the pan and cook for 3 to 4 minutes, until slightly browned and softened.

4. Add the chicken and ½ cup of the green onions and stir to combine with the carrots and broccoli. Sauté for 1 to 2 minutes, until the chicken starts to brown slightly.

5. Add the remaining tablespoon of oil, then add the rice, coconut aminos, sesame oil, salt, red pepper flakes, and scrambled eggs. Mix together, then cook, undisturbed, for 2 to 3 minutes. Stir once more, then cook for an additional 2 to 3 minutes.

6. Taste and adjust the seasoning, if needed, then remove from the heat. Garnish with the remaining 2 tablespoons of green onions and the cilantro and serve!

GROUND BEEF, ZUCCHINI, and MUSHROOMS

If you're like me, when you first read "ground beef, zucchini, and mushrooms," you may think, "That doesn't exactly sound delicious." Hang in there! I'm going to show you how to transform these basic components into three killer dinners. First up is a Spinach Artichoke Meatza that will knock your socks right off, and then we have Enchilada-Stuffed Zucchini Boats, and finally a killer Ground Beef Stroganoff served over zucchini noodles. This is another naturally low-carb–friendly week! It's great for those following a low-carb plan—or who just like delicious food. I hope you enjoy! If you'd like to supplement this week's three main dinner recipes with two additional meals, see the suggested "Bonus Dinner Options" on the next page.

Weekly Ingredients

FRESH PRODUCE

Cauliflower, 1 large head (about 3 pounds), or 18 ounces frozen riced cauliflower

Cilantro, ½ small bunch

Garlic, 6 cloves

Lemon, 1 small

Lime, 1

Onion, white, 1

Sliced baby bella (aka cremini) mushrooms, 16 ounces

Spinach, 8 ounces

Zucchini, 6 medium (about 2½ pounds) and 3 large (about 1½ pounds)

MEAT/DAIRY

Butter, salted, 1 tablespoon

Cream cheese, 1 (8-ounce) package

Ground beef, 5 pounds

Shredded Mexican cheese blend, 2 ounces (½ cup)

Sour cream, 6 ounces (¾ cup)

PANTRY

Artichoke hearts, quartered, 1 (14-ounce) can

Chicken broth, 16 fluid ounces (2 cups)

Coconut aminos, Coconut Secret brand, 1 tablespoon

Dijon mustard, 1 tablespoon

Extra-virgin olive oil, 2 fluid ounces (¼ cup)

Tomato paste, 1 tablespoon

Tomato sauce, 1 (8-ounce) can

SEASONINGS

Chili powder, 1 tablespoon

Dried oregano leaves, 1 teaspoon

Dried parsley, 1 teaspoon

Garlic powder, ½ teaspoon

Ground cumin, 1 teaspoon

Italian seasoning, 2 tablespoons

Red pepper flakes, ½ teaspoon (optional)

Ingredient Subs

To make this week PALEO and/or DAIRY-FREE:

· *Replace the butter with ghee or oil of choice.*

· *Use dairy-free cream cheese–style spread (such as Kite Hill brand) in place of the cream cheese.*

· *Use the cream from 2 (13½-ounce) cans of full-fat coconut milk in place of the sour cream.*

· *Omit the cheese.*

Bonus Dinner Options

Dinner 1

Easy Tuna Steak
(page 353)

Crispy Brussels Sprouts
(page 356)

Spinach Salad
(page 362)

Bonus Dinner Ingredients

Balsamic vinegar, 2 tablespoons

Brussels sprouts, 12 ounces

Extra-virgin olive oil, 2½ fluid ounces
(5 tablespoons)

Lemon, 1

Pecans, raw, 2 ounces (½ cup)

Spinach, fresh, 8 ounces (about 6 cups)

Strawberries, fresh, ½ pint

Tuna steaks, about 1 inch thick, 4
(6 to 8 ounces each)

Dinner 2

Jerk Pork Tenderloin
(page 351)

Braised Collards
(page 358)

Basic Cauliflower Rice
(page 363)

Bonus Dinner Ingredients

Cauliflower, 1 large head (about 3 pounds), or 18 ounces frozen
riced cauliflower

Collard greens, 1 small bunch (about 1 pound)

Extra-virgin olive oil, 2 fluid ounces (¼ cup)

Jerk Seasoning, 1 tablespoon (see page 375 for ingredients)

Lemon, ½

Pork tenderloin, 1 (1¼ pounds)

Prep Day

This is going to be a fun day in the kitchen! I like to start with the ground beef: A portion of the beef heads to the stove for browning while the rest is seasoned, formed into a crust, and then baked as the base for the meatza. While the beef cooks, I turn my attention to the zucchini: Some of the zucchini is spiral-sliced for use as noodles, and the rest is sliced in half and hollowed out for boats. From there, I cook the mushrooms, make the enchilada sauce and cauliflower rice, and finally prep the cilantro, onion, and garlic!

note: *To save myself a step, I purchase presliced mushrooms; if you are using whole mushrooms, add the step of cleaning and slicing the mushrooms to this week's prep day tasks.*

Brown some of the ground beef

Yield: 8 scant cups

Cook Time: 15 minutes

In a large sauté pan over medium heat, combine 3½ pounds of ground beef and 1 teaspoon of coarse sea salt. (You will add more seasoning later.) Cook, crumbling the meat as it cooks, for 10 to 15 minutes, until fully browned. Put 4½ cups in a container and label it "Stroganoff," then put the remaining 3¼ cups in another container and label it "Zucchini Boats." Store in the refrigerator for use later in the week.

Make the meatza crust

Prep Time: 10 minutes

Cook Time: 15 minutes

1½ pounds ground beef

1 tablespoon Italian seasoning

1 teaspoon coarse sea salt

½ teaspoon ground black pepper

1. Preheat the oven to 375°F.

2. In a medium-sized bowl, combine the ground beef, Italian seasoning, salt, and pepper using your hands.

3. Place the meat mixture on a sheet of parchment paper and spread it as thinly as possible into a circle using either your hands or a rolling pin, then transfer to a rimmed pizza pan and par-bake for 15 minutes.

4. Once cool, drain the fat, cover, and store in the pizza pan in the refrigerator for use later in the week.

note: *If you don't have a large enough rimmed pizza pan, form the meatza crust into a rectangle to fit on a rimmed baking sheet instead!*

Prep the zucchini

Yield: about 6 cups
Prep Time: 10 minutes

FOR THE ZUCCHINI NOODLES:

1. Spiral-slice six medium-sized zucchini into noodles, then toss the zucchini noodles with 1½ teaspoons of coarse sea salt.

2. Line two rimmed baking sheets with tea towels or triple layers of paper towels, then spread the zucchini noodles across the towels. Let sit for 30 minutes to 1 hour while you prep the rest of the components, then gather the zucchini in the towels and wring them to squeeze out as much water as possible.

3. Line a container with paper towels (the zucchini will continue to release water), then place the zucchini in it. Store in the refrigerator for use later in the week.

Yield: 6 boats
Prep Time: 10 minutes

FOR THE ZUCCHINI BOATS:

1. Cut three large zucchini in half lengthwise and scoop out the seeds and pulp, leaving a ¼-inch-thick wall of squash; discard the seeds and pulp.

2. Store in the refrigerator for use later in the week.

Cook the mushrooms

Yield: 1½ cups
Prep Time: 5 minutes
Cook Time: 10 minutes

1 tablespoon extra-virgin olive oil

16 ounces sliced baby bella (aka cremini) mushrooms

½ teaspoon coarse sea salt

¼ teaspoon ground black pepper

1. Heat the oil in a large skillet over medium heat. Once hot, add the sliced mushrooms. Season with the salt and pepper.

2. Sauté for 8 to 10 minutes, until the mushrooms are fully cooked through and slightly browned.

3. Put two-thirds of the cooked mushrooms, about 1 cup, in a container and label it "Stroganoff," then put the remainder, about ½ cup, in a separate container and label it "Meatza." Store in the refrigerator for use later in the week.

Make the enchilada sauce

Prep Time: 2 minutes

Cook Time: 5 minutes

1 (8-ounce) can tomato sauce

1 tablespoon tomato paste

½ cup chicken broth

½ teaspoon coarse sea salt

1 tablespoon chili powder

1 teaspoon ground cumin

1 teaspoon dried oregano leaves

¼ teaspoon ground black pepper

In a saucepan over medium heat, whisk together the tomato sauce and tomato paste until no lumps remain. Stir in the broth, salt, and spices. Simmer for 4 to 5 minutes, until the sauce is bubbling and warmed through. Store in the refrigerator for use later in the week.

Make the cauliflower rice

Make a batch of Basic Cauliflower Rice (page 363), then store in the refrigerator for use later in the week.

Chop the cilantro

Wash and dry half of a small bunch of cilantro, then chop enough to equal ½ cup plus 2 tablespoons of chopped cilantro. Store in the refrigerator for use later in the week.

Dice an onion

Dice a white onion and store in the refrigerator for use later in the week.

Mince the garlic

Mince six cloves of garlic, or until you have 6 teaspoons of minced garlic. Store in the refrigerator for use later in the week.

Spinach Artichoke Meatza

Yield: 4 servings   Prep Time: 5 minutes   Cook Time: 20 minutes

1 (8-ounce) package cream cheese or dairy-free cream cheese–style spread

½ teaspoon garlic powder

¾ teaspoon coarse sea salt, divided

1 tablespoon extra-virgin olive oil

3 teaspoons minced garlic ✓

8 ounces fresh spinach

1 (14-ounce) can quartered artichoke hearts

½ cup cooked mushrooms ✓

1 tablespoon Italian seasoning

1 par-baked meatza crust ✓

½ teaspoon red pepper flakes, for garnish (optional)

1. Preheat the oven to 400°F.

2. Place the cream cheese in a small microwave-safe bowl and microwave for 20 to 30 seconds, until softened. Stir in the garlic powder and ¼ teaspoon of the salt. Set aside.

3. Heat the oil in a large skillet over medium-high heat. Once hot, add the garlic and sauté for 30 seconds, or until fragrant. Then add the spinach and sauté for 1 minute, until the spinach is wilted.

4. Drain the artichoke hearts and add them to the skillet, along with the mushrooms. Sprinkle with the Italian seasoning and the remaining ½ teaspoon of salt. Sauté for 2 to 3 minutes, until warmed through.

5. Meanwhile, pull the meatza crust out of the refrigerator and spread the cream cheese mixture evenly over the crust, then top with the spinach and artichoke mixture.

6. Bake the meatza for 15 minutes, until slightly browned. Let rest for 5 minutes, then sprinkle with the red pepper flakes, if using. Cut into 8 slices and serve!

Enchilada-Stuffed Zucchini Boats

Yield: 4 servings   Prep Time: 5 minutes   Cook Time: 25 minutes

FOR THE STUFFED ZUCCHINI:

3¼ cups cooked ground beef ✓

Enchilada sauce ✓

6 hollowed-out zucchini halves ✓

1 tablespoon extra-virgin olive oil

½ teaspoon coarse sea salt

¼ teaspoon ground black pepper

½ cup shredded Mexican cheese blend (omit for dairy-free)

2 tablespoons chopped fresh cilantro, for garnish ✓

FOR THE CILANTRO-LIME CAULIFLOWER RICE:

Cooked cauliflower rice ✓

½ cup chopped fresh cilantro ✓

2 tablespoons fresh lime juice (about 1 lime)

1. Preheat the oven to 375°F.

2. Stir the ground beef into the enchilada sauce.

3. Place the zucchini halves in a 3-quart casserole dish or on a rimmed baking sheet. Brush the boats on all sides with the oil, then season with the salt and pepper.

4. Fill each zucchini half with an equal amount of the meat sauce, then top with the cheese.

5. Bake for 25 minutes, or until the cheese is browned and bubbling and the zucchini is cooked through.

6. About 10 minutes before the zucchini boats are done, make the cilantro-lime rice: Reheat the cauliflower rice in a saucepan over medium heat, covered, for 3 to 4 minutes, or microwave it for 1½ minutes, until warmed through. Stir in the ½ cup of cilantro and the lime juice.

7. Garnish the baked zucchini boats with 2 tablespoons of cilantro. To serve, place one zucchini boat on each plate, then cut the remaining two boats in half and add an additional half boat to each plate (for a total of 1½ boats per serving). Divide the rice among the plates and enjoy!

Ground Beef Stroganoff

Yield: 4 servings   Prep Time: 5 minutes   Cook Time: 20 minutes

FOR THE BEEF STROGANOFF:

1 tablespoon salted butter or ghee

1 white onion, diced ✓

3 teaspoons minced garlic ✓

1 cup cooked mushrooms ✓

1½ cups chicken broth

1 tablespoon coconut aminos

1 tablespoon Dijon mustard

1 teaspoon coarse sea salt

½ teaspoon ground black pepper

4½ cups cooked ground beef ✓

¾ cup sour cream, or the cream from 2 (13½-ounce) cans of full-fat coconut milk

2 tablespoons fresh lemon juice (about 1 small lemon)

FOR THE ZUCCHINI NOODLES:

1 tablespoon extra-virgin olive oil

6 cups zucchini noodles (from 6 medium zucchini) ✓

½ teaspoon coarse sea salt

¼ teaspoon ground black pepper

1 teaspoon dried parsley, for garnish

1. Begin making the stroganoff: Melt the butter in a 10-inch cast-iron pan or similar-sized sauté pan over medium-high heat. Once hot, add the onion and garlic. Cook for 3 to 4 minutes, until the onion is translucent.

2. Add the mushrooms, broth, coconut aminos, mustard, salt, and pepper. Stir until fully combined, then add the ground beef. Simmer for 5 to 7 minutes, until the sauce is slightly thickened and reduced.

3. While the stroganoff is reducing, start the zucchini noodles: Heat the oil in a large sauté pan or pot over medium heat. Once hot, add the zucchini noodles and season with the salt and pepper. Cook for 5 to 7 minutes, until softened, stirring occasionally.

4. Stir the sour cream and lemon juice into the stroganoff mixture, cook for 1 additional minute to warm everything through, then remove from the heat.

5. Serve the stroganoff alongside the zucchini noodles and garnish with the parsley.

ROASTED CHICKEN
and CAULIFLOWER

Whether or not you follow a low-carb diet, I need you to make this week's meals. Even as a carb lover, I can say that this low-carb week includes some of my favorite recipes in this book! With just a few strategic add-on ingredients, you're going to transform just two main components—chicken and cauliflower—into some epically tasty dishes. First up is a Loaded Cauliflower Casserole. (I want to make this dish every day.) Then we have a Balsamic Chicken Sheet Pan Dinner (simple, but BIG flavors here) and some luscious Buffalo Chicken–Stuffed Avocados! If you'd like to supplement this week's three main dinner recipes with two additional meals, see the suggested "Bonus Dinner Options" on the next page.

Weekly Ingredients

FRESH PRODUCE

Avocados, 4 medium

Cauliflower, 3 medium heads (1½ to 2 pounds each), or 3 pounds precut florets

Green onions, 4

MEAT/DAIRY

Bacon, 10 strips (about 12 ounces)

Butter, salted, 2 tablespoons

Chickens, 2 whole (4 to 5 pounds each)

Shredded cheddar cheese, 6 ounces (1½ cups)

Sour cream, 2 ounces (¼ cup)

PANTRY

Avocado oil, 2 tablespoons

Avocado oil mayonnaise, store-bought or homemade (page 372), 3 tablespoons

Balsamic vinegar, 2 fluid ounces (¼ cup)

Coconut aminos, Coconut Secret brand, 1 tablespoon

Dijon mustard, 1 tablespoon

Extra-virgin olive oil, 4 fluid ounces (½ cup)

Medium-hot hot sauce, such as Frank's RedHot, 2⅔ fluid ounces (⅓ cup)

SEASONINGS

Dried parsley, 1 teaspoon

Garlic powder, 1 teaspoon

Italian seasoning, 1 tablespoon

Ingredient Subs

To make this week PALEO and/or DAIRY-FREE:

· *Replace the butter with ghee or oil of choice.*

· *Omit the cheese.*

· *Replace the sour cream with cream from a can of full-fat coconut milk.*

To make this week EGG-FREE:

· *Replace the avocado oil mayo with butter or oil of choice.*

Bonus Dinner Options

Dinner 1

Simple Seared Pork Chops
(page 349)

Lemony Kale
(page 359)

Roasted Asparagus
(page 360)

Bonus Dinner Ingredients

Asparagus, fresh, 1 pound

Extra-virgin olive oil, 2 tablespoons plus 2 teaspoons

Kale, 1 small bunch (about 1 pound)

Lemon, ½

Pork chops, boneless, about 1 inch thick, 1½ pounds

Texas Grill Rub, 2 tablespoons (see page 374 for ingredients)

Dinner 2

Lemon-Garlic Shrimp
(page 354)

Roasted Cherry Tomatoes
(page 360)

Wilted Spinach
(page 358)

Bonus Dinner Ingredients

Cherry tomatoes, 2 pints

Extra-virgin olive oil, 2 tablespoons plus 2 teaspoons

Garlic powder, ½ teaspoon

Lemons, 1½

Shrimp, large, 1½ pounds, peeled and deveined

Spinach, fresh, 1 pound

Prep Day

Your prep for this week's dinners is really straightforward! To start, you need to get those chickens in the oven. Once the chickens are roasting, you can prep the cauliflower, turning some of it into mashed "potatoes" and storing the rest as florets for later in the week. As soon as the chicken comes out of the oven, you can bake the bacon while at the same time have the cauliflower cooking for the mash. Once the chicken is cool enough to handle, you shred the breast meat and break the rest of the chicken down into thigh and leg quarters and wings. Finally, you'll make the balsamic sauce, then pack up everything and store it in the fridge!

note: *If you're planning to make homemade mayonnaise rather than use store-bought, I recommend that you add it to your prep day tasks so that it's ready for use later in the week. To save myself a step, I purchase preshredded cheese; if you are using block cheese, add the step of shredding the cheddar to today's tasks as well.*

Roast and break down the chickens

Yield: 5 cups shredded breast meat, 4 quarters, 4 wings
Prep Time: 5 minutes
Cook Time: 1 hour 15 minutes

2 (4- to 5-pound) whole chickens

2 tablespoons avocado oil

2 teaspoons coarse sea salt

1 teaspoon ground black pepper

1. Preheat the oven to 375°F.

2. Place the chickens on a rimmed baking sheet and pat dry with paper towels.

3. Rub the chickens with the avocado oil, then season with the salt and pepper.

4. Bake for 1 hour 15 minutes, until a thermometer inserted into the thickest part of a chicken breast registers 165°F.

5. Let cool for at least 30 minutes, then separate the chicken breasts from the bone and shred the meat with two forks, discarding the skin. You should have about 5 cups of shredded chicken breast. Put 3 cups of the shredded meat in a container and label it "Cauli Casserole"; put the remaining 2 cups in a second container and label it "Stuffed Avocados." Store in the refrigerator for use later in the week.

6. Cut away the leg quarters (consisting of the thighs and drumsticks) and wings, leaving the skin on, and store in the refrigerator for use later in the week.

Prep the cauliflower

If you've purchased bagged cauliflower florets, skip ahead to the next paragraph. Otherwise, cut three medium-sized heads of cauliflower into florets, discarding the stems.

Put 3 cups of the florets in a container and store in the refrigerator for use later in the week. Set the rest of the florets aside to use for making the mashed cauliflower (up next!).

Make the mashed cauliflower

Prep Time: 2 minutes

Cook Time: 10 to 15 minutes, depending on method

Cauliflower florets set aside for the mash *(from earlier in prep day)*

¼ cup sour cream or coconut cream

2 tablespoons salted butter, ghee, or oil of choice

1 teaspoon coarse sea salt

¼ teaspoon ground black pepper

1. Steam the cauliflower using one of these two methods:

- **Microwave Option** (Cook Time: 10 minutes)
  Place the cauliflower in a microwave-safe bowl with ¼ cup of water. Cover and microwave on high for 10 minutes, until cooked through. Let cool slightly, then drain.

- **Stovetop Option** (Cook Time: 15 minutes)
  Pour ¼ cup of water into a large skillet or sauté pan over medium heat. Once hot, add the cauliflower and cover the pan. Reduce the heat to medium-low and let the cauliflower steam for 12 to 15 minutes, until cooked through. Let cool slightly, then drain.

2. Place the cooked cauliflower in a food processor or large mixing bowl, along with the sour cream, butter, salt, and pepper. Pulse or blend using an immersion blender until smooth.

3. Store in the refrigerator for use later in the week.

Cook and slice or crumble the bacon

Prep Time: 3 minutes

Cook Time: 18 minutes

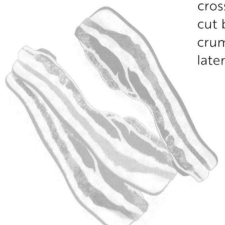

1. Preheat the oven to 400°F.

2. Lay ten strips of bacon on a rimmed baking sheet and bake until crisp, 12 to 18 minutes. The total cooking time will depend on the thickness of your bacon.

3. Transfer the bacon to a paper towel–lined plate and let cool. When the bacon is cool enough to handle, slice it crosswise into ¼-inch pieces or crumble it. (if you used thick-cut bacon, slicing it will be easier; if you used regular bacon, crumbling it will be easier.) Store in the refrigerator for use later in the week.

Make the balsamic sauce

½ cup extra-virgin olive oil

¼ cup balsamic vinegar

1 tablespoon coconut aminos

1 tablespoon Dijon mustard

1 tablespoon Italian seasoning

1 teaspoon garlic powder

¼ teaspoon ground black pepper

In a small bowl, whisk together all of the ingredients. Store in the refrigerator for use later in the week.

Slice the green onions

Slice four green onions, then divide them evenly between two containers. Store in the refrigerator for use later in the week.

Loaded Cauliflower Casserole

Yield: 6 servings   Prep Time: 5 minutes   Cook Time: 20 minutes

Mashed cauliflower ✓

1½ cups shredded cheddar cheese

3 cups shredded cooked chicken breast ✓

10 strips bacon, cooked and sliced or crumbled ✓

2 green onions, sliced, for garnish ✓

1. Preheat the oven to 400°F.

2. Evenly spread the mashed cauliflower in an 8-inch round casserole dish or 3½-quart cast-iron braiser.

3. Sprinkle the cheese over the cauliflower, then top with the chicken and bacon.

4. Bake for 20 minutes, until the cheese is browned and bubbling.

5. Let cool slightly, garnish with the green onions, and serve!

Balsamic Chicken Sheet Pan Dinner

Yield: 4 servings   Prep Time: 10 minutes   Cook Time: 40 minutes

3 cups cauliflower florets ✓

½ teaspoon coarse sea salt

Balsamic sauce, divided ✓

4 roasted chicken leg quarters plus 4 chicken wings ✓

1 teaspoon dried parsley, for garnish

1. Preheat the oven to 400°F.

2. In a large bowl, toss the cauliflower with the salt and ¼ cup of the balsamic sauce. (If the sauce has separated in the refrigerator, simply whisk it back together.) Spread the cauliflower on a rimmed baking sheet and bake for 20 minutes.

3. Dip the chicken leg quarters and wings in the remaining sauce and place on the baking sheet with the cauliflower. Bake for an additional 20 minutes, until the chicken is browned and slightly crisp. Remove from the oven and garnish with dried parsley.

Buffalo Chicken–Stuffed Avocados

Yield: 4 servings   Prep Time: 10 minutes   Cook Time: 15 minutes

4 medium avocados

⅓ cup medium-hot hot sauce

3 tablespoons avocado oil mayonnaise or salted butter

2 cups shredded chicken breast ✓

2 green onions, sliced, divided ✓

1. Preheat the oven to 400°F.

2. Halve the avocados and remove the pits, then slice ¼ inch off of the bottom of each avocado to make a flat surface for the avocado to sit on. Place the avocados on a rimmed baking sheet.

3. In a bowl, whisk together the hot sauce and mayonnaise, then add the shredded chicken and about 2 tablespoons of the sliced green onions, reserving some for garnish. Toss to coat the chicken.

4. Stuff each avocado with an equal amount of the chicken mixture, then bake the stuffed avocados for 15 minutes, or until the chicken is slightly browned on top.

5. Let cool slightly, garnish with the reserved sliced green onions, and serve!

GROUND BEEF, BROCCOLI, and YUKON GOLD POTATOES

If you're anything like me, ground beef, broccoli, and potatoes are three ingredients that can almost always be found in your kitchen. I have good news for you! This week gives you the opportunity to reinvent the ways in which these basic components come together on your dinner table. You're going to make three incredible dinners: Bacon Burgers (bunless!) with Broccoli and Twice-Baked Fries, Picadillo Tacos (this is a Tex-Mex-style picadillo!), and a luscious Cottage Pie. If you'd like to supplement this week's three main dinner recipes with two additional meals, see the suggested "Bonus Dinner Options" on the next page.

Weekly Ingredients

FRESH PRODUCE

Avocado, 1 small (optional)

Broccoli, 3 medium heads (about 2 pounds), or about 1½ pounds precut florets

Butter lettuce, 1 head (optional)

Cilantro, 10 sprigs

Flat-leaf parsley, 8 sprigs (optional)

Garlic, 2 cloves

Onion, white, 1 small

Tomato, 1 (or 4 cherry tomatoes)

Yukon gold potatoes, 5 pounds

FROZEN FOODS

Peas and carrots, 1 (10-ounce) package

MEAT/DAIRY

Bacon, 4 strips

Butter, salted, 2 ounces (¼ cup)

Ground beef, 5 pounds

Heavy cream, 2 fluid ounces (¼ cup)

White cheddar cheese or other semi-firm cheese of choice, 4 slices

PANTRY

Beef broth, 4 fluid ounces (½ cup)

Coconut aminos, Coconut Secret brand, 1½ teaspoons

Corn tortillas (about 6 inches in diameter), 8

Dijon mustard, 1½ teaspoons

Extra-virgin olive oil, 3 tablespoons plus 1 teaspoon

Red wine, 8 fluid ounces (1 cup)

Tomato paste, 1 (6-ounce) can

Tomato sauce, 1 (8-ounce) can

SEASONINGS

Chili powder, 1 tablespoon

Dried oregano leaves, 1 teaspoon

Garlic powder, 1½ teaspoons

Ground cumin, 2 teaspoons

Italian seasoning, 1 tablespoon

Onion powder, 1 teaspoon

Ingredient Subs

To make this week PALEO:

· *Use the substitutions listed below for making the week grain-free and dairy-free.*

To make this week GRAIN-FREE:

· *Use grain-free tortillas in place of the corn tortillas.*

To make this week DAIRY-FREE:

· *Use extra-virgin olive oil in place of the butter.*

· *Use full-fat coconut milk in place of the heavy cream.*

· *Omit the cheese.*

Bonus Dinner Options

Dinner 1

Paprika Lime Chicken Breasts
(page 347)

Steamed Green Beans
(page 361)

Basic White Rice
(page 368)

Bonus Dinner Ingredients

Chicken breasts, boneless, skinless, 1½ pounds

Extra-virgin olive oil, 2 tablespoons plus 2 teaspoons

Green beans, fresh, 1 pound

Lime, 1

Paprika, 1 tablespoon

White rice, 6½ ounces (1 cup)

Bonus Dinner Ingredient Subs

To make this meal Paleo and/or grain-free, replace the white rice with 1 large head cauliflower (about 3 pounds) or 18 ounces frozen riced cauliflower; make Basic Cauliflower Rice (page 363) instead of the Basic White Rice.

Dinner 2

Basic Pork Tenderloin
(page 350)

Spinach Salad
(page 362)

Basic Polenta
(page 369)

Bonus Dinner Ingredients

Balsamic vinegar, 2 tablespoons

Chicken broth, 20 fluid ounces (2½ cups)

Extra-virgin olive oil, 2½ fluid ounces (5 tablespoons)

Pecans, raw, 2 ounces (½ cup)

Polenta meal or corn grits, 4½ ounces (¾ cup)

Pork tenderloin, 1 (1¼ pounds)

Spinach, fresh, 8 ounces

Strawberries, fresh, ½ pint

Texas Grill Rub, 2 tablespoons (see page 374 for ingredients)

Bonus Dinner Ingredient Subs

To make this meal Paleo and/or grain-free, replace the polenta meal (or corn grits) with 1 large head cauliflower (about 3 pounds) or 18 ounces frozen riced cauliflower, omit the broth, and reduce the total amount of olive oil by 1 tablespoon; make Basic Cauliflower Rice (page 363) instead of the Basic Polenta.

Prep Day

Today's prep efforts are going to be smooth sailing! First, you're going to steam and peel 3½ pounds of potatoes, then dice some and set the rest aside for mashing later. While the potatoes are steaming, you'll cut the remaining 1½ pounds of potatoes into fries, prep the broccoli, and get them into the oven at the same time (they cook at the same temperature). Then you'll mash the steamed potatoes, cook some of the ground beef, and shape the rest of the meat into burger patties. Lastly, you'll whip up the picadillo sauce. I like to start by popping the designated amount of potatoes into the Instant Pot for steaming. This method cooks them the fastest, which means that they will be cool enough to handle sooner, and I spend less time in the kitchen.

Steam the potatoes

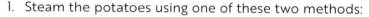

Prep Time: 5 minutes

Cook Time: 13 to 30 minutes, depending on method

1. Steam the potatoes using one of these two methods:

- **Stovetop Method** (Cook Time: 30 minutes)
  Place a steamer insert inside a large pot and pour in 1 cup of water. Turn the heat to high. Once the water starts to boil, add 3½ pounds of Yukon gold potatoes to the pot and cover. Cook for 25 to 30 minutes, until the potatoes are easily pierced with a fork. Remove the steamer insert and let the potatoes cool.

- **Instant Pot Method** (Cook Time: 13 minutes)
  Place 1 cup of water in a 6-quart Instant Pot, then add the steamer insert and 3½ pounds of Yukon gold potatoes. Seal the lid onto the Instant Pot, press the Pressure Cook or Manual button, and set the timer for 13 minutes. Once the cooking is finished, release the pressure manually by slowly turning the pressure valve to "venting." Remove the lid and make sure the potatoes are easily pierced with a fork. If they are still hard in the middle, seal the lid onto the pot again, press Pressure Cook or Manual, and set the timer for an additional 1 to 2 minutes. If they are fully cooked through, remove the potatoes from the pot and let cool.

2. Once the potatoes are cool to the touch, remove the peels. Set aside about three-quarters of the potatoes for use later in the prep day. Cut the remaining potatoes into ½-inch cubes, then store in the refrigerator for use later in the week.

Bake the fries

Prep Time: 10 minutes

Cook Time: 50 minutes

1½ pounds Yukon gold potatoes, cut into ½-inch-thick wedges

2 tablespoons extra-virgin olive oil

½ teaspoon coarse sea salt

Pinch of ground black pepper

1. Preheat the oven to 400°F. Line a rimmed baking sheet with parchment paper.

2. Place the potato wedges, olive oil, salt, and pepper in a medium-sized bowl and toss to coat. Spread the potato wedges on the lined baking sheet so that they're not touching.

3. Bake for 30 minutes, then flip and bake for an additional 15 to 20 minutes, until cooked through and golden brown.

4. Store in the refrigerator for use later in the week.

Roast the broccoli

Yield: about 5 cups

Prep Time: 10 minutes

Cook Time: 25 minutes

3 medium heads broccoli, or 1½ pounds precut fresh florets

1 tablespoon extra-virgin olive oil

½ teaspoon coarse sea salt

1. Preheat the oven to 400°F. Line a rimmed baking sheet with parchment paper.

2. If using precut broccoli florets, skip ahead to Step 3. To prep the heads of broccoli, cut the florets away from the large center stalks, then discard the stalks.

3. Place the florets in a large bowl. Add the olive oil and salt and toss to combine. Spread the broccoli on the lined baking sheet.

4. Roast for 25 minutes, or until the tops are brown.

5. Place 3 cups of the roasted broccoli in a container and label it "Burgers" and the remaining 2 cups in another container and label it "Cottage Pie." Store in the refrigerator for use later in the week.

Make the mashed potatoes

Steamed and peeled whole potatoes *(from earlier in prep day)*

3 tablespoons salted butter, ghee, or other fat of choice

¼ cup heavy cream or full-fat coconut milk

½ to 1 teaspoon coarse sea salt

¼ teaspoon ground black pepper

1. Place the potatoes in a medium-sized pot over medium-low heat and mash with a potato masher.

2. Add the butter, cream, ½ teaspoon of salt, and pepper and stir until smooth. Taste for seasoning and add up to ½ teaspoon more salt, if needed.

3. Store in the refrigerator for use later in the week.

Cook the ground beef

Yield: 8 scant cups

Cook Time: 15 minutes

1. In a large skillet over medium heat, combine 3½ pounds of ground beef and 1 teaspoon of coarse sea salt. (You will add more seasoning later.) Cook for 10 to 15 minutes, until fully browned and crumbled, then drain the fat.

2. Place 3½ cups in a container labeled "Tacos" and the remaining 4½ cups in a container labeled "Cottage Pie." Store in the refrigerator for use later in the week.

Shape the burger patties

1½ pounds ground beef

1½ teaspoons coconut aminos

1½ teaspoons Dijon mustard

½ teaspoon garlic powder

½ teaspoon coarse sea salt

¼ teaspoon ground black pepper

Put all of the ingredients in a large bowl and mix together with your hands, then shape the meat mixture into 4 equal-sized patties, about ¾ inch thick. Store in the refrigerator for use later in the week.

Cook the bacon

Prep Time: 1 minute

Cook Time: 6 minutes

Cut four strips of bacon in half crosswise. Cook in a medium-sized skillet over medium heat until crisp, about 6 minutes. Store in the refrigerator for use later in the week.

Make the picadillo sauce

Prep Time: 5 minutes

Cook Time: 10 minutes

1 small white onion

2 cloves garlic

1 tablespoon salted butter or extra-virgin olive oil

1 (8-ounce) can tomato sauce

½ teaspoon coarse sea salt

1 tablespoon chili powder

2 teaspoons ground cumin

1 teaspoon dried oregano leaves

½ teaspoon ground black pepper

1. Dice the onion and mince the garlic.

2. Melt the butter in a large saucepan over medium heat. Once melted, add the onion and cook for 3 to 4 minutes, until the onion is translucent and has begun to brown. Then add the garlic and cook for 30 seconds, until fragrant.

3. Pour the tomato sauce and 2 cups of water into the pan and stir to combine with the onion and garlic, then season with the salt and spices. Cook for 3 to 4 minutes, until the sauce begins to bubble and becomes fragrant, then remove from the heat.

4. Store in the refrigerator for use later in the week.

Bacon Burgers with Broccoli and Twice-Baked Fries

Yield: 4 servings   Prep Time: 20 minutes   Cook Time: 15 minutes

Baked potato wedges ✓

3 cups roasted broccoli ✓

1 teaspoon extra-virgin olive oil

4 premade burger patties ✓

4 slices white cheddar cheese or other cheese of choice (omit for dairy-free)

4 strips bacon, halved and cooked ✓

1 tomato, or 4 cherry tomatoes

1 small avocado (optional)

8 butter lettuce leaves (optional)

For the broccoli and fries:

1. Preheat the oven to 400°F. Line a rimmed baking sheet with parchment paper.

2. Spread out the fries on one half of the lined baking sheet and toss with the olive oil. On the other half of the baking sheet, spread out the broccoli.

3. Bake for 15 minutes, until both the fries and the broccoli are warmed through and slightly crisp.

For the burgers:

1. While the fries and broccoli are baking, preheat a grill to high heat. Once the grill is at temperature, sear the burger patties for 4 to 5 minutes on each side, until they develop char marks and are medium to medium-well done. (Alternatively, you can cook the burgers in a skillet over medium-high heat for 4 to 5 minutes per side.) After flipping, top the burgers with cheese and bacon. Once cooked, transfer to a plate to rest.

2. While the burgers are resting, slice the tomato(es) and avocado, if using. Plate the burgers, top with the tomato and avocado slices, and serve alongside the fries and broccoli! If desired, use butter lettuce leaves as "buns."

Picadillo Tacos

Yield: 4 servings   Prep Time: 5 minutes   Cook Time: 15 minutes

Picadillo sauce ✓

3¼ cups cooked ground beef ✓

Diced steamed potatoes ✓

8 corn tortillas or grain-free tortillas

2 tablespoons chopped fresh cilantro, for garnish

1. Place the picadillo sauce in a large saucepan over medium-low heat, then stir in the ground beef and potatoes. Cover and cook for 15 minutes, until warmed through.

2. While the picadillo mixture is warming, set a cast-iron or other heavy-bottomed skillet over medium heat. Once hot, put one tortilla in the pan at a time and warm for about 30 seconds per side, until the tortilla is pliable and begins to brown slightly. Repeat with the remaining tortillas. To keep the tortillas warm while you are heating the remaining ones, you can wrap them in a kitchen towel.

3. Spoon equal portions of the picadillo mixture into the tortillas, garnish with the cilantro, and serve!

Cottage Pie

Yield: 6 servings   Prep Time: 10 minutes   Cook Time: 30 minutes

4½ cups cooked ground beef ✓

2 cups roasted broccoli ✓

1 (10-ounce) package frozen peas and carrots

1 (6-ounce) can tomato paste

1 cup red wine

½ cup beef broth

1 teaspoon coarse sea salt

1 tablespoon Italian seasoning

1 teaspoon garlic powder

1 teaspoon onion powder

¼ teaspoon ground black pepper

Mashed potatoes ✓

2 tablespoons chopped fresh flat-leaf parsley, for garnish (optional)

1. Preheat the oven to 350°F.

2. Put the ground beef, broccoli, and peas and carrots in a large saucepan or enameled 3½-quart Dutch oven and stir to combine. Cook over medium heat for 2 minutes, until warmed through.

3. Stir the tomato paste into the beef mixture. Once fully combined, add the wine, broth, salt, and spices. Bring to a boil, then slide the pan off the heat. If you used a saucepan, transfer the beef mixture to a deep 9-inch round or similar-sized casserole dish.

4. Warm the mashed potatoes either by placing them in a medium-sized saucepan over medium heat, stirring occasionally, for 3 to 5 minutes, or by microwaving them for about 3 minutes, until hot. Spread the potatoes evenly over the beef mixture.

5. Bake for 30 minutes, until the top is slightly browned and the pie is fully warmed through.

6. Remove from the oven, let cool slightly, garnish with the parsley, if using, and serve!

BAKED CHICKEN BREAST, TOMATOES, and RICE

If you like Italian, Cajun, and Mexican food, this week is a good fit! You'll be transforming chicken breast, tomatoes, and rice into three craveable dinners. First up, to make use of homemade pico de gallo when it's super fresh, is a Green Chili Chicken Casserole, then a Chicken Parmesan Bake, and finally a Cajun Chicken and Rice Skillet. Though rice is a mainstay for this week and the Chicken Parmesan does call for pasta, I have included instructions for modifying these recipes to make them low-carb and grain-free! If you'd like to supplement this week's three main dinner recipes with two additional meals, see the suggested "Bonus Dinner Options" on the next page.

Weekly Ingredients

FRESH PRODUCE

Bell pepper, green, 1

Bell pepper, red, 1

Cilantro, 1 small bunch

Flat-leaf parsley, 8 sprigs (optional)

Garlic, 5 cloves

Jalapeño pepper, ½

Lemons, 2½

Limes, 3

Onion, yellow, 1

Tomatoes, 2 medium

MEAT/DAIRY

Andouille sausage, 12 ounces

Butter, salted, 3 tablespoons

Chicken breasts, boneless, skinless, 5 pounds

Shredded Mexican cheese blend, 4 ounces (1 cup)

Shredded Parmesan cheese, 1½ ounces (½ cup)

Sour cream, 4 ounces (½ cup)

PANTRY

Chicken broth, 2 fluid ounces (¼ cup)

Crushed tomatoes, 1 (28-ounce) can

Extra-virgin olive oil, 2 tablespoons

Gluten-free noodles, 1 (9-ounce) package

Green chilis, whole, 1 (10-ounce) can

Pork rinds, ½ (5-ounce) package

White rice, 13 ounces (2 cups)

SEASONINGS

Dried oregano leaves, 1 teaspoon

Dried parsley, 1 tablespoon plus 1 teaspoon

Garlic powder, 2 teaspoons

Ground cumin, 1 teaspoon

Italian seasoning, 1 tablespoon

Paprika, ½ teaspoon

Ingredient Subs

To make this week LOW-CARB and/or GRAIN-FREE:

· *Replace the gluten-free noodles with 6 medium zucchini and add 2 teaspoons oil of choice.*

· *Replace the white rice with 2 medium heads cauliflower (about 4 pounds) or 2 (12-ounce) packages frozen riced cauliflower and add 1½ tablespoons extra-virgin olive oil.*

To make this week PALEO:

· *Make the substitutions listed above for making the week low-carb and/or grain-free and below for making it dairy-free.*

To make this week DAIRY-FREE:

· *Replace the butter with avocado oil.*

· *Omit the cheeses.*

· *Replace the sour cream with cream from a can of full-fat coconut milk.*

Bonus Dinner Options

Dinner 1

Southwestern Pork Chops
(page 350)

Sautéed Squash
(page 356)

Basic Polenta
(page 369)

Bonus Dinner Ingredients

Chicken broth, 20 fluid ounces (2½ cups)

Extra-virgin olive oil, 3 tablespoons plus 2 teaspoons

Polenta meal or corn grits, 4½ ounces (¾ cup)

Pork chops, boneless, about 1 inch thick, 1½ pounds

Texas Chili Spice Blend, 2 tablespoons (see page 374 for ingredients)

Zucchini or yellow squash, 4

Bonus Dinner Ingredient Subs

To make this meal LOW-CARB, PALEO, and/or GRAIN-FREE:

Omit the broth. Replace the polenta meal (or corn grits) with 1 large head cauliflower (about 3 pounds) or 18 ounces frozen riced cauliflower; make Basic Cauliflower Rice (page 363) instead of the Basic Polenta.

Dinner 2

Pan-Seared Steak
(page 352)

Spinach Salad
(page 362)

Baked Sweet Potatoes
(page 365)

Bonus Dinner Ingredients

Balsamic vinegar, 2 tablespoons

Extra-virgin olive oil, 2 fluid ounces (¼ cup)

Pecans, raw, 2 ounces (½ cup)

Sirloin or rib-eye steaks, boneless, about 1 inch thick, 4 (4 to 6 ounces each)

Spinach, fresh, 8 ounces (about 6 cups)

Strawberries, fresh, ½ pint

Sweet potatoes, 4 small to medium (about 1 pound)

Texas Grill Rub, 2 tablespoons (see page 374 for ingredients)

Bonus Dinner Ingredient Subs

To make this meal LOW-CARB:

Omit the sweet potatoes.

To make this meal NUT-FREE:

Omit the pecans.

Prep Day

Today you're going to knock out the majority of your kitchen time for the week! I like to start off by getting the main protein, the versatile chicken breast, into the oven. Once cooked and cooled to the touch, it just needs a quick dice. While the chicken is baking, I recommend starting on the rice and then the noodles. From there, I get the red sauce going. While it's simmering, I get the other odds and ends underway, like crushing the pork rinds, chopping the veggies, and making the pico de gallo and green chili sauce.

note: *To save myself a step, I purchase preshredded Parmesan cheese; if you are using block cheese, add the step of shredding the Parmesan to this week's prep day tasks.*

Bake and cube the chicken

Yield: 10 cups

Prep Time: 5 minutes

Cook Time: 40 minutes

5 pounds boneless, skinless chicken breasts

1 tablespoon extra-virgin olive oil

1 teaspoon coarse sea salt

½ teaspoon ground black pepper

1. Preheat the oven to 375°F.

2. Brush the chicken breasts with the olive oil, then sprinkle with the salt and pepper.

3. Bake for 40 minutes, until the internal temperature reaches 165°F and the juices run clear when cut.

4. Let the chicken cool, then cut into ½-inch cubes. Put 4 cups of the diced chicken in each of two containers and the remaining 2 cups in a third container. Label the 4-cup quantities "Casserole" and "Parmesan" and the 2-cup quantity "Cajun Skillet." Refrigerate for use later in the week.

Cook the rice

Yield: 6 cups

Prep Time: 1 minute

Cook Time: about 20 minutes

Cook 2 cups of white rice according to the package instructions. Place 3½ cups of the cooked rice in a container labeled "Casserole" and the remaining 2½ cups in another container labeled "Cajun Skillet." Store in the refrigerator for use later in the week.

LOW CARB **P** **LOW-CARB/PALEO/GRAIN-FREE RICE SUBSTITUTE**
Make 1½ batches of Basic Cauliflower Rice (page 363), then follow the storage instructions for the white rice above.

Cook the noodles

Cook a 9-ounce package of gluten-free noodles according to the package instructions. Store in the refrigerator for use later in the week.

Yield: 6 cups
Prep Time: 10 minutes
Cook Time: 5 minutes

6 medium zucchini
1 teaspoon coarse sea salt
2 teaspoons oil of choice

 LOW-CARB/PALEO/GRAIN-FREE NOODLE SUBSTITUTE

1. Spiral-slice the zucchini to make about 6 cups of zucchini noodles.

2. Toss the zucchini noodles with the salt. Line two rimmed baking sheets with a thick layer of paper towels and place the zucchini noodles on them.

3. Let the zucchini sit for 15 minutes, then gather the zucchini in the towels and wring them to squeeze out as much water as possible.

4. To cook the zucchini noodles, heat the oil in a large skillet over medium heat. Once hot, add the zucchini noodles and sauté for 4 to 5 minutes, until the noodles are reduced in volume and cooked through. Drain off any excess water, then store in the refrigerator for use later in the week.

Make the red sauce

Place all of the ingredients in a medium-sized saucepan over medium heat. Cook for 4 to 5 minutes, until bubbling. Store in the refrigerator for use later in the week.

Prep Time: 3 minutes
Cook Time: 7 minutes

1 (28-ounce) can crushed tomatoes
1 tablespoon Italian seasoning
1 teaspoon garlic powder
¼ teaspoon coarse sea salt
¼ teaspoon ground black pepper
Juice of 1 lemon

Crush the pork rinds

Crush 2½ ounces of pork rinds to make 1 cup of crushed pork rinds. Store in a resealable plastic bag or other airtight container for use later in the week.

Slice the bell peppers

Thinly slice a red bell pepper and a green bell pepper, then store in the refrigerator for use later in the week.

Mince the garlic and dice the half onion

Mince three cloves of garlic, then place in a container.

Dice half of a yellow onion, then add it to the container with the garlic. Store in the refrigerator for use later in the week.

Prep the cilantro

Wash and thoroughly dry a small bunch of cilantro. Divide the bunch in half and set one half aside. Chop the leaves of the other half bunch and set aside for making the pico de gallo (your next prep day task). Take the other half bunch and tear off enough leaves (leaving a little stem is okay) to equal ¼ cup and set aside for making the green chili sauce later in the day. Store the remaining cilantro in the refrigerator for use later in the week.

Make the pico de gallo

Prep Time: 10 minutes

2 medium tomatoes

½ yellow onion

½ jalapeño pepper

½ small bunch cilantro, chopped *(from earlier in prep day)*

2 tablespoons fresh lime juice (about 1 lime)

¼ teaspoon coarse sea salt

Dice the tomatoes and onion and put them in a small bowl. Remove the seeds from the jalapeño and finely chop it, then add it, along with the rest of the ingredients, to the tomatoes and onion. Toss to combine, then cover and store in the refrigerator for use later in the week.

Make the green chili sauce

1 (10-ounce) can whole green chilis

½ cup sour cream or cream from a can of full-fat coconut milk

2 tablespoons fresh lime juice (about 1 lime)

2 cloves garlic

¼ cup fresh cilantro leaves *(from earlier in prep day)*

½ teaspoon coarse sea salt

¼ teaspoon ground black pepper

Place the green chilis, sour cream, lime juice, garlic, cilantro, salt, and pepper in a blender and blend until smooth. Store in the refrigerator for use later in the week.

Slice the sausage

Cut 12 ounces of andouille sausage into ½-inch slices. Store in the refrigerator for use later in the week.

Green Chili Chicken Casserole

Yield: 6 servings   Prep Time: 5 minutes   Cook Time: 30 minutes

3½ cups cooked white rice or cauli-rice ✓

4 cups cubed cooked chicken breast ✓

Green chili sauce ✓

Pico de gallo ✓

2 tablespoons fresh lime juice (about 1 lime)

1 teaspoon ground cumin

½ teaspoon coarse sea salt

1 cup shredded Mexican cheese blend (omit for Paleo and dairy-free)

2 tablespoons chopped fresh cilantro, for garnish ✓

1. Preheat the oven to 350°F.

2. Reheat the rice either by placing it in a medium-sized saucepan, covered, over low heat for 5 minutes or by microwaving it for about 2 minutes, until hot.

3. Meanwhile, put the chicken and green chili sauce in a bowl and toss to coat.

4. Put the warmed rice in a 3-quart casserole dish along with the pico de gallo, lime juice, cumin, and salt and stir to combine. Spread the rice mixture evenly in the dish.

5. Place the chicken mixture on top of the rice, making sure to spoon all of the green chili sauce out of the bowl, then top with the cheese.

6. Bake for 25 minutes, until the cheese is browned and bubbling. Garnish with the cilantro and serve!

Chicken Parmesan Bake

Yield: 5 servings   Prep Time: 15 minutes   Cook Time: 20 minutes

1 (9-ounce) package gluten-free noodles, or 6 cups zucchini noodles, cooked ✓

1 tablespoon extra-virgin olive oil

1 teaspoon garlic powder

¼ teaspoon coarse sea salt

¼ teaspoon ground black pepper

4 cups cubed cooked chicken breast ✓

Red sauce ✓

1 cup crushed pork rinds ✓

1 tablespoon plus 1 teaspoon dried parsley, divided

½ cup shredded Parmesan cheese (omit for Paleo and dairy-free)

1. Preheat the oven to 350°F.

2. Toss the noodles with the olive oil, garlic powder, salt, and pepper, then layer in a 10-inch cast-iron skillet or an 8-inch square baking dish.

3. Layer the chicken on top of the noodles. Pour the red sauce over the chicken.

4. In a small bowl, toss together the pork rinds, 1 tablespoon of the parsley, and the cheese, then sprinkle on top of the red sauce.

5. Bake for 20 minutes, until the cheese on top is bubbling. Remove from the oven and sprinkle with the remaining teaspoon of parsley. Let cool slightly, then serve!

Cajun Chicken and Rice Skillet

Yield: 5 servings   Prep Time: 5 minutes   Cook Time: 15 minutes

FOR THE CAJUN CHICKEN:

1 tablespoon salted butter or avocado oil

1 green bell pepper, thinly sliced ✓

1 red bell pepper, thinly sliced ✓

½ yellow onion, diced ✓

3 cloves garlic, minced ✓

1 lemon

Sliced andouille sausage ✓

2 cups cubed cooked chicken breast ✓

FOR THE RICE:

2 tablespoons salted butter or avocado oil

2½ cups cooked white rice or cauli-rice ✓

1 tablespoon fresh lemon juice (about ½ small lemon)

¼ cup chicken broth

½ teaspoon fine sea salt

¼ teaspoon ground black pepper

1 teaspoon dried oregano leaves

½ teaspoon paprika

FOR GARNISH:

2 tablespoons chopped fresh flat-leaf parsley (optional)

Charred lemon halves (from above)

1. To make the Cajun chicken, melt the butter in a large sauté pan over medium heat. Once melted, add the peppers, onion, and garlic and cook for 5 to 6 minutes, until browned, then transfer the vegetables to a large bowl and set aside.

2. Cut the lemon in half and place the halves cut side down in the pan for 1 to 2 minutes, until browned, then set aside.

3. Add the sausage and chicken to the pan and cook until slightly browned, 3 to 5 minutes, then transfer to the bowl with the vegetables.

4. To make the rice, melt the butter in the same pan. Once melted, add the rest of the ingredients for the rice and stir to combine. Cook until warmed through, scraping the bottom of the pan with a wooden spoon to release the charred bits.

5. Top the rice with the veggies, sausage, and chicken and garnish with the parsley and charred lemon halves, then serve.

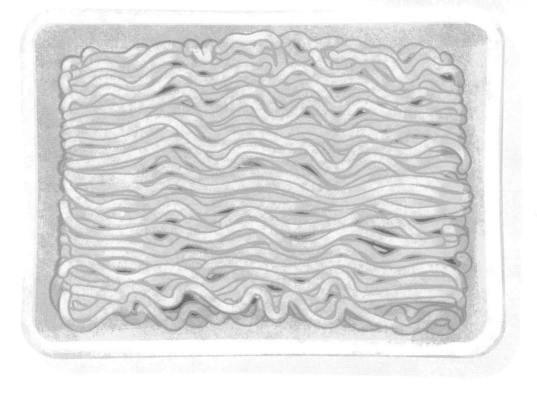

GROUND CHICKEN, BELL PEPPERS, and RICE

I know that at first glance, ground chicken, bell peppers, and rice don't sound like the most inspiring ingredients, but hang in there. These unassuming components really show off in three fabulous recipes this week! We start with one of my husband's favorite meals, Curried Chicken Lettuce Cups. Then we move on to Firecracker Meatballs (think: honey and Sriracha) and Chicken Burrito Bowls (think: Chipotle at home). If you'd like to supplement this week's three main dinner recipes with two additional meals, see the suggested "Bonus Dinner Options" on the next page.

Weekly Ingredients

FRESH PRODUCE

Avocado, 1

Bell peppers, red, 4

Butter lettuce, 1 head

Cilantro, 1 small bunch

Garlic, 2 cloves

Green onions, 1 large bunch

Limes, 5

Onion, red, ½ small

Onion, yellow, 1

MEAT/DAIRY

Butter, salted, 2 tablespoons

Ground chicken, 5 pounds

PANTRY

Avocado oil, 1 tablespoon

Chicken broth, 4 fluid ounces (½ cup)

Coconut aminos, Coconut Secret brand, 2 fluid ounces (¼ cup)

Fish sauce, ¼ teaspoon

Ghee or avocado oil, 1 tablespoon

Honey, 3 ounces (¼ cup)

Sriracha sauce, 2 fluid ounces (¼ cup)

White rice, 13 ounces (2 cups)

SEASONINGS

Chili powder, 2 teaspoons

Curry powder, 1 tablespoon

Dried oregano leaves, 1 teaspoon

Garlic powder, 1 teaspoon

Ginger powder, ½ teaspoon

Ground cumin, 1 teaspoon

Ingredient Subs

To make this week PALEO:

· Use the substitutions listed below for making the week grain-free and dairy-free.

To make this week GRAIN-FREE:

· Replace the white rice with 2 medium heads cauliflower (about 4 pounds total) or 2 (12-ounce) bags frozen riced cauliflower and add 1½ tablespoons extra-virgin olive oil.

To make this week DAIRY-FREE:

· Substitute ghee or oil of choice for the butter.

Bonus Dinner Options

Dinner 1

Southwestern Pork Chops
(page 350)

Lemony Kale
(page 359)

Easy Baked Beets
(page 367)

Bonus Dinner Ingredients

Beets, 3 or 4 large

Dried thyme leaves, 1 teaspoon

Extra-virgin olive oil, 2 tablespoons plus 2 teaspoons

Kale, 1 small bunch (about 1 pound)

Lemon, ½

Pork chops, boneless, about 1 inch thick, 1½ pounds

Texas Chili Spice Blend, 2 tablespoons (see page 374 for ingredients)

Dinner 2

Salmon Bake
(page 354)

Steamed Green Beans
(page 361)

Basic Quinoa
(page 369)

Bonus Dinner Ingredients

Extra-virgin olive oil, 1 tablespoon plus 2 teaspoons

Green beans, fresh, 1 pound

Quinoa, 6 ounces (1 cup)

Ranch dressing, store-bought or homemade (page 372), 2 fluid ounces (¼ cup)

Salmon fillet, 1 (1½ pounds)

Bonus Dinner Ingredient Subs

To make this meal PALEO:

Use the substitutions listed below for making the meal grain-free and dairy-free.

To make this meal GRAIN-FREE:

Replace the quinoa with 1 large head cauliflower (about 3 pounds) or 18 ounces frozen riced cauliflower; make Basic Cauliflower Rice (page 363) instead of the Basic Quinoa.

To make this meal DAIRY-FREE:

Use a dairy-free ranch dressing.

To make this meal EGG-FREE:

Use an egg-free ranch dressing.

Prep Day

The prep work for this week is pretty simple. I like to start off by browning the designated portion of the ground chicken. Once that's going, I prep the green onions (some of which are used in the meatballs) and then use the remaining chicken to make the meatballs. Once the meatballs are in the oven, I start the rice on the stove. Next, I whip up the Sriracha-lime sauce and prep the rest of the veggies and the cilantro for the week. Then everything gets placed in containers and stored in the refrigerator!

Cook some of the chicken

Yield: about 7 cups
Cook Time: 10 minutes

1. Place 3½ pounds of ground chicken, 1 teaspoon of coarse sea salt, and ¼ teaspoon of ground black pepper in a large sauté pan over medium heat. Cook, crumbling the meat as it cooks, for 7 to 10 minutes, until fully cooked through and slightly browned.

2. Transfer 4 cups of the cooked chicken to a container and label it "Burrito Bowls." Place the remaining cooked chicken (about 3 cups) in a separate container and label it "Lettuce Cups." Store in the refrigerator for use later in the week.

Slice the green onions

Thinly slice 10 to 12 green onions, or enough to equal ¾ cup. Set aside 2 tablespoons of the sliced onions for making the meatballs, which is your next task. Store the remainder of the sliced onions in the refrigerator for use later in the week, placing ½ cup in a container labeled "Lettuce Cups" and the rest, about 2 tablespoons, in a separate container labeled "Meatballs" (this portion will be used for garnish).

Make the meatballs

Prep Time: 15 minutes
Cook Time: 18 minutes

1½ pounds ground chicken

2 tablespoons sliced green onions
(from earlier in prep day)

1 tablespoon coconut aminos

¼ teaspoon fish sauce

¼ teaspoon coarse sea salt

¼ teaspoon ground black pepper

½ teaspoon garlic powder

1. Preheat the oven to 400°F. Line a rimmed baking sheet with parchment paper.

2. In a large mixing bowl, combine all of the ingredients with your hands.

3. Roll the meat mixture into 1-inch balls using either your hands or a 1-tablespoon scoop. Place the meatballs on the lined baking sheet.

4. Bake for 18 minutes, or until browned. Store in the refrigerator for use later in the week.

Cook the rice

Yield: 6 cups
Prep Time: 1 minute
Cook Time: about 20 minutes

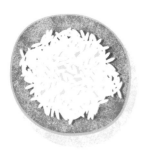

Cook 2 cups of white rice according to the package instructions. Divide the rice between two containers, putting 3 cups in each, then store in the refrigerator for use later in the week.

 PALEO/GRAIN-FREE RICE SUBSTITUTE
Make 1½ batches of Basic Cauliflower Rice (page 363), then follow the storage instructions for the white rice above.

Make the Sriracha-lime sauce

Prep Time: 3 minutes
Cook Time: 5 minutes

¼ cup Sriracha sauce

¼ cup fresh lime juice (about 2 limes)

¼ cup honey

2 tablespoons salted butter, ghee, or oil of choice

2 tablespoons coconut aminos

Pinch of coarse sea salt

Place all of the ingredients in a small saucepan over medium heat. Whisk until the butter is melted, then cook for 3 to 4 minutes, until the sauce comes to a light simmer. Store in the refrigerator for use later in the week.

Slice and dice the bell peppers

Remove the ribs and seeds from four red bell peppers. Slice two of the peppers into thin strips. Dice the other two.

Place the diced peppers in a container and label it "Lettuce Cups." Place the pepper strips in another container and label it "Burrito Bowls." Store in the refrigerator for use later in the week.

Slice the onion

Cut a yellow onion in half and thinly slice both halves. Store in the refrigerator for use later in the week.

Mince the garlic

Mince two cloves of garlic and store in the refrigerator for use later in the week.

Chop the cilantro

Wash and dry a small bunch of cilantro, then chop enough leaves and stems to equal ½ cup. Divide the chopped cilantro evenly between two containers, putting ¼ cup in each; label one container "Lettuce Cups" and the other "Burrito Bowls." Store in the refrigerator for use later in the week.

Wash and dry the lettuce leaves

Remove the leaves from a head of butter lettuce, then wash and dry them. Store in the refrigerator for use later in the week.

Curried Chicken Lettuce Cups

Yield: 4 servings   Prep Time: 5 minutes   Cook Time: 12 minutes

FOR THE CURRIED CHICKEN FILLING:

1 tablespoon ghee or avocado oil

2 red bell peppers, diced ✓

1 lime

2 cloves garlic, minced ✓

3 cups cooked ground chicken ✓

½ cup sliced green onions ✓

1 tablespoon curry powder

½ teaspoon ginger powder

½ teaspoon coarse sea salt

¼ cup chicken broth

1 tablespoon coconut aminos

¼ cup chopped fresh cilantro ✓

FOR SERVING:

½ lime

Butter lettuce leaves ✓

1. To make the chicken filling, heat the ghee in a large sauté pan over medium-high heat. Once hot, add the bell peppers and cook, stirring occasionally, for 3 to 4 minutes, until slightly browned.

2. Meanwhile, juice the lime and set aside.

3. Add the garlic to the pan with the bell peppers and cook for 30 seconds, or until fragrant.

4. Add the chicken, green onions, curry powder, ginger powder, and salt to the pan and stir to combine. Add the broth, coconut aminos, and lime juice and cook for 5 to 6 minutes, until the chicken is warmed through and the broth has evaporated. Meanwhile, cut ½ lime into wedges for serving.

5. Stir the cilantro into the chicken mixture, then remove from the heat. Spoon the chicken into the lettuce leaves and serve with lime wedges!

Firecracker Meatballs

Yield: 4 servings   Cook Time: 5 minutes

Precooked meatballs ✓

Sriracha-lime sauce ✓

3 cups cooked white rice or cauli-rice, for serving ✓

2 tablespoons sliced green onions, for garnish ✓

1. Place the meatballs and sauce in a large saucepan over medium heat and toss to coat. Cover and cook for 5 minutes, or until the meatballs are warmed through.

2. Meanwhile, reheat the rice either by placing it in a medium-sized saucepan, covered, over low heat for 5 minutes or by microwaving it for about 2 minutes, until hot.

3. Serve the meatballs alongside the rice and garnish with the sliced green onions.

Chicken Burrito Bowls

Yield: 5 servings   Prep Time: 5 minutes   Cook Time: 20 minutes

FOR THE PEPPER/ONION AND CHICKEN TOPPINGS:

1 tablespoon avocado oil

2 red bell peppers, sliced into thin strips ✓

1 yellow onion, thinly sliced ✓

1 teaspoon coarse sea salt, divided

4 cups cooked ground chicken ✓

¼ cup chicken broth

1 tablespoon fresh lime juice (about ½ lime)

2 teaspoons chili powder

1 teaspoon ground cumin

1 teaspoon dried oregano leaves

½ teaspoon garlic powder

FOR THE RICE:

3 cups cooked white rice or cauli-rice ✓

½ teaspoon coarse sea salt

1 tablespoon fresh lime juice (about ½ lime)

¼ cup chopped fresh cilantro ✓

FOR SERVING:

1 avocado

½ small red onion

1 lime

1. To make the pepper and onion topping, heat the oil in a large sauté pan over medium heat. Once hot, add the peppers and onion and season with ½ teaspoon of the salt. Cook, stirring occasionally, for 7 to 8 minutes, until the peppers and onion are limp and slightly browned.

2. Meanwhile, prepare the ingredients for serving: Slice the avocado, dice the red onion, and cut the lime into five wedges.

3. When the peppers and onion are done, remove them from the pan and set aside.

4. To make the chicken topping, add the chicken to the sauté pan along with the broth, lime juice, spices, and remaining ½ teaspoon of salt. Cook for 5 to 6 minutes, until the broth has evaporated, then remove from the heat.

5. Meanwhile, reheat the rice either by placing it in a medium-sized saucepan, covered, over low heat for 5 minutes or by microwaving it for about 2 minutes, until hot. Stir the salt, lime juice, and cilantro into the rice.

6. To assemble the burrito bowls, divide the rice among five bowls, then add the pepper/onion and chicken toppings. Garnish with the avocado slices and diced red onion and serve with lime wedges!

TURKEY BREAST TENDERLOINS, CHERRY TOMATOES, and YUKON GOLD POTATOES

This week shows how a few unlikely food pairings can work together beautifully in three delicious dinners. You're going to make Roasted Tomato Soup with Grilled Turkey and Cheese Sandwiches (SO GOOD), a Buffalo Turkey Casserole (a crowd favorite), and a Turkey Pizza Sheet Pan Dinner (one of my favorite SPDs ever). If you'd like to supplement this week's three main dinner recipes with two additional meals, see the suggested "Bonus Dinner Options" on the next page.

Weekly Ingredients

FRESH PRODUCE

Basil, 1 ounce

Bell pepper, green, ½

Cherry tomatoes, 2½ pints

Flat-leaf parsley, 8 sprigs

Garlic, 3 cloves

Green onions, 2

Onion, white, ½ medium

Sliced baby bella (aka cremini) mushrooms, 4 ounces

Yukon gold potatoes, 3 pounds

MEAT/DAIRY

Bacon, 6 strips

Butter, salted, 6 ounces (1½ sticks)

Cheddar cheese, white (or other semi-hard cheese of choice), 8 slices

Heavy cream, 2 fluid ounces (¼ cup)

Shredded mozzarella cheese, 4 ounces (1 cup)

Sliced pepperoni, 2 ounces

Turkey breast tenderloins, 5 pounds

PANTRY

Black olives, sliced, 2 tablespoons

Bread, gluten-free, 8 slices

Chicken broth, 8 fluid ounces (1 cup)

Extra-virgin olive oil, 2¼ fluid ounces (4½ tablespoons)

Medium-hot hot sauce, such as Frank's RedHot, 2½ fluid ounces (⅓ cup)

Ranch dressing, store-bought or homemade (page 372), 4 fluid ounces (½ cup)

SEASONINGS

Red pepper flakes, ½ teaspoon

Ingredient Subs

To make this week EGG-FREE:

· *Use an egg-free ranch dressing.*

Bonus Dinner Options

Dinner 1

Simple Seared Pork Chops
(page 349)

Roasted Asparagus
(page 360)

Roasted Carrots
(page 364)

Bonus Dinner Ingredients

Asparagus, fresh, 1 pound

Carrots, slender, 2 bunches (about 1 pound)

Extra-virgin olive oil, 2 tablespoons plus
1 teaspoon

Lemon, ½

Pork chops, boneless, 1 inch thick, 1½ pounds

Texas Grill Rub, 2 tablespoons (see page 374
for ingredients)

Dinner 2

Pan-Seared White Fish
(page 353)

Steamed Green Beans
(page 361)

Roasted Butternut Squash
Cubes
(page 366)

Bonus Dinner Ingredients

Butternut squash, 1 medium (about 2 pounds)

Extra-virgin olive oil, 3 tablespoons plus 2 teaspoons

Green beans, fresh, 1 pound

Lemon, 1

White fish fillets (such as snapper), 4 (6 ounces each)

Prep Day

Today's meal prep efforts are really straightforward! You're going to roast the turkey breast, bake the potatoes, roast the tomatoes, cook the bacon, and then prep a handful of fresh veggies. To start, I like to get the turkey in the oven. While the turkey roasts, I get the potatoes and tomatoes ready for the oven. Once the turkey comes out, I up the oven temperature to 400°F and then roast the potatoes and tomatoes at the same time. While those are in the oven, I cook the bacon on the stovetop, dice the onion, mince the garlic, and slice the bell pepper. When it is cool enough to handle, I slice one-third of the turkey breast and cut the rest into cubes.

note: *If you're planning to make homemade ranch dressing rather than use store-bought, I recommend that you add it to your prep day tasks so that it's ready for use later in the week. A half batch will be plenty for this week. To save myself a couple of steps, I purchase presliced mushrooms and preshredded mozzarella cheese; if you are using whole mushrooms and/ or block cheese, add the steps of cleaning and slicing the mushrooms and/or shredding the mozzarella to this week's tasks as well.*

Roast the turkey breast

Yield: 6 cups cubed cooked turkey; 1¼ pounds sliced cooked turkey

Prep Time: 10 minutes

Cook Time: 45 minutes

5 pounds turkey breast tenderloins

1 tablespoon extra-virgin olive oil

1 teaspoon coarse sea salt

¼ teaspoon ground black pepper

1. Preheat the oven to 375°F. Line a rimmed baking sheet with parchment paper.

2. Rub the turkey tenderloins with the olive oil and season with the salt and pepper, then place on the lined baking sheet.

3. Bake for 45 minutes, or until the juices run clear and a meat thermometer registers a temperature of 165°F when inserted in the thickest part of a tenderloin.

4. Let cool, then thinly slice one-third of the turkey and place in a container labeled "Sandwiches." Cut the remaining turkey into 1-inch cubes. Place 4 cups of the cubed turkey in a container labeled "Casserole" and the remaining 2 cups in a container labeled "SPD." Store in the refrigerator for use later in the week.

Roast the potatoes

Prep Time: 10 minutes

Cook Time: 50 minutes

3 pounds Yukon gold potatoes

1½ tablespoons extra-virgin olive oil

1 teaspoon coarse sea salt

1. If you are planning to roast the potatoes and tomatoes at the same time (my suggestion!), place one oven rack in the middle to top third of the oven (for the potatoes) and a second rack in the bottom third of the oven (for the tomatoes).

2. Preheat the oven to 400°F. Line a rimmed baking sheet with parchment paper.

3. Cut the potatoes into 1-inch cubes, then toss with the olive oil and salt. Spread the potatoes on the lined baking sheet.

4. Roast for 30 minutes, then flip the potatoes over and roast for an additional 20 to 30 minutes, until golden brown and easily pierced with a fork.

5. Store in the refrigerator for use later in the week.

Roast the tomatoes

Prep Time: 5 minutes

Cook Time: 35 minutes

2 pints cherry tomatoes

1 tablespoon extra-virgin olive oil

1 teaspoon coarse sea salt

1. Preheat the oven to 400°F. Line a rimmed baking sheet with parchment paper.

2. Toss the tomatoes with the olive oil and salt. Spread the tomatoes on the lined baking sheet.

3. Roast for 30 to 35 minutes, until the tomatoes are wrinkled and slightly browned. (*Note:* If roasting the tomatoes at the same time as the potatoes, slide them onto the rack below the potatoes.)

4. Store in the refrigerator for use later in the week.

Cook and chop or crumble the bacon

Prep Time: 3 minutes

Cook Time: 6 minutes

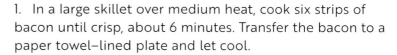

1. In a large skillet over medium heat, cook six strips of bacon until crisp, about 6 minutes. Transfer the bacon to a paper towel–lined plate and let cool.

2. When the bacon is cool enough to handle, chop or crumble it. (If you used thick-cut bacon, chopping it will be easier; if you used regular bacon, crumbling it will be easier.) Store in the refrigerator for use later in the week.

Dice the onion

Dice half of a medium-sized white onion, then store in the refrigerator for use later in the week.

Mince the garlic

Mince three cloves of garlic, then store in the refrigerator for use later in the week.

Slice the bell pepper

Cut half of a green bell pepper into thin strips. Store in the refrigerator for use later in the week.

Roasted Tomato Soup and Grilled Turkey and Cheese Sandwiches

Yield: 4 servings   Prep Time: 5 minutes   Cook Time: 15 minutes

FOR THE SOUP:

1 tablespoon extra-virgin olive oil

½ medium white onion, diced ✓

3 cloves garlic, minced ✓

⅓ cup fresh basil leaves, divided

Roasted cherry tomatoes (about 3 cups) ✓

1 cup chicken broth

¼ cup heavy cream

½ teaspoon coarse sea salt

¼ teaspoon ground black pepper

FOR THE SANDWICHES:

8 slices white cheddar cheese or other cheese of choice

Sliced roasted turkey breast ✓

8 slices gluten-free bread

8 tablespoons (1 stick) salted butter, softened

To make the soup:

1. Heat the olive oil in a medium-sized saucepan over medium-high heat. Once hot, add the onion and garlic. Sauté for 3 to 4 minutes, until the onion starts to brown and the garlic is fragrant.

2. Measure out ¼ cup of the basil leaves and tear each leaf in half, setting the rest aside for garnish. Add the torn basil leaves to the pan along with the remaining soup ingredients and stir to combine. Simmer for 1 to 2 minutes, then either blend in the pan with an immersion blender or transfer the soup to a blender and carefully blend until smooth.

3. Return the soup to the pan, then taste for seasoning and add more salt, if needed. Reduce the heat to low to keep the soup warm while you make the sandwiches.

To make the grilled cheese sandwiches:

1. Place a skillet large enough to fit at least two sandwiches over medium-low heat.

2. For each sandwich, layer a slice of cheese, one-quarter of the turkey, and another slice of cheese between two slices of bread.

3. Spread 1 tablespoon of butter on the outside of each slice of bread. Place two sandwiches in the skillet and cook for about 2 minutes, until the cheese is starting to melt and the bread is golden brown.

4. Carefully flip the sandwiches and cook for an additional 2 minutes, until the cheese is fully melted and the bread is golden brown. Repeat with the remaining bread, butter, cheese, and turkey to make two more sandwiches.

5. While the second set of sandwiches is toasting, cut the remaining basil into ribbons: Stack the leaves, then roll them up and thinly slice them.

6. Cut the sandwiches in half and serve alongside the hot tomato soup garnished with the sliced basil. Enjoy!

Buffalo Turkey Casserole

Yield: 6 servings   Prep Time: 10 minutes   Cook Time: 30 minutes

4 cups roasted potatoes ✓

⅓ cup medium-hot hot sauce

¼ cup (½ stick) salted butter, melted

4 cups cubed roasted turkey breast ✓

6 strips bacon, cooked and chopped or crumbled ✓

2 green onions, for garnish

Leaves from 8 sprigs flat-leaf parsley, for garnish

¼ cup ranch dressing, for serving

1. Preheat the oven to 350°F.

2. Spread the potatoes in a 3-quart casserole dish or 2½-quart Dutch oven.

3. In a large bowl, whisk together the hot sauce and melted butter. Add the turkey and toss to coat.

4. Layer the turkey and sauce on top of the potatoes in the casserole dish, then top with the bacon.

5. Bake the casserole for 30 minutes, until completely warmed through. While the casserole is in the oven, thinly slice the green onions and chop the parsley.

6. Remove the casserole from the oven and allow to cool slightly. Drizzle with the ranch dressing, then garnish with the sliced green onions and chopped parsley and serve!

Turkey Pizza Sheet Pan Dinner

Yield: 4 servings   Prep Time: 8 minutes   Cook Time: 20 minutes

2 cups cubed roasted turkey breast ✓

¼ cup ranch dressing

1 cup cherry tomatoes

2 cups roasted potatoes ✓

1 cup shredded mozzarella cheese

2 ounces sliced pepperoni

1 cup sliced mushrooms

2 tablespoons sliced black olives

½ green bell pepper, sliced ✓

½ teaspoon red pepper flakes, for garnish

1. Preheat the oven to 375°F. Line a rimmed baking sheet with parchment paper.

2. Toss the turkey with the ranch dressing, then spread the turkey on the lined baking sheet.

3. Cut the tomatoes in half and sprinkle them on top of the turkey. Follow with the potatoes and then the cheese. Layer the pepperoni, mushrooms, black olives, and bell pepper on top of the cheese.

4. Bake for 20 minutes, until the toppings are browned and the cheese is bubbly. Garnish with the red pepper flakes and serve!

08 LOW CARB P 🌾 🥛 🥚 🐚

GROUND BEEF, CARROTS, and RICE

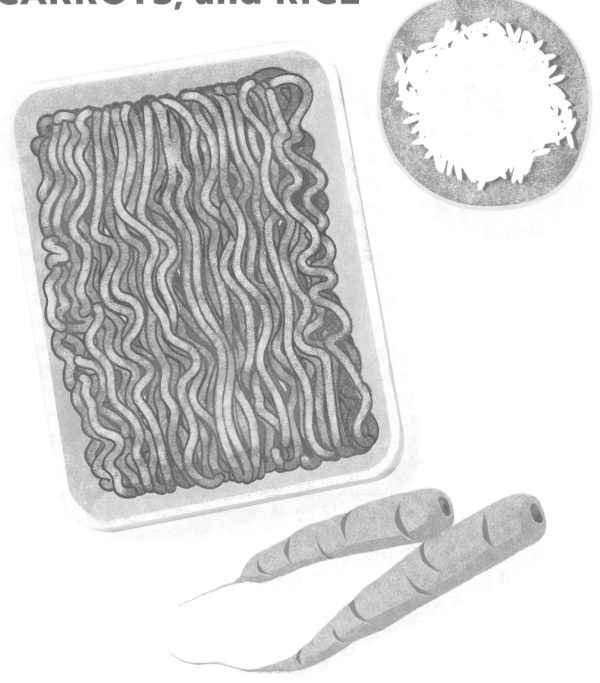

When I was developing the plan for this week, I wanted to reinvent the way we think about ground beef. With that in mind, I transformed ground beef, carrots, and rice into three craveable and compelling dinners that I just know you're going to love! Get ready for some BBQ Mini Meatloaves with the tastiest carrot fries, a flavor-packed Taco Casserole, and Korean Beef Bowls with a delicious Sriracha mayo and quick-pickled carrots. For those who want a low-carb or Paleo option, this week has you covered with some straightforward swaps. If you'd like to supplement this week's three main dinner recipes with two additional meals, see the suggested "Bonus Dinner Options" on the next page.

Weekly Ingredients

FRESH PRODUCE

Avocado, 1

Carrots, 1½ pounds

Cilantro, ⅓ bunch

Green onions, 1½ bunches (about 10 onions)

Jalapeño pepper, 1

Limes, 1½

Onion, red, 1 small

Romaine lettuce, ½ head

Tomato, 1

MEAT/EGGS

Bacon, 8 strips (about 9½ ounces)

Eggs, large, 5

Ground beef, 5 pounds

PANTRY

Avocado oil mayonnaise, store-bought or homemade (page 372), 4 fluid ounces (½ cup)

BBQ sauce, store-bought or homemade (page 373), 6 fluid ounces (¾ cup)

Coconut aminos, Coconut Secret brand, 1 (8-ounce) bottle

Extra-virgin olive oil, 1 tablespoon

Fish sauce, ½ teaspoon

Ghee or avocado oil, 1 tablespoon

Mild diced tomatoes and green chilis, 1 (10-ounce) can

Sriracha sauce, 2 tablespoons

Toasted sesame oil, 2 teaspoons

Unseasoned rice wine vinegar, 1 tablespoon

Vinegar, apple cider, white wine, or red wine, 16 fluid ounces (2 cups)

White rice, 20 ounces (3 cups)

SEASONINGS

Black peppercorns, 1 teaspoon

Chili powder, 1 tablespoon

Dried oregano leaves, 1 teaspoon

Dried parsley, 1 teaspoon

Garlic powder, 1½ teaspoons

Ginger powder, ½ teaspoon

Ground cumin, 1 teaspoon

Onion powder, 1 teaspoon

Red pepper flakes, ¼ teaspoon

Sesame seeds, 1 teaspoon

Ingredient Subs

To make this week LOW-CARB:

· *Use a low-carb BBQ sauce.*

· *Replace the white rice with 3 medium heads cauliflower (5 to 6 pounds total) or 3 (12-ounce) bags frozen riced cauliflower and add 3 tablespoons extra-virgin olive oil.*

· *Make the Low-Carb Teriyaki Sauce on page 373.*

To make this week PALEO:

· *Use the homemade BBQ sauce on page 373.*

· *Replace the white rice with 3 medium heads cauliflower (5 to 6 pounds total) or 3 (12-ounce) bags frozen riced cauliflower and add 3 tablespoons extra-virgin olive oil.*

To make this week GRAIN-FREE:

· *Replace the white rice with 3 medium heads cauliflower (5 to 6 pounds total) or 3 (12-ounce) bags frozen riced cauliflower and add 3 tablespoons extra-virgin olive oil.*

To make this week EGG-FREE:

· *Omit the eggs and substitute vegan mayo for the avocado oil mayonnaise.*

Bonus Dinner Options

Dinner 1

Lemon Pepper Chicken Breasts (page 347)

Braised Collards (page 358)

Baked Russet Potatoes (page 366)

Bonus Dinner Ingredients

Chicken breasts, boneless, skinless, 1½ pounds

Collard greens, 1 small bunch (about 1 pound)

Extra-virgin olive oil, 2 tablespoons

Lemons, 1½

Russet potatoes, 4 small to medium (about 1 pound)

Bonus Dinner Ingredient Subs

To make this meal low-carb:

Omit the potatoes.

Dinner 2

Jerk Pork Tenderloin (page 351)

Crispy Brussels Sprouts (page 356)

Pan-Fried Plantains (page 368)

Bonus Dinner Ingredients

Brussels sprouts, 12 ounces

Extra-virgin olive oil, 2½ fluid ounces (5 tablespoons)

Jerk Seasoning, 1 tablespoon (see page 375 for ingredients)

Lemon, 1

Plantains, yellow, 2 large (about 1 pound)

Pork tenderloin, 1 (1¼ pounds)

Bonus Dinner Ingredient Subs

To make this meal low-carb:

Omit the plantains.

Prep Day

Today you'll be prepping some components so that this week's dinners come together easily. I like to get the ground beef started first, and then I chop the carrots into fries and stick them in the oven. From there, I get the quick-pickled carrots in their mason jar and into the fridge, assemble the meatloaves (which are only assembled today, not baked), and get the rice cooking on the stove. While all of that is underway, I whip up the sauces for the Korean Beef Bowls and chop the veggies.

note: *If you're planning to make homemade mayonnaise rather than use store-bought, I recommend that you add it to your prep day tasks so that it's ready for use in the Sriracha mayo. If you're planning to make homemade BBQ sauce, add it to your list of tasks so that it's ready for use later in the week.*

Brown some of the ground beef

Yield: 8 scant cups

Cook Time: 15 minutes

1. Place 3½ pounds of ground beef and 1 teaspoon of coarse sea salt in a large skillet over medium heat. (You will add more seasoning later.) Cook for 10 to 15 minutes, crumbling the meat as it cooks, until fully browned. Let cool completely.

2. Once cool, drain the fat and divide the browned beef evenly between two containers, putting about 3¾ cups in each. Label one container "Casserole" and the other "Bowls." Store in the refrigerator for use later in the week.

Bake the carrot fries

Prep Time: 10 minutes

Cook Time: 30 minutes

1 pound carrots

1½ tablespoons extra-virgin olive oil

½ teaspoon coarse sea salt

1 teaspoon dried parsley

1. Preheat the oven to 400°F. Line a rimmed baking sheet with parchment paper.

2. Peel the carrots and slice off the tops and bottoms. Cut the carrots in half lengthwise, then slice them in half crosswise and cut each piece lengthwise into thirds. Each carrot fry should be about 3 inches long by ½ inch thick.

3. Place the carrots, olive oil, and salt on the lined baking sheet and toss to coat.

4. Bake for 30 minutes, flipping halfway through, until the fries are slightly wrinkled and browned. Remove from the oven and toss with the parsley.

5. Store in the refrigerator for use later in the week.

Pickle 8 ounces of carrots

Prep Time: 20 minutes, plus time to pickle

8 ounces carrots

2 cups apple cider vinegar, white wine vinegar, or red wine vinegar

2 teaspoons fine sea salt

1 teaspoon black peppercorns

1. Peel the carrots, then shave them into wide ribbons, discarding the cores. The easiest way to do so is to lay the carrots flat on a cutting board and peel them into thin strips down to the core.

2. In a glass bowl or 32-ounce mason jar, whisk together the vinegar, salt, and peppercorns. Add the carrots to the brine, toss or shake to coat the carrots in the brine, then cover and refrigerate. The pickled carrots are ready to eat after 1 day.

Assemble the BBQ mini meatloaves

1½ pounds ground beef

¾ cup BBQ sauce, divided

1 large egg

1 teaspoon garlic powder

1 teaspoon onion powder

½ teaspoon coarse sea salt

½ teaspoon ground black pepper

8 strips bacon, cut in half crosswise

1. Place the ground beef, ½ cup of the BBQ sauce, the egg, garlic powder, onion powder, salt, and pepper in a large bowl and work the ingredients with your hands until thoroughly combined.

2. Line a rimmed baking sheet with parchment paper, then shape the meat mixture into four small loaves. Brush the tops of the loaves with the remaining ¼ cup of BBQ sauce, then top each loaf with two half-strips of bacon.

3. Cover and refrigerate for use later in the week.

Cook the rice

Yield: 9 cups
Prep Time: 1 minute
Cook Time: about 20 minutes

Cook 3 cups of white rice according to the package instructions. Divide the rice evenly between two containers, putting about 4½ cups in each. Label one container "Casserole" and the other "Fried Rice." Store in the refrigerator for use later in the week.

LOW CARB · P · LOW-CARB/PALEO/GRAIN-FREE RICE SUBSTITUTE
Make a double batch of Basic Cauliflower Rice (page 363), then follow the storage instructions for the white rice above.

Make the sauce for the Korean Beef Bowls

Prep Time: 2 minutes

Cook Time: 10 minutes

1 (8-ounce) bottle coconut aminos

1 tablespoon unseasoned rice wine vinegar

2 teaspoons toasted sesame oil

½ teaspoon fish sauce

½ teaspoon garlic powder

½ teaspoon ginger powder

¼ teaspoon red pepper flakes

Place the coconut aminos in a medium-sized saucepan over medium heat. Cook, stirring occasionally, for 8 to 10 minutes, until it thickens enough to coat the back of a spoon. Remove from the heat, then stir in the remaining ingredients. Store in the refrigerator for use later in the week.

Make the Sriracha mayo

½ cup avocado oil mayonnaise or vegan mayo

1 tablespoon fresh lime juice (about ½ lime)

1 to 2 tablespoons Sriracha sauce, depending on heat preference

Place all of the ingredients in a bowl and whisk until fully combined. Store in the refrigerator for use later in the week.

Chop the cilantro

Wash one-third of a bunch of cilantro, thoroughly dry it, and coarsely chop it. You should get about ¼ cup of chopped cilantro. Store in the refrigerator for use later in the week.

Slice the lettuce

Cut half of a head of romaine lettuce lengthwise into two long pieces, then slice the pieces crosswise into ½-inch-thick strips, until you have about 1 cup of sliced lettuce. Store in the refrigerator for use later in the week.

Dice the tomato

Dice a tomato and store in the refrigerator for use later in the week.

Slice the jalapeño

Thinly slice a jalapeño pepper and store in the refrigerator for use later in the week.

Slice the onions

Thinly slice a small red onion. Thinly slice ten green onions, placing ½ cup in a container labeled "½ cup green onions" and the remainder (about 4 onions' worth) in a separate container labeled "4 green onions." Store the onions in the refrigerator for use later in the week.

BBQ Mini Meatloaves with Carrot Fries

Yield: 4 servings   Cook Time: 30 minutes

4 assembled BBQ mini
meatloaves ✓

Baked carrot fries ✓

1. Preheat the oven to 350°F.

2. Bake the mini meatloaves for 20 minutes. While the meatloaves are baking, line a rimmed baking sheet with parchment paper and spread out the carrot fries on the baking sheet.

3. After the meatloaves have cooked for 20 minutes, place the carrot fries in the oven on the bottom rack. Bake the meatloaves and fries for an additional 10 minutes, until the tops of the meatloaves are browned and the fries are warmed through. Remove from the oven and serve!

Taco Casserole

Yield: 6 servings   Prep Time: 5 minutes   Cook Time: 20 minutes

FOR THE RICE LAYER:

4½ cups cooked white rice or cauli-rice ✓

1 (10-ounce) can mild diced tomatoes and green chilis

¼ cup chopped fresh cilantro ✓

1 tablespoon fresh lime juice (about ½ lime)

1 teaspoon coarse sea salt

FOR THE BEEF LAYER:

3¾ cups cooked ground beef ✓

1 tablespoon chili powder

1 teaspoon ground cumin

1 teaspoon garlic powder

1 teaspoon onion powder

1 teaspoon dried oregano leaves

½ teaspoon coarse sea salt

TOPPINGS:

1 cup sliced romaine lettuce ✓

1 avocado

1 tomato, diced ✓

1 jalapeño pepper, thinly sliced ✓

1 red onion, thinly sliced ✓

1. Preheat the oven to 350°F.

2. Put all of the ingredients for the rice layer in a large bowl and mix to combine, then spread the mixture in an 8 by 11-inch or similar-sized baking dish.

3. Mix together the ingredients for the beef layer, then layer the beef mixture on top of the rice.

4. Bake for 20 minutes, until the casserole is hot and the beef is browned on top. While the casserole is baking, dice the avocado.

5. Remove the casserole from the oven, top it with the lettuce, avocado, tomato, jalapeño, and red onion, and serve!

Korean Beef Bowls

Yield: 5 servings   Prep Time: 5 minutes   Cook Time: 15 minutes

1½ tablespoons ghee or avocado oil, divided

3¾ cups cooked ground beef ✓

½ cup thinly sliced green onions ✓

Korean beef bowl sauce ✓

5 large eggs (omit for egg-free)

4½ cups cooked white rice or cauli-rice ✓

Pickled carrots ✓

FOR TOPPING THE BOWLS:

4 green onions, thinly sliced ✓

Sriracha mayo ✓

1 teaspoon sesame seeds

Red pepper flakes (optional)

1. Heat 1 tablespoon of the ghee in a large skillet over medium heat. Once hot, add the ground beef and green onions. Cook for 3 to 4 minutes, until the onions have wilted, then pour the Korean sauce over the beef mixture. Cook for an additional 4 to 5 minutes, until warmed through.

2. Meanwhile, fry the eggs: Heat the remaining ½ tablespoon of ghee in a large skillet over medium heat. Crack the eggs into the skillet and fry for about 4 minutes, or until done to your liking.

3. Reheat the rice either by placing it in a medium-sized saucepan, covered, over low heat for 5 minutes or by microwaving it for about 2 minutes, until hot.

4. To serve, divide the warmed rice, beef mixture, and pickled carrots evenly among five bowls. Top each bowl with a fried egg, some green onions, Sriracha mayo, sesame seeds, and a sprinkle of red pepper flakes, if using, and serve!

BAKED CHICKEN BREAST, KALE, and CORN

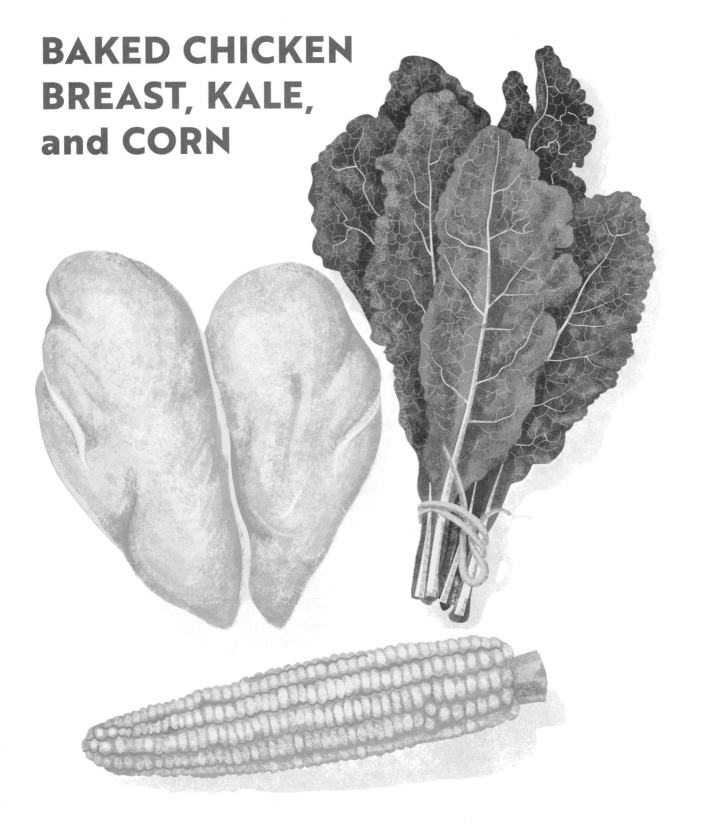

Though I have been known to whip up these recipes at just about any time of the year, I love to make this week of meals in summer when fresh corn is in season. When it's not in season, or if I find myself particularly short on time and in need of a shortcut, I use frozen corn. You're going to transform humble chicken breast, kale, and corn into three stunning dinners. First up is a Confetti Chicken Casserole (that my whole family loves), then we have Mexican Chicken and Corn Street Tacos (taco night!), and lastly a Green Goddess Salad made with kale. This week is entirely gluten-free, and I have included considerations for how to make it dairy-free as well! If you'd like to supplement this week's three main dinner recipes with two additional meals, see the suggested "Bonus Dinner Options" on the next page.

Weekly Ingredients

FRESH PRODUCE

Avocado, 1

Bell peppers, red, 2

Chives, 4

Corn, 6 large ears (or use 24 ounces frozen corn kernels)

Flat-leaf parsley, 1 small bunch

Garlic, 3 cloves

Green onion, 1 large

Lacinato (aka dinosaur) kale, 2 bunches

Lemon, 1 small

Limes, 2

Onion, red, 1

Tarragon, ¼ ounce

MEAT/DAIRY

Bacon, 10 strips (about 12 ounces)

Butter, salted, 2 tablespoons

Chicken breasts, boneless, skinless, 5 pounds

Cotija cheese, 1 ounce (¼ cup crumbled)

Shredded cheddar cheese, 2 ounces (½ cup)

Sour cream, 2 ounces (¼ cup)

PANTRY

Avocado oil mayonnaise, store-bought or homemade (page 372), 10 fluid ounces (1¼ cups)

Extra-virgin olive oil, 1 teaspoon

Corn tortillas, miniature (about 4½ inches in diameter), 12, or regular-size (about 6 inches in diameter), 8

SEASONINGS

Chili powder, ½ teaspoon

Chipotle chili powder, ¼ teaspoon

Garlic powder, ½ teaspoon

Paprika, ½ teaspoon

Ingredient Subs

To make this week DAIRY-FREE:

· *Replace the butter with avocado oil.*

· *Omit the cheeses.*

· *Substitute the cream from a can of full-fat coconut milk for the sour cream.*

Bonus Dinner Options

Dinner 1

Mocha Coffee Steak
(page 352)

Sautéed Bell Peppers
(page 361)

Baked Russet Potatoes
(page 366)

Bonus Dinner Ingredients

Bell peppers, red, 1 pound

Cocoa powder, 1 teaspoon

Extra-virgin olive oil, 2 tablespoons plus
2 teaspoons

Instant coffee powder, 1 teaspoon

Russet potatoes, 4 small to medium (about 1 pound)

Sirloin or rib-eye steaks, boneless, about 1 inch thick,
4 (4 to 6 ounces each)

Dinner 2

Simple Seared Pork Chops
(page 349)

Wilted Spinach
(page 358)

Basic White Rice
(page 368)

Bonus Dinner Ingredients

Extra-virgin olive oil,
3 tablespoons

Lemon, ½

Pork chops, boneless, about
1 inch thick, 1½ pounds

Spinach, fresh, 1 pound

Texas Grill Rub, 2 tablespoons
(see page 374 for ingredients)

White rice, 6½ ounces (1 cup)

Bonus Dinner Ingredient Subs

To make this meal PALEO and/or GRAIN-FREE:

Replace the white rice with 1 large head cauliflower (about 3 pounds) or 18 ounces frozen riced cauliflower; make Basic Cauliflower Rice (page 363) instead of the Basic White Rice.

Prep Day

This week's prep day is really straightforward! I like to start by getting the chicken into the oven. While the chicken is baking, I cook the corn. (Using frozen corn eliminates a task here.) From there, I cook the veggies for the Confetti Casserole and prep the kale. When the chicken comes out of the oven, I increase the oven temperature and then bake the bacon. Lastly, I whisk up the two dressings for the week, stashing them in the refrigerator as I go! Once the chicken is cool just enough so that I can handle it, I cut it up and store it in the refrigerator.

note: *If you're planning to make homemade mayonnaise rather than use store-bought, I recommend that you add it to your prep day tasks so that it's ready for use later in the day and later in the week. To save myself a step, I purchase preshredded cheddar cheese; if you are using block cheese, add the step of shredding the cheese to this week's tasks as well.*

Bake and cube the chicken

Yield: 10 cups

Prep Time: 5 minutes

Cook Time: 40 minutes

5 pounds boneless, skinless chicken breasts

1 tablespoon extra-virgin olive oil

1 teaspoon coarse sea salt

½ teaspoon ground black pepper

1. Preheat the oven to 375°F. Line a rimmed baking sheet with parchment paper.

2. Place the chicken on the lined baking sheet. Brush with the olive oil and sprinkle with the salt and pepper.

3. Bake for 40 minutes, until the chicken reaches an internal temperature of 165°F and the juices run clear when cut.

4. When cool enough to handle, cut the chicken into ½-inch cubes. Place 4 cups in a container and label it "Casserole." Place 3 cups in another container and label it "Tacos." Place the remaining 3 cups in a third container and label it "Salad." Store in the refrigerator for use later in the week.

Cook the ears of corn and remove the kernels

Yield: 4½ cups
Prep Time: 5 minutes
Cook Time: 5 minutes

Bring a large pot of water to a boil. Meanwhile, husk six ears of corn. When the water reaches a boil, add the corn. Boil for 5 minutes, then remove from the pot. Let the corn cool, then slice the kernels off of the cobs. Place 1 cup of the kernels in a container and label it "Salad"; put 1½ cups of kernels in another container and label it "Tacos"; and put the remaining kernels, about 2 cups, in a third container and label it "Casserole." Store in the refrigerator for use later in the week.

Prep the kale

Wash and dry two bunches of kale, then remove the stems from the leaves. Chop one bunch and place it in a container labeled "Salad." Slice the remaining kale leaves into ½-inch-wide strips. Put two-thirds of the sliced kale, about 2 cups, in a container and label it "Casserole"; put the remaining third, about 1 cup, in a separate container and label it "Tacos." Store in the refrigerator for use later in the week.

Prep and cook the Confetti Casserole veggies

Prep Time: 10 minutes
Cook Time: 6 minutes

1 red onion
2 red bell peppers
3 cloves garlic
1 teaspoon extra-virgin olive oil

1. Dice the onion and bell peppers, then mince the garlic.

2. Heat the olive oil in a large sauté pan over medium-high heat. When hot, add the onion, peppers, and garlic. Cook, stirring occasionally, for 5 to 6 minutes, until the vegetables are wilted and slightly browned.

3. Store in the refrigerator for use later in the week.

Cook and slice or crumble the bacon

Prep Time: 3 minutes
Cook Time: 18 minutes

1. Preheat the oven to 400°F.

2. Lay ten strips of bacon on a rimmed baking sheet and bake until crisp, 12 to 18 minutes. The total cooking time will depend on the thickness of your bacon.

3. Transfer the bacon to a paper towel–lined plate and let cool. When the bacon is cool enough to handle, slice six strips crosswise into ¼-inch pieces or crumble them. (If you used thick-cut bacon, slicing it will be easier; if you used regular bacon, crumbling it will be easier.) Place the sliced or crumbled bacon in a container and label it "Casserole." Slice or crumble the remaining four strips of bacon, place in a separate container, and label it "Salad." Store in the refrigerator for use later in the week.

Make the chipotle-lime dressing

¼ cup avocado oil mayonnaise

2 teaspoons fresh lime juice

¼ teaspoon chipotle chili powder

Place all of the ingredients in a bowl and whisk until fully combined. Transfer to a jar and seal the lid. Store in the refrigerator for use later in the week.

Make the green goddess dressing

½ cup fresh flat-leaf parsley (leaves and stems)

¼ cup fresh tarragon leaves

4 fresh chives

2 tablespoons fresh lemon juice (about 1 small lemon)

½ cup avocado oil mayonnaise

¼ cup sour cream or coconut cream

Place all of the ingredients in a blender and blend until smooth. Transfer to a jar and seal the lid. Store in the refrigerator for use later in the week.

Confetti Chicken Casserole

Yield: 6 servings   Prep Time: 5 minutes   Cook Time: 30 minutes

Cooked onion, bell peppers, and garlic ✓

2 cups cooked fresh corn kernels ✓ or frozen corn kernels

2 cups sliced kale ✓

4 cups cubed baked chicken breast ✓

½ cup avocado oil mayonnaise

1 teaspoon coarse sea salt

½ teaspoon ground black pepper

½ cup shredded cheddar cheese (omit for dairy-free)

6 strips bacon, cooked and sliced or crumbled ✓

1 large green onion, for garnish

1. Preheat the oven to 350°F.

2. In a large bowl, stir together the onion and bell pepper mixture, corn, kale, chicken, mayonnaise, salt, and pepper until combined.

3. Transfer the chicken mixture to a 3-quart rectangular casserole dish, then top with the cheese and bacon.

4. Bake for 30 minutes, until the cheese is browned and bubbling.

5. Meanwhile, slice the green onion and set aside.

6. Let the casserole cool slightly, then garnish with green onion and serve!

Mexican Chicken and Corn Street Tacos

Yield: 4 servings   Prep Time: 5 minutes   Cook Time: 14 minutes

FOR THE KALE SLAW:

1 cup sliced kale ✓

Chipotle-lime dressing ✓

FOR THE CHICKEN FILLING:

2 tablespoons salted butter or avocado oil

3 cups cubed baked chicken breast ✓

1½ cups cooked fresh corn kernels ✓ or frozen corn kernels

2 tablespoons fresh lime juice (about 1 lime)

1 teaspoon coarse sea salt

½ teaspoon chili powder

½ teaspoon garlic powder

½ teaspoon paprika

12 miniature corn tortillas, or 8 regular-size corn tortillas

¼ cup crumbled Cotija cheese (omit for dairy-free)

4 lime wedges, for serving

1. Make the slaw: In a small bowl, toss the kale with the chipotle-lime dressing until it is fully coated. Set aside.

2. Make the chicken filling: Melt the butter in a large skillet over medium-high heat. Once melted, add the chicken and corn and cook for 2 minutes to warm through.

3. Add the lime juice, salt, chili powder, garlic powder, and paprika and toss to coat the chicken and corn. Sauté for 3 to 4 minutes, until the chicken is slightly browned.

4. Place a small skillet over medium-high heat. Once hot, put one tortilla in the pan at a time and warm for about 30 seconds per side, until the tortilla is pliable and begins to brown slightly. Repeat with the remaining tortillas. To keep the tortillas warm while you are heating the remaining ones, you can wrap them in a kitchen towel.

5. To assemble the tacos, top the warmed tortillas with the kale slaw and chicken filling and garnish with the Cotija cheese. Serve with lime wedges.

Green Goddess Salad

Yield: 4 servings   Prep Time: 10 minutes

1 bunch Lacinato (aka dinosaur) kale, destemmed and chopped ✓

Green goddess dressing, divided ✓

1 avocado

1 cup cooked fresh corn kernels ✓ or frozen corn kernels, thawed

3 cups cubed baked chicken breast ✓

4 strips bacon, cooked and sliced or crumbled ✓

1. Toss the kale with ⅓ cup of the dressing until well coated.

2. Cube the avocado.

3. Divide the dressed kale among four plates. Top each serving evenly with the corn, chicken, avocado, and bacon. Serve with the remaining dressing on the side.

BRISKET,
BELL PEPPERS, and
RUSSET POTATOES

Hold on to your seat, my friend; this week is going to blow you away! Okay, maybe that's a slight exaggeration. But if you love food like I love food, I have a feeling you're going to love these dinners. Brisket is an often overlooked protein, but it's ideal for meal prepping because it usually yields a lot of food. You'll ride that wave this week by making use of brisket, bell peppers, and russet potatoes. These humble components are transformed into Philly Cheesesteak Loaded Fries (they're as good as they sound), Pepper Steak Stir-Fry (a killer recipe crafted by the Fed + Fit team's very own Amber Goulden), and Gyro Salad with Garlic Fries (So. Dang. Delicious.). If you'd like to supplement this week's three main dinner recipes with two additional meals, see the suggested "Bonus Dinner Options" on the next page.

Weekly Ingredients

FRESH PRODUCE

Bell peppers, green, 2

Bell peppers, red, 2

Cucumber, 1 medium

Garlic, 1 clove

Grape tomatoes, 5 ounces (about ½ pint or 1 cup)

Lemons, 2

Onion, red, ½ small

Onions, yellow, 2

Romaine lettuce, 1 head

Russet potatoes, 3 pounds

MEAT/DAIRY

Brisket, 1 (6 to 7 pounds)

Feta cheese, 1 ounce (¼ cup crumbled)

Greek yogurt, plain, full-fat, 6 ounces (¾ cup)

Provolone cheese, 8 or more slices

PANTRY

Arrowroot powder, 1 teaspoon

Avocado oil or other oil of choice, 2 tablespoons

Beef broth, 8 to 16 fluid ounces (1 to 2 cups, depending on brisket cooking method)

Chicken broth, 4 fluid ounces (½ cup)

Coconut aminos, Coconut Secret brand, 4 fluid ounces (½ cup)

Extra-virgin olive oil, 5¾ fluid ounces (½ cup plus 3½ tablespoons)

Kalamata olives, pitted, 3 ounces (½ cup)

Red wine vinegar, 2 fluid ounces (¼ cup)

Toasted sesame oil, 1 teaspoon

Unseasoned rice wine vinegar, 1½ teaspoons

White rice, 10 ounces (1½ cups)

SEASONINGS

Dried basil, 1 tablespoon

Dried oregano leaves, 1 tablespoon

Dried parsley, 2 teaspoons

Garlic powder, 2 teaspoons

Ginger powder, ½ teaspoon

Red pepper flakes, ½ teaspoon

Ingredient Subs

To make this week PALEO:

· Use the substitutions listed below for making the week grain-free and dairy-free.

To make this week GRAIN-FREE:

· Replace the white rice with 1 large head cauliflower (about 3 pounds) or 18 ounces frozen riced cauliflower and add 1 tablespoon extra-virgin olive oil.

To make this week DAIRY-FREE:

· Omit the cheeses.

· Substitute plain, unsweetened dairy-free Greek-style yogurt (such as Kite Hill brand) for the Greek yogurt.

Bonus Dinner Options

Dinner 1

Simple Seared Pork Chops
(page 349)

Roasted Cherry Tomatoes
(page 360)

Easy Baked Beets
(page 367)

Bonus Dinner Ingredients

Beets, 3 or 4 large

Cherry tomatoes, 2 pints

Dried thyme leaves, 1 teaspoon

Extra-virgin olive oil, 2 tablespoons plus
1 teaspoon

Pork chops, boneless, about 1 inch thick,
1½ pounds

Texas Grill Rub, 2 tablespoons (see page 374
for ingredients)

Dinner 2

Pan-Seared White Fish
(page 353)

Baked Okra
(page 359)

Pan-Fried Plantains
(page 368)

Bonus Dinner Ingredients

Extra-virgin olive oil, 2⅓ fluid ounces (¼ cup plus
2 teaspoons)

Lemon, 1

Okra, fresh, 1 pound

Plantains, yellow, 2 large (about 1 pound)

White fish fillets (such as snapper), 4 (6 ounces each)

Prep Day

Today in the kitchen you're going to prep a few strategic components so that your week of dinners comes together really quickly! I like to start with the brisket. You just trim it and then cook it. You'll slice it another day after it's cool and easier to handle. Once the brisket is cooking, I like to get the potatoes into the oven, put the rice on the stove, and start on the sauces. Once all those pots are simmering away, I prepare all of the fresh veggies.

Cook the brisket

Prep Time: 5 minutes

Cook Time: 1 hour 10 minutes to 8 hours, depending on method

1 (6- to 7-pound) brisket

1½ teaspoons coarse sea salt

1 tablespoon avocado oil (Instant Pot method only)

1 to 2 cups beef broth (depending on method)

1. Trim most of the excess fat off of the brisket, leaving a ¼-inch layer of fat. If using the Instant Pot method, cut the brisket into three equal pieces; otherwise, leave it whole. Rub the meat with the salt.

2. Cook the brisket using one of these three methods:

- **Oven Method** (Cook Time: 4½ to 5 hours)
  Preheat the oven to 275°F. Place the seasoned brisket in a roasting pan or 9 by 13-inch casserole dish. Add 1½ cups of beef broth to the pan, then cover with aluminum foil. Bake for 4½ to 5 hours, until the beef pulls apart easily with a fork.

- **Instant Pot Method** (Cook Time: 1 hour 25 minutes)
  Place the oil in a 6-quart Instant Pot and set to Sauté mode. Once the oil is hot, add the seasoned brisket to the pot in batches, searing the meat for 2 to 3 minutes per side, until browned. (If you're in a hurry, feel free to skip this step.) Once all of the beef is seared, return all of the pieces to the pot along with 1 cup of beef broth. Seal the lid onto the Instant Pot, press the Meat/Stew button, and set the timer for 70 minutes. Once the brisket is finished cooking, let the pressure release naturally until the lid opens easily, about 15 minutes.

- **Slow Cooker Method** (Cook Time: 4 or 8 hours)
  Place the seasoned brisket in a 6-quart slow cooker along with 2 cups of beef broth. Cook on low for 8 hours or on high for 4 hours, until the beef pulls apart easily with a fork.

3. Refrigerate the brisket whole (or in three pieces if cooked in an Instant Pot) overnight to make it easier to slice later in the week.

Bake the potato wedges

Prep Time: 10 minutes

Cook Time: 50 minutes

3 pounds russet potatoes, cut into ½-inch-thick wedges

1 tablespoon extra-virgin olive oil

1 teaspoon coarse sea salt

¼ teaspoon ground black pepper

1. Preheat the oven to 400°F. Line a rimmed baking sheet with parchment paper.

2. Place the potato wedges, olive oil, salt, and pepper in a medium-sized bowl and toss to coat. Spread the potato wedges on the lined baking sheet so that they're not touching. (You may need to use two baking sheets to ensure there's no overlap.)

3. Bake for 30 minutes, then turn the potatoes over and bake for an additional 15 to 20 minutes, until cooked through and golden brown.

4. Store in the refrigerator for use later in the week.

Cook the rice

Yield: 4½ cups

Prep Time: 1 minute

Cook Time: about 20 minutes

Cook 1½ cups of white rice according to the package instructions. Store in the refrigerator for use later in the week.

  PALEO/GRAIN-FREE RICE SUBSTITUTE
Make a batch of Basic Cauliflower Rice (page 363), then follow the storage instructions for the white rice above.

Make the stir-fry sauce

Prep Time: 5 minutes

Cook Time: 7 minutes

½ cup chicken broth

½ cup coconut aminos

1½ teaspoons unseasoned rice wine vinegar

1 teaspoon toasted sesame oil

½ teaspoon garlic powder

½ teaspoon ginger powder

½ teaspoon red pepper flakes

1 teaspoon arrowroot powder

Coarse sea salt

1. Place all of the ingredients, except for the arrowroot powder and salt, in a small saucepan. Bring to a simmer over medium heat, then cook for 5 minutes more, until the sauce is slightly reduced.

2. In a small bowl, whisk together the arrowroot powder and 1 tablespoon of water, then whisk this mixture into the sauce. Bring the sauce to a boil, stir, then taste for seasoning and add salt, if needed.

3. Store in the refrigerator for use later in the week.

Make the Greek dressing

¼ cup fresh lemon juice (about 2 lemons)

¼ cup red wine vinegar

½ cup extra-virgin olive oil

½ teaspoon fine sea salt

1 tablespoon dried basil

1 tablespoon dried oregano leaves

½ teaspoon garlic powder

½ teaspoon ground black pepper

1. Place the lemon juice and vinegar in a medium-sized bowl. Slowly drizzle in the olive oil while whisking constantly. Once combined, whisk in the seasonings.

2. Pour the dressing into a jar, seal the lid, and store in the refrigerator for use later in the week. Shake before using.

Sauté the bell peppers and yellow onions

Prep Time: 10 minutes

Cook Time: 15 minutes

2 green bell peppers

2 red bell peppers

2 yellow onions

1 tablespoon avocado oil

½ teaspoon coarse sea salt

1. Thinly slice the bell peppers and onions.

2. Heat the oil in a large skillet over medium heat. Once hot, add the bell peppers, onions, and salt. Sauté for 12 to 15 minutes, until the vegetables are slightly browned and cooked through.

3. Store in the refrigerator for use later in the week.

Chop the lettuce

Chop a head of romaine lettuce and store in the refrigerator for use later in the week.

Dice the cucumber

Cut two-thirds of a medium-sized cucumber into ½-inch dice, to make 1 cup of diced cucumbers. Store the diced cucumbers and remaining one-third of the cucumber in the refrigerator for use later in the week.

Halve the olives

Halve 3 ounces of pitted Kalamata olives, then store in the refrigerator for use later in the week.

Thinly slice the red onion

Thinly slice half of a small red onion, then store in the refrigerator for use later in the week.

Philly Cheesesteak Loaded Fries

Yield: 5 servings   Prep Time: 5 minutes   Cook Time: 15 minutes

Two-thirds of the roasted potato wedges ✓

1 tablespoon extra-virgin olive oil, divided

One-third of the cooked brisket, thinly sliced (about 3 cups) ✓

1 teaspoon coarse sea salt

½ teaspoon ground black pepper

½ teaspoon garlic powder

Half of the sautéed bell peppers and yellow onions ✓

8 slices provolone cheese (omit for Paleo/dairy-free)

1 teaspoon dried parsley, for garnish

1. Preheat the oven to 400°F.

2. Place the potato wedges and 1½ teaspoons of the olive oil in a medium-sized bowl and toss to coat. Spread the potato wedges on a rimmed baking sheet.

3. In another medium-sized bowl, toss the brisket with the remaining oil, salt, pepper, and garlic powder. Arrange the seasoned beef on top of the fries.

4. Spread the peppers and onions on top of the beef, then top with the cheese.

5. Bake for 15 minutes, until the cheese is browned and bubbling. Sprinkle with the dried parsley and serve!

Pepper Steak Stir-Fry

Yield: 5 servings   Prep Time: 3 minutes   Cook Time: 10 minutes

1 tablespoon extra-virgin olive oil or other oil of choice

One-third of the cooked brisket, thinly sliced (about 3 cups) ✓

Half of the sautéed bell peppers and yellow onions ✓

Stir-fry sauce ✓

4½ cups cooked white rice or cauli-rice, for serving ✓

1. Heat a large wok or sauté pan over medium-high heat. Once hot, pour in the oil and swirl it around the pan. Add the brisket and cook for 2 to 3 minutes, then flip and cook for an additional 2 to 3 minutes, until warmed through and slightly crispy.

2. Add the sautéed peppers and onions to the pan and stir to combine with the beef. Pour the sauce over the beef mixture and cook for 3 to 4 minutes, until completely warmed through.

3. While the stir-fry is warming, reheat the rice, either by placing it in a medium-sized saucepan, covered, over low heat for 5 minutes or by microwaving it for about 2 minutes, until hot.

4. Plate the stir-fry with the rice and serve!

Gyro Salad with Garlic Potato Wedges

Yield: 4 servings   Prep Time: 10 minutes   Cook Time: 10 minutes

One-third of the baked potato wedges ✓

1½ teaspoons extra-virgin olive oil

½ teaspoon garlic powder

One-third of cooked brisket, thinly sliced (about 3 cups) ✓

Greek dressing, divided ✓

1 head romaine lettuce, chopped ✓

1 cup diced cucumbers ✓

½ cup halved Kalamata olives ✓

¼ red onion, sliced ✓

¼ cup crumbled feta cheese (omit for Paleo/dairy-free)

1 cup grape tomatoes (optional)

FOR THE TZATZIKI:

⅓ cucumber

¾ cup plain full-fat Greek yogurt or dairy-free Greek-style yogurt

1 clove garlic, grated

Pinch of fine sea salt

1. Preheat the oven to 400°F.

2. Toss the potato wedges with the olive oil and garlic powder and lay on one-half of a rimmed baking sheet.

3. Toss the brisket with one-third of the Greek dressing, then lay the beef on the other half of the baking sheet. Bake the potatoes and brisket for 10 minutes, until warmed through and slightly browned.

4. While the potatoes and beef are baking, make the salad: Put the lettuce, diced cucumbers, olives, red onion, and feta in a large serving bowl. If using grape tomatoes, slice them in half and add them to the bowl. Toss the salad and set aside.

5. To make the tzatziki, peel and shred the cucumber, then roll it up in a dish towel or cheesecloth and squeeze until all of the moisture is released. Place the drained cucumber in a small bowl along with the yogurt, garlic, and salt. Stir to combine and set aside.

6. When the potatoes and beef are finished baking, place them on top of the salad, then drizzle with the remaining dressing. Serve with the tzatziki for dipping!

ROASTED CHICKEN, GREEN BEANS, and YUKON GOLD POTATOES

This week, you're going to transform the humble roasted chicken, green beans, and Yukon gold potatoes into three flavorful all-star dishes. First up is a Chicken Bacon Ranch Casserole, which I have a hunch you're going to love. Next is a Lemon Ginger Chicken Stir-Fry, and then a delicious Chicken Vesuvio rounds out our trio of dinners. If you'd like to supplement this week's three main dinner recipes with two additional meals, see the suggested "Bonus Dinner Options" on the next page.

Weekly Ingredients

FRESH PRODUCE

Chives, 3 (optional)

Flat-leaf parsley, 8 sprigs

Garlic, 6 cloves

Green beans, 1 pound

Lemons, 2 medium and 2 small

Onion, yellow, 1

Yukon gold potatoes, 4 pounds

FROZEN FOODS

Peas, 2½ ounces (½ cup)

MEAT/DAIRY

Bacon, 8 strips (about 9½ ounces)

Butter, salted, 3½ ounces (7 tablespoons)

Chickens, whole, 2 (4 to 5 pounds each)

Whole milk, 2⅔ fluid ounces (⅓ cup)

PANTRY

Arrowroot powder, 1 tablespoon

Avocado oil, 2 fluid ounces (¼ cup)

Chicken broth, 12 fluid ounces (1½ cups)

Coconut aminos, Coconut Secret brand, 1 tablespoon

Coconut sugar, 2½ tablespoons

Extra-virgin olive oil, 3 tablespoons

Pork rinds, 1 (2½-ounce) package

Ranch dressing, store-bought or homemade (page 372), 8 fluid ounces (1 cup)

White wine, 8 fluid ounces (1 cup)

SEASONINGS

Garlic powder, ½ teaspoon

Ginger powder, ½ teaspoon

Sesame seeds, 1 teaspoon

Ingredient Subs

To make this week PALEO and/or DAIRY-FREE:

· *Substitute ghee, avocado oil, or other fat of choice for the butter.*

· *Use full-fat coconut milk in place of the whole milk.*

· *Use a dairy-free ranch dressing.*

To make this week EGG-FREE:

· *Use an egg-free ranch dressing. If making homemade, use vegan mayo.*

Bonus Dinner Options

Dinner 1

Simple Seared Pork Chops
(page 349)

Baked Okra
(page 359)

Basic Polenta
(page 369)

Bonus Dinner Ingredients

Chicken broth, 20 fluid ounces
(2½ cups)

Extra-virgin olive oil,
3 tablespoons plus 2 teaspoons

Okra, fresh, 1 pound

Polenta meal or corn grits,
4 ounces (¾ cup)

Pork chops, boneless, about
1 inch thick, 1½ pounds

Texas Grill Rub, 2 tablespoons
(see page 374 for ingredients)

Bonus Dinner Ingredient Subs

To make this meal PALEO and/or GRAIN-FREE:

Replace the polenta meal (or corn grits) with 1 large head cauliflower (about 3 pounds) or 18 ounces frozen riced cauliflower, omit the chicken broth, and reduce the total amount of olive oil by 1 tablespoon; make Basic Cauliflower Rice (page 363) instead of the Basic Polenta.

Dinner 2

Mocha Coffee Steak
(page 352)

Roasted Broccoli
(page 357)

Easy Baked Beets
(page 367)

Bonus Dinner Ingredients

Beets, 3 or 4 large

Broccoli, fresh, 2 medium to large heads

Cocoa powder, 1 teaspoon

Dried thyme leaves, 1 teaspoon

Extra-virgin olive oil, 3 tablespoons plus 2 teaspoons

Garlic powder, ½ teaspoon

Instant coffee powder, 1 teaspoon

Sirloin or rib-eye steaks, boneless, about 1 inch thick,
4 (4 to 6 ounces each)

Prep Day

Today you will be roasting chickens, cooking potatoes (in two ways), cooking bacon, making the lemon-ginger sauce, prepping some veggies, and assembling the casserole. I find it most efficient to get the chickens and designated portion of the potatoes into the oven first since they can roast at the same temperature. Then I start on the mashed potatoes. Once the potatoes are boiling, I cook and then slice or crumble the bacon. By the time the bacon is finished, I can mash the boiled potatoes. While the roasted chickens and potatoes cool, I prepare the sauce, crush the pork rinds, cut up the green beans, and slice the onion and garlic. Once the chickens are cool enough to handle, I can break them down. Lastly, I assemble the casserole using the components prepped earlier in the day.

note: *If you're planning to make homemade ranch dressing rather than use store-bought, I recommend that you add it to your prep day tasks so that it's ready for use later in the week. You'll need a half batch.*

Roast and break down the chickens

Yield: 6 cups cubed breast meat, 4 leg quarters, 4 wings
Prep Time: 15 minutes
Cook Time: 1 hour 15 minutes

2 (4- to 5-pound) whole chickens

2 tablespoons extra-virgin olive oil

2 teaspoons coarse sea salt

1 teaspoon ground black pepper

1. If you are planning to roast the chickens and potatoes at the same time (my suggestion!), place one oven rack in the middle of the oven (for the chickens) and a second rack in the bottom third of the oven (for the potatoes).

2. Preheat the oven to 375°F. Line a rimmed baking sheet with parchment paper.

3. Place the chickens on the lined baking sheet and pat dry with paper towels. Rub the chickens with the oil, then season all over with the salt and pepper.

4. Bake for 1 hour 15 minutes, until a thermometer inserted into the thickest part of a chicken breast registers 165°F.

5. Let cool for at least 30 minutes, then separate the breasts from the bones of both chickens. Cut the breasts into ½-inch cubes, discarding the skin. Set aside half of the chicken breast (about 3 cups) for use later in the prep day, then place the other half in a container labeled "Stir-Fry" and store in the refrigerator for use later in the week.

6. Cut the leg quarters and wings from both chickens, place in a container labeled "Vesuvio," and store in the refrigerator for use later in the week.

Roast 1½ pounds of potatoes

Prep Time: 10 minutes
Cook Time: 45 minutes

1½ pounds Yukon gold potatoes

1 tablespoon extra-virgin olive oil

1 teaspoon coarse sea salt

1. Preheat the oven to 375°F. (If you are planning to roast the potatoes along with the chickens, the oven will already be hot.) Line a rimmed baking sheet with parchment paper.

2. Scrub the potatoes, then cut them into ½-inch cubes. Place the potatoes on the lined baking sheet and toss with the oil and salt.

3. Roast the potatoes on the lower rack of the oven for 1 hour, until browned. Remove from the oven, leaving the chickens in to roast for another 15 minutes.

4. Store in the refrigerator for use later in the week.

Cook and mash 2½ pounds of potatoes

Prep Time: 15 minutes
Cook Time: 20 minutes

2½ pounds Yukon gold potatoes

5 tablespoons salted butter, ghee, avocado oil, or other fat of choice

⅓ cup whole milk or full-fat coconut milk

1 to 1½ teaspoons coarse sea salt

½ teaspoon ground black pepper

½ teaspoon garlic powder

1. Place the potatoes in a large pot and cover with water. Bring to a boil over high heat, then reduce the heat and simmer for 15 to 20 minutes, until the potatoes are easily pierced with a fork.

2. Drain the potatoes and place them in a large bowl with the butter, milk, 1 teaspoon of salt, pepper, and garlic powder. Using a potato masher, mash until the ingredients are well incorporated and the potatoes are smooth. Taste for seasoning and add up to ½ teaspoon more salt, if desired.

3. Set aside for use later in the prep day.

Cook and slice or crumble the bacon

Prep Time: 3 minutes
Cook Time: 6 minutes

1. In a large skillet over medium heat, cook eight strips of bacon until crisp, about 6 minutes. Transfer the bacon to a paper towel–lined plate and let cool.

2. When the bacon is cool enough to handle, slice it crosswise into ¼-inch pieces or crumble it. (If you used thick-cut bacon, chopping it will be easier; if you used regular bacon, crumbling it will be easier.) Set aside for use later in the prep day.

Make the lemon-ginger sauce

Prep Time: 5 minutes

Cook Time: 5 minutes

1 cup chicken broth

¼ cup fresh lemon juice (about 2 lemons)

2½ tablespoons coconut sugar

1 tablespoon coconut aminos

½ teaspoon coarse sea salt

½ teaspoon ginger powder

1 tablespoon arrowroot powder

1. Place 1 cup of water, the broth, lemon juice, coconut sugar, coconut aminos, salt, and ginger powder in a small saucepan over medium heat. Cook for 1 minute, or until the sugar has dissolved.

2. In a small bowl, mix together the arrowroot powder and 2 tablespoons of water, then stir the mixture into the lemon sauce.

3. Bring the sauce to a boil, then continue to boil for 1 minute to thicken it, watching carefully to make sure the sauce doesn't spill over. Whisk the sauce and remove from the heat.

4. Store in the refrigerator for use later in the week.

Crush the pork rinds

Crush a 2½-ounce package of pork rinds until they have the texture of breadcrumbs. You can either pour the pork rinds into a gallon-sized plastic bag and crush them by hand or place them in a food processor and pulse until they're crushed. You should get about 1 cup of crushed pork rinds. Transfer to a container and store on the counter or in the pantry for use later in the week.

Cut the green beans

Trim the ends off of 1 pound of green beans.

Place 8 ounces of the green beans in a container labeled "Stir-Fry." Cut the remaining 8 ounces of green beans into 1-inch pieces, then place in a container labeled "Vesuvio." Store in the refrigerator for use later in the week.

Slice the onion and garlic

Thinly slice a yellow onion and six cloves of garlic. Store in the refrigerator for use later in the week.

Assemble the casserole

Mashed potatoes *(from earlier in prep day)*

Half of the cubed roasted chicken breast (about 3 cups) *(from earlier in prep day)*

1 cup ranch dressing

8 strips bacon, cooked and sliced or crumbled *(from earlier in prep day)*

1. Spread the mashed potatoes in an 8-inch square casserole dish.

2. In a medium-sized bowl, toss the chicken with the ranch dressing, then spread on top of the mashed potatoes.

3. Layer the bacon over the chicken, then cover either with the lid or with aluminum foil and store in the refrigerator for use later in the week.

Chicken Bacon Ranch Casserole

Yield: 6 servings   Prep Time: 1 minute   Cook Time: 30 minutes

1 (2½-ounce) package pork rinds, crushed (about 1 cup) ✓

Assembled, unbaked Chicken Bacon Ranch Casserole ✓

1 tablespoon snipped fresh chives, for garnish (optional)

1. Preheat the oven to 350°F.

2. Sprinkle the crushed pork rinds over the top of the casserole.

3. Bake for 30 minutes, until the casserole is warmed through and the top is slightly browned. Garnish with the snipped chives, if using.

Lemon Ginger Chicken Stir-Fry

Yield: 4 servings   Prep Time: 2 minutes   Cook Time: 12 minutes

2 tablespoons avocado oil

8 ounces green beans, trimmed ✓

Half of the cubed roasted chicken breast (about 3 cups) ✓

Lemon-ginger sauce ✓

1 teaspoon sesame seeds, for garnish

½ small lemon, cut into wedges, for garnish

1. Heat the oil in a large sauté pan or wok over medium-high heat. Once hot, add the green beans and stir-fry for 3 to 4 minutes, until bright green and crisp-tender. Remove the beans from the pan and set aside.

2. Add the chicken to the pan and cook, stirring occasionally, for 4 to 5 minutes, until warmed through and slightly browned.

3. Return the green beans to the pan with the chicken, then pour the sauce over the beans and chicken and stir to combine. Cook for 1 to 2 minutes, until the sauce is warmed, then remove from the heat.

4. Garnish with the sesame seeds and serve with lemon wedges.

Chicken Vesuvio

Yield: 4 servings   Prep Time: 8 minutes   Cook Time: 20 minutes

2 tablespoons avocado oil, divided

6 cloves garlic, thinly sliced ✓

1 cup white wine

½ cup chicken broth

4 roasted chicken leg quarters ✓

4 roasted chicken wings ✓

1 yellow onion, thinly sliced ✓

8 ounces green beans, cut into 1-inch pieces ✓

Roasted potatoes ✓

½ cup frozen peas

1 teaspoon coarse sea salt

¼ teaspoon ground black pepper

2 tablespoons salted butter

2 tablespoons fresh lemon juice (about 1 small lemon)

½ small lemon, thinly sliced, for garnish

2 tablespoons chopped fresh parsley, for garnish

1. Heat 1 teaspoon of the oil in a medium-sized saucepan over medium heat. Once hot, add the garlic and cook for 30 seconds to 1 minute, until browned. Add the white wine and broth and bring to a simmer. Continue to simmer for 5 minutes, until reduced slightly, then remove the pan from the heat. Meanwhile, recrisp the chicken and cook/reheat the vegetables.

2. Heat the remaining 1 tablespoon plus 2 teaspoons of oil in a large cast-iron skillet or heavy sauté pan over medium-high heat. Sear the chicken pieces, skin side down, for 5 to 7 minutes, or until crisp. If the chicken skin sticks to the pan, add more oil as needed to prevent sticking. Remove the chicken from the pan and set aside.

3. Add the onion to the cast-iron skillet and cook for 3 minutes, or until translucent. Then add the green beans, potatoes, peas, salt, and pepper and toss to combine.

4. Whisk the butter and lemon juice into the thickened wine and garlic sauce, then pour it over the green bean and potato mixture. Nestle the chicken into the pan, skin side up, and reduce the heat to medium. Cook for 5 minutes, until everything is fully reheated and the sauce is bubbling.

5. Garnish with the lemon slices and parsley, then serve!

SHREDDED BEEF, COLLARD GREENS, and ACORN SQUASH

This week, you're going to transform versatile shredded beef, nutrient-dense collard greens, and comforting acorn squash into three delicious dinners. The recipes include a Rustic Beef–Stuffed Acorn Squash, Italian Beef Rolls with Vodka Sauce (one of my favorite dishes in the whole book), and a Red Curry Acorn Squash Soup with Crispy Beef. If you'd like to supplement this week's three main dinner recipes with two additional meals, see the suggested "Bonus Dinner Options" on the next page.

Weekly Ingredients

FRESH PRODUCE

Acorn squash, 4 medium

Basil, 1 ounce

Cilantro, 10 sprigs

Collard greens, 2 bunches

Cranberries, 4 ounces (1 cup) (or use frozen cranberries)

Lemons, 1½

Limes, 2

Onions, yellow, 3 large

Thyme, 4 sprigs

MEAT/DAIRY

Butter, salted, 2 tablespoons

Chuck roast, 1 (5 to 6 pounds)

Heavy cream, 4 fluid ounces (½ cup)

Shredded Parmesan cheese, 1½ ounces (½ cup)

PANTRY

Avocado oil mayonnaise, store-bought or homemade (page 372), 4 fluid ounces (½ cup)

Chicken broth, 8 fluid ounces (1 cup)

Coconut aminos, Coconut Secret brand, 1 tablespoon

Coconut milk, full-fat, 8 fluid ounces (1 cup)

Crushed tomatoes, 1 (28-ounce) can

Extra-virgin olive oil, 1½ tablespoons

Ghee, 2 tablespoons

Red curry paste, 1 (4-ounce) jar

Vodka, 4 fluid ounces (½ cup)

SEASONINGS

Garlic powder, ¾ teaspoon

Ginger powder, ¼ teaspoon

Italian seasoning, 1 teaspoon

Red pepper flakes, ¼ teaspoon

Ingredient Subs

To make this week PALEO and/or DAIRY-FREE:

· *Substitute ghee or another fat for the butter.*

· *Use canned full-fat coconut milk in place of the heavy cream.*

· *Omit the Parmesan cheese.*

To make this week EGG-FREE:

· *Use vegan mayo in place of egg-based mayonnaise.*

Bonus Dinner Options

Dinner 1

Seared Chicken Breasts
(page 346)

Crispy Brussels Sprouts
(page 356)

Roasted Butternut Squash
Cubes (page 366)

Bonus Dinner Ingredients

Brussels sprouts, fresh, 12 ounces

Butternut squash, 1 medium (about 2 pounds)

Chicken breasts, boneless, skinless, 1½ pounds

Extra-virgin olive oil, 3 tablespoons

Lemon, 1

Texas Grill Rub, 2 tablespoons (see page 374
for ingredients)

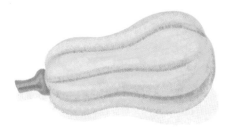

Dinner 2

Pan-Seared Salmon
(page 355)

Roasted Asparagus
(page 360)

Easy Baked Beets
(page 367)

Bonus Dinner Ingredients

Asparagus, fresh, 1 pound

Beets, 3 or 4 large

Dried thyme leaves, 1 teaspoon

Extra-virgin olive oil, 2 tablespoons plus 1 teaspoon

Salmon fillets, 4 (6 ounces each)

Prep Day

Today you're going to make the shredded beef, roast the squash, caramelize the onions, make the vodka sauce (yum), prep the collard greens, and then quickly whip up the lemon-thyme cream sauce. Because I want to spend as little time prepping as possible, I opt for the Instant Pot method to cook the beef. This keeps my oven free so that I can start roasting the squash at the same time. While the beef and squash cook, I start on the onions. Fabulous caramelized onions take time, so I try to get those cooking as soon as possible on prep day. Next, I make the vodka sauce (you're going to want to pour it over everything), and then I prep the collards. Lastly, I whisk together the cream sauce. Once the beef is cooked, I shred it with two forks.

note: *If you're planning to make homemade mayonnaise rather than use store-bought, I recommend that you add it to your prep day tasks so that it's ready for use in the cream sauce later in the day. To save myself a step, I purchase preshredded Parmesan cheese; if you are using block cheese, add the step of shredding the Parmesan to today's tasks as well.*

Cook and shred the beef

Yield: 10 cups

Prep Time: 10 minutes

Cook Time: 1 to 8 hours, depending on method

1. If using the Instant Pot method, cut a 5- to 6-pound chuck roast into three or four equal pieces; otherwise, leave it whole. Season the meat with 1½ teaspoons of coarse sea salt.

2. Cook the roast using one of these three methods:

- **Oven Method** (Cook Time: 4 to 5 hours)
  Preheat the oven to 325°F. Place the seasoned roast in a Dutch oven or other large oven-safe pot with a lid along with 2 cups of water. Bake, covered, for 4 to 5 hours, until the meat pulls apart easily with a fork.

- **Instant Pot Method** (Cook Time: 1½ hours)
  Place the seasoned pieces of beef in a 6-quart Instant Pot along with ½ cup of water. Seal the lid onto the pot, press the Meat/Stew button, and set the timer for 60 minutes. When the timer goes off, allow the pressure to release naturally (meaning, do not manually move the pressure release knob). This should take about 30 minutes; the lid will automatically unlock when the pressure is fully released.

- **Slow Cooker Method** (Cook Time: 4 to 8 hours)
  Place the seasoned roast in a 6-quart slow cooker along with 1 cup of water. Cover and cook on low for 6 to 8 hours or on high for 4 hours, until the meat easily pulls apart.

3. Transfer the cooked beef to a bowl and shred with two forks. Place 4 cups in a container labeled "Stuffed Squash," 3 cups in a container labeled "Beef Rolls," and the remaining 3 cups in a container labeled "Soup." Store in the refrigerator for use later in the week.

Roast the squash

Prep Time: 10 minutes

Cook Time: 1 hour

4 medium acorn squash

1 tablespoon extra-virgin olive oil

1. Preheat the oven to 400°F. Line a rimmed baking sheet with parchment paper.

2. Cut the squash in half and scoop out the seeds and stringy membranes with a spoon.

3. Lay the squash halves cut side up on the lined baking sheet. Brush the halves with the olive oil and roast for 40 minutes to 1 hour, until the squash is easily pierced with a fork.

4. Place four of the squash halves in one container, then scoop the pulp out of the remaining four halves and put the pulp in a separate container; discard the shells. Store in the refrigerator for use later in the week.

Caramelize the onions

Prep Time: 10 minutes

Cook Time: 1 hour

3 large yellow onions

2 tablespoons salted butter, ghee, or other fat of choice

1 teaspoon coarse sea salt

1. Thinly slice the onions.

2. Melt the butter in a large heavy skillet (cast iron is a good choice) over medium-low heat. Add the onions and salt and stir. Cook, stirring occasionally, for 45 minutes to 1 hour, until the onions have reduced significantly in size and have developed a deep caramel color. Store in the refrigerator for use later in the week.

Make the vodka sauce

Prep Time: 10 minutes

Cook Time: 8 minutes

1 (28-ounce) can crushed tomatoes

½ cup vodka

½ teaspoon coarse sea salt

¼ teaspoon ground black pepper

¼ teaspoon red pepper flakes

¼ cup fresh basil leaves

½ cup heavy cream or coconut cream

½ cup shredded Parmesan cheese (omit for dairy-free)

1. In a saucepan over medium heat, bring the tomatoes, vodka, salt, black pepper, and red pepper flakes to a simmer. Meanwhile, chop the basil and set aside.

2. Once the tomato mixture has reached a simmer, stir in the cream, Parmesan cheese, and chopped basil. Bring the sauce back up to a simmer, then remove from the heat. Store in the refrigerator for use later in the week.

Prep the collard greens

Prep Time: 15 minutes

Cook Time: 5 minutes

2 bunches collard greens

1½ teaspoons extra-virgin olive oil

Juice of ½ lemon

Pinch of coarse sea salt

Shave the stems of 12 collard leaves:

1. Sort through the two bunches of collards and pull out the 12 largest leaves; set the remaining leaves aside to be wilted.

2. Wash and dry the 12 collard leaves.

3. Lay one of the leaves on a cutting board so that the side with the prominent spine (the outer, or convex, side of the leaf) is facing up. Cut the stem off of the leaf at the base of the collard. Then slide the knife carefully across the raised part of the stem, keeping the knife parallel to your cutting board and the leaf. Slide the knife down the length of the stem to "shave" it. Your goal is not to remove the stem, but to shave it until it is about as thin as the leaf itself. This will make the leaves more pliable and easier to roll around the beef filling when making the Italian Beef Rolls.

4. Repeat this process with the remaining 11 collard leaves, then store in a container in the refrigerator for use later in the week.

Wilt the remaining collard greens:

1. Wash and destem the remaining collard leaves (from above), then coarsely chop them. Put the olive oil in a skillet that has a lid over medium heat. Once hot, add the collards and toss in the oil.

2. Cover and allow the collards to wilt, 3 to 4 minutes. Once completely wilted, remove the lid and stir in the lemon juice and salt. Store in a separate container in the refrigerator for use later in the week.

Make the lemon-thyme cream sauce

½ cup avocado oil mayonnaise or vegan mayo

1 tablespoon fresh lemon juice (about ½ small lemon)

2 teaspoons chopped fresh thyme

In a small bowl, whisk together all of the ingredients until smooth. Store in the refrigerator for use later in the week.

Rustic Beef–Stuffed Acorn Squash

Yield: 4 servings   Prep Time: 10 minutes   Cook Time: 25 minutes

4 roasted acorn squash halves ✓

4 cups shredded beef ✓

Wilted collard greens ✓

Caramelized onions ✓

1 cup cranberries, fresh or frozen

½ teaspoon coarse sea salt

⅛ teaspoon ground black pepper

Lemon-thyme cream sauce ✓
(omit for egg-free)

1 teaspoon fresh thyme leaves, for garnish (optional)

1. Preheat the oven to 375°F. Line a rimmed baking sheet with parchment paper.

2. Place the squash halves cut side up on the lined baking sheet.

3. Put the beef, collard greens, onions, cranberries, salt, and pepper in a large bowl and toss to combine. Stuff equal portions of the beef mixture into the squash halves.

4. Bake for 25 minutes, until the beef is slightly browned and the squash and stuffing are fully warmed through.

5. Drizzle the sauce over the stuffed squash, sprinkle with the thyme leaves, if using, and serve!

Italian Beef Rolls with Vodka Sauce

Yield: 4 servings   Prep Time: 20 minutes   Cook Time: 20 minutes

3 cups shredded beef ✓

1 teaspoon Italian seasoning

½ teaspoon garlic powder

½ teaspoon coarse sea salt

¼ teaspoon ground black pepper

12 collard leaves, stems shaved ✓

Vodka sauce ✓

2 tablespoons chopped fresh basil, for garnish

1. Preheat the oven to 350°F.

2. Put the beef in a bowl and toss with the Italian seasoning, garlic powder, salt, and pepper.

3. Place about ¼ cup of the seasoned beef on the bottom third of a collard leaf, then fold the sides of the leaf over the beef filling and roll. Place the collard roll, folded side down, in a 3-quart rectangular casserole dish. Repeat with the remaining collard leaves and beef.

4. Pour the vodka sauce over the collard rolls, then bake for 20 minutes, until the sauce has browned slightly on top. Garnish with the chopped basil and serve!

Red Curry Acorn Squash Soup with Crispy Beef

Yield: 4 servings   Prep Time: 10 minutes   Cook Time: 10 minutes

FOR THE SOUP:

Pulp from 4 roasted acorn squash halves ✓

1 cup full-fat coconut milk

1 cup chicken broth

1 (4-ounce) jar red curry paste

¼ cup fresh lime juice (about 2 limes)

½ teaspoon coarse sea salt

¼ teaspoon ground black pepper

FOR THE CRISPY BEEF:

2 tablespoons ghee, avocado oil, or other fat of choice

3 cups shredded beef ✓

¼ teaspoon garlic powder

¼ teaspoon ginger powder

¼ teaspoon coarse sea salt

1 tablespoon coconut aminos

2 tablespoons chopped fresh cilantro, for garnish

1. Put all of the soup ingredients in a blender and blend until smooth, then pour the soup into a large pot. Cook over medium heat for 5 minutes or until fully warmed through.

2. While the soup is heating, prepare the beef: Place the ghee in a large skillet over medium-high heat. Put the beef, spices, salt, and coconut aminos in a medium-sized bowl and toss to combine. Once the ghee is hot, add the seasoned beef to the pan, spreading it across the surface of the pan. Cook for 3 to 4 minutes, until crisp, then flip and cook for an additional 3 to 4 minutes, until browned and crisp on the other side.

3. Serve the soup in bowls topped with the shredded beef and garnished with the cilantro.

BAKED CHICKEN BREAST, BELL PEPPERS, and SPAGHETTI SQUASH

This week shows you how chicken breast, bell peppers, and spaghetti squash can be show-stoppers with just a little strategy. You're going to transform these humble components into a Sweet-and-Sour Chicken Chow Mein, Chicken Souvlaki Bowls, and a fabulous Chicken Tetrazzini. If you'd like to supplement this week's three main dinner recipes with two additional meals, see the suggested "Bonus Dinner Options" on the next page.

Weekly Ingredients

FRESH PRODUCE

Bell peppers, red, 4

Cucumber, 1 medium

Flat-leaf parsley, 12 sprigs

Garlic, 5 cloves

Green cabbage, ¼ head (or 1 cup preshredded cabbage)

Green onions, 2

Lemons, 2 small

Onions, white, 1 medium and 1 small

Pineapple chunks, 8 ounces (1 cup) (or use frozen)

Romaine lettuce, 1 head

Sliced baby bella (aka cremini) mushrooms, 8 ounces

Spaghetti squash, 2 (about 4½ pounds each)

Tomato, 1 large

FROZEN FOODS

Peas, 4½ ounces (1 cup)

MEAT/DAIRY

Butter, salted, 2 tablespoons

Chicken breasts, boneless, skinless, 5 pounds

Greek yogurt, plain, full-fat, 6 ounces (¾ cup)

Heavy cream, 4 fluid ounces (½ cup)

PANTRY

Apple cider vinegar, 2 fluid ounces (¼ cup)

Arrowroot powder, 1½ teaspoons

Chicken broth, 21 fluid ounces (2½ cups plus 2 tablespoons)

Coconut aminos, Coconut Secret brand, 10 fluid ounces (1¼ cups)

Coconut sugar, 2 tablespoons

Extra-virgin olive oil, 5 fluid ounces (½ cup plus 2 tablespoons) plus 1 teaspoon

Fish sauce, ½ teaspoon

Ghee or avocado oil, 2 tablespoons

Gluten-free flour blend, 2 tablespoons

Kalamata olives, pitted, 3 ounces (½ cup)

Pineapple juice, 4 fluid ounces (½ cup)

Red wine vinegar, 2 fluid ounces (¼ cup)

Toasted sesame oil, 2 teaspoons

Unseasoned rice wine vinegar, 1 tablespoon

White rice, 6½ ounces (1 cup)

SEASONINGS

Dried basil, 1 tablespoon

Dried oregano leaves, 1 tablespoon

Garlic powder, 1 teaspoon

Ginger powder, ½ teaspoon

Sesame seeds, 1 teaspoon

Ingredient Subs

To make this week PALEO:

· Use the substitutions listed below for making the week grain-free and dairy-free.

To make this week GRAIN-FREE:

· Substitute 1 tablespoon arrowroot powder for the gluten-free flour blend. Omit the butter (you won't need it).

· Replace the white rice with 1 medium to large head cauliflower (about 2 pounds) or 1 (12-ounce) bag frozen riced cauliflower. Add 2 teaspoons extra-virgin olive oil.

To make this week DAIRY-FREE:

· Use ghee or another fat in place of the butter.

· Substitute plain, unsweetened dairy-free Greek-style yogurt (such as Kite Hill brand) for the Greek yogurt.

· Use full-fat coconut milk in place of the heavy cream.

Bonus Dinner Options

Dinner 1

Mocha Coffee Steak
(page 352)

Braised Collards
(page 358)

Baked Sweet Potatoes
(page 365)

Bonus Dinner Ingredients

Cocoa powder, 1 teaspoon

Collard greens, 1 small bunch (about 1 pound)

Extra-virgin olive oil, 3 tablespoons

Instant coffee powder, 1 teaspoon

Lemon, ½

Sirloin or rib-eye steaks, boneless, 1 inch thick, 4
(4 to 6 ounces each)

Sweet potatoes, small to medium, 4 (about 1 pound)

Dinner 2

Lemon-Garlic Shrimp
(page 354)

Baked Okra
(page 359)

Basic Quinoa
(page 369)

Bonus Dinner Ingredients

Extra-virgin olive oil,
2 tablespoons plus 2 teaspoons

Garlic powder, ½ teaspoon

Lemon, 1

Okra, fresh, 1 pound

Quinoa, 6 ounces (1 cup)

Shrimp, large, 1½ pounds,
peeled and deveined

Bonus Dinner Ingredient Subs

To make this meal PALEO and/or GRAIN-FREE, *replace the quinoa with 1 large head cauliflower (about 3 pounds) or 18 ounces frozen riced cauliflower; make Basic Cauliflower Rice (page 363) instead of the Basic Quinoa.*

Prep Day

The list of today's meal prep efforts may seem long, but it moves quickly. You're going to bake chicken breasts, bake spaghetti squash, make a teriyaki and a sweet-and-sour sauce, cook some rice, make a quick Greek dressing, prep bell peppers (storing one portion raw and cooking another portion), cook mushrooms with onion and garlic, and then chop the rest of the fresh veggies. I like to get the chicken in the oven first. While the chicken is baking, I make the sauces and the dressing and get the onions, mushrooms, and garlic started in a pan. As soon as the chicken comes out of the oven, I put the squash in and then the bell peppers (the squash and peppers bake at the same temperature, so if your oven is large enough to fit them both, bake them all at once to save yourself some time). Then I chop, cut, slice, and shred the remaining veggies. Once the chicken and squash are cool enough to handle, I finish prepping those, cutting the chicken into cubes and removing the strands from the squash for storage.

note: *To save myself a step, I purchase presliced mushrooms. If you are using whole mushrooms, add the step of cleaning and slicing the mushrooms to this week's prep day tasks.*

Bake and cube the chicken

Yield: about 10 cups
Prep Time: 5 minutes
Cook Time: 40 minutes

5 pounds boneless, skinless chicken breasts

1 tablespoon extra-virgin olive oil

1 teaspoon coarse sea salt

½ teaspoon ground black pepper

1. Preheat the oven to 375°F. Line a rimmed baking sheet with parchment paper.

2. Place the chicken on the lined baking sheet. Brush with the olive oil and season with the salt and pepper.

3. Bake for 40 minutes, until the chicken reaches an internal temperature of 165°F.

4. Let the chicken cool, then cut into ½-inch cubes.

5. Place 3 cups of the cubed chicken in a container labeled "Chow Mein," 3 cups in a container labeled "Bowls," and the remaining 4 cups in a container labeled "Tetrazzini." Store in the refrigerator for use later in the week.

Make the Teriyaki Sauce

Follow the recipe on page 373 to make a full batch of Teriyaki Sauce.

Make the sweet-and-sour sauce

Prep Time: 5 minutes

Cook Time: 5 minutes

1 cup plus 2 tablespoons chicken broth, divided

½ cup pineapple juice

¼ cup apple cider vinegar

¼ cup coconut aminos

2 tablespoons coconut sugar

½ teaspoon coarse sea salt

¼ teaspoon fish sauce

1½ teaspoons arrowroot powder

1. Place 1 cup of the broth, the pineapple juice, vinegar, coconut aminos, coconut sugar, salt, and fish sauce in a saucepan over medium-high heat. Let the mixture come to a boil, then cook for 3 to 4 minutes, until slightly reduced.

2. In a small bowl, whisk together the arrowroot powder and the remaining 2 tablespoons of broth to make a slurry, then pour the slurry into the saucepan, whisking constantly. Bring the sauce to a boil again. Continue to simmer until thickened, then remove from the heat. Store in the refrigerator for use later in the week.

Cook the rice

Yield: 3 cups

Prep Time: 1 minute

Cook Time: about 20 minutes

Cook 1 cup of white rice according to the package instructions. Store in the refrigerator for use later in the week.

🅿 🌿 **PALEO/GRAIN-FREE RICE SUBSTITUTE**
Using the method outlined on page 363, make a small batch of Basic Cauliflower Rice using the following quantities: 1 medium to large head cauliflower (about 2 pounds) or 1 (12-ounce) bag frozen riced cauliflower, 2 teaspoons of extra-virgin olive oil, and ¼ heaping teaspoon of coarse sea salt. Follow the storage instructions for the white rice above.

Make the Greek dressing

Yield: about 1 cup

Prep Time: 5 minutes

¼ cup fresh lemon juice (about 2 small lemons)

¼ cup red wine vinegar

½ cup extra-virgin olive oil

1 tablespoon dried basil

1 tablespoon dried oregano leaves

½ teaspoon garlic powder

¼ teaspoon fine sea salt

½ teaspoon ground black pepper

Place all of the ingredients in a jar, then seal and shake to combine. Store in the refrigerator for use later in the week.

Cook the mushrooms, onion, and garlic

Prep Time: 10 minutes

Cook Time: 7 minutes

1 small white onion	8 ounces sliced baby bella (aka cremini) mushrooms
4 cloves garlic	
1 tablespoon extra-virgin olive oil	

1. Dice the onion and mince the garlic.

2. Heat the olive oil in a large skillet over medium heat. Once hot, add the mushrooms, onion, and garlic. Cook, stirring occasionally, for 5 to 7 minutes, until the mushrooms and onion have started to brown.

3. Store in the refrigerator for use later in the week.

Bake the squash

Prep Time: 10 minutes

Cook Time: 1 hour

1. Preheat the oven to 400°F.

2. Cut two spaghetti squash in half lengthwise, scoop out the seeds and stringy membranes with a spoon, and lay the halves cut side up on two rimmed baking sheets. Bake for 45 to 60 minutes, until the squash strands easily pull away from the shells with a fork.

3. Once cool enough to handle, remove the squash strands with a fork, discarding the shells. Store the strands in the refrigerator for use later in the week.

Prep the bell peppers

Prep Time: 10 minutes

Cook Time: 20 minutes

1. Cut four red bell peppers in half and remove the seeds.

2. Chop two of the peppers into 1-inch pieces, then store in the refrigerator for use later in the week.

3. Preheat the oven to 400°F. Slice the two remaining peppers into ½-inch strips, then place on a rimmed baking sheet. Toss the pepper strips with 1 teaspoon of extra-virgin olive oil and roast for 20 minutes, or until wilted and slightly browned. Store in the refrigerator for use later in the week.

Cut the white onion

Cut a medium-sized white onion into 1-inch pieces. Store in the refrigerator for use later in the week.

Shred the cabbage

Thinly slice one-quarter head of green cabbage, or enough to equal 1 cup. Store in the refrigerator for use later in the week.

Slice the green onions

Thinly slice two green onions, or enough to equal 2 tablespoons. Store in the refrigerator for use later in the week.

Chop the lettuce

Chop a head of romaine lettuce into 1-inch pieces. Store in the refrigerator for use later in the week.

Prep the cucumber

Slice two-thirds of a medium-sized cucumber. Store the cucumber slices and the remaining third of the cucumber in the refrigerator for use later in the week.

Sweet-and-Sour Chicken Chow Mein

Yield: 4 servings   Prep Time: 5 minutes   Cook Time: 15 minutes

FOR THE SWEET-AND-SOUR CHICKEN:

1 tablespoon ghee or avocado oil

2 red bell peppers, chopped ✓

1 medium-sized white onion, chopped ✓

3 cups cubed baked chicken breast ✓

1 cup pineapple chunks, fresh or frozen

Sweet-and-sour sauce ✓

FOR THE CHOW MEIN:

1 tablespoon ghee or avocado oil

1 cup shredded green cabbage ✓

Half of the baked spaghetti squash strands ✓

Teriyaki sauce ✓

2 tablespoons sliced green onions ✓

1 teaspoon sesame seeds, for garnish

For the sweet-and-sour chicken:

1. Put the ghee in a large skillet or wok over medium-high heat. Once hot, add the bell peppers and onion. Cook, stirring occasionally, for 4 to 5 minutes, until the onion is translucent and the peppers are slightly browned and wilted.

2. Add the chicken and pineapple, then pour in the sauce and cook for an additional 2 to 3 minutes, until fully heated. Reduce the heat to low while you prepare the chow mein.

For the chow mein:

1. Place the ghee in a large skillet over medium-high heat. Once hot, add the cabbage and cook for 2 to 3 minutes, until wilted, then add the squash and teriyaki sauce and toss to coat. Cook for an additional 2 to 3 minutes, until warmed through.

2. Add the green onions and stir to combine, then garnish with the sesame seeds.

3. Serve the sweet-and-sour chicken alongside the chow mein.

Chicken Souvlaki Bowls

Yield: 5 servings   Prep Time: 10 minutes   Cook Time: 8 minutes

FOR THE TZATZIKI:

⅓ cucumber

¾ cup plain full-fat Greek yogurt or dairy-free Greek-style yogurt

1 clove garlic, minced

Pinch of fine sea salt

FOR THE SOUVLAKI BOWLS:

3 cups cubed baked chicken breast ✓

Greek dressing ✓, divided

Roasted red bell pepper strips ✓

3 cups cooked white rice ✓

Leaves from 8 sprigs fresh flat-leaf parsley

1 tomato

1 head romaine lettuce, chopped ✓

⅔ cucumber, sliced ✓

½ cup pitted Kalamata olives

1. To make the tzatziki, peel and shred the cucumber, or until you have about 3 tablespoons, then roll it up in a dish towel or cheesecloth and squeeze until all of the excess moisture is released from the cucumber.

2. Place the drained cucumber in a small bowl along with the yogurt, garlic, and salt. Stir to combine, then store in the refrigerator until ready to serve.

3. Put the chicken in a large skillet over medium heat, then pour in half of the dressing; reserve the other half for serving. Toss to coat the chicken with the dressing. Cook for 2 to 3 minutes, then flip the chicken.

4. Add the roasted peppers to the skillet and cook for an additional 2 to 3 minutes, until the peppers are warmed and the chicken is browned, then remove from the heat.

5. While the peppers are warming, reheat the rice either by placing it in a medium-sized saucepan, covered, over low heat for 5 minutes or by microwaving it for about 2 minutes, until hot.

6. Meanwhile, chop the parsley leaves and cut the tomato into four wedges. When the rice is warmed, stir in the chopped parsley.

7. To assemble the bowls, divide the lettuce evenly among five bowls, then top the lettuce evenly with the rice, chicken and peppers, cucumber slices, tomato wedges, and olives. Serve with the tzatziki and the remaining Greek dressing on the side.

Chicken Tetrazzini

Yield: 6 servings   Prep Time: 8 minutes   Cook Time: 35 minutes

2 tablespoons salted butter or ghee

2 tablespoons gluten-free flour blend, or 1 tablespoon arrowroot powder (see note below)

1½ cups chicken broth

½ cup heavy cream or full-fat coconut milk

½ teaspoon coarse sea salt

¼ teaspoon ground black pepper

4 cups cubed baked chicken breast ✓

1 cup frozen peas

Cooked mushrooms, onion, and garlic ✓

Half of the baked spaghetti squash strands ✓

2 tablespoons chopped fresh parsley, for garnish

1. Preheat the oven to 350°F.

2. Place the butter in a medium-sized saucepan over medium heat. Once melted, add the flour and whisk until smooth.

3. Slowly pour in the broth, whisking constantly to smooth out any lumps, then whisk in the heavy cream, salt, and pepper.

4. Bring the mixture to a boil, then stir in the chicken, peas, and cooked mushroom mixture. Simmer for 2 minutes to thicken the sauce.

5. Layer the squash strands in a 9 by 13-inch baking dish, then spoon the chicken mixture over the squash.

6. Bake for 30 minutes, until the top is slightly bubbly, then remove from the oven.

7. Let cool slightly, then garnish with the parsley and serve!

note: *If using arrowroot powder, omit the butter and skip Steps 2 and 3. Instead, combine the broth, cream, salt, and pepper in a medium-sized saucepan and bring to a boil over medium-high heat. In a small bowl, mix together 1 tablespoon arrowroot powder and 2 tablespoons water. Once the broth mixture is boiling, pour in the arrowroot slurry and bring back up to a boil. Reduce the heat and simmer until thickened, 1 to 2 minutes, then proceed with Step 4.*

SHREDDED BEEF, KALE, and POLENTA

I know I'm not supposed to play favorites, but if I had to choose just one week's worth of meals to make over and over again, it would undoubtedly be this one. If you're game to include some corn in your diet, you're going to love this week! It artfully combines shredded beef, kale, and polenta into the most delicious Rustic Polenta and Beef Casserole (with the tastiest red wine reduction), Barbacoa-Stuffed Poblanos (possibly my favorite dish in the whole book), and a classic Beef Ragu. If you'd like to supplement this week's three main dinner recipes with two additional meals, see the suggested "Bonus Dinner Options" on the next page.

Weekly Ingredients

FRESH PRODUCE

Cilantro, 4 sprigs

Flat-leaf parsley, 8 sprigs (optional)

Garlic, 3 cloves

Lacinato (aka dinosaur) kale, 2 bunches

Lemon, ½

Limes, 3

Onions, yellow, 3 large plus ½ medium

Poblano peppers, 6

Zucchini, 5 large

MEAT/DAIRY

Butter, salted, 3 ounces (¾ stick)

Chuck roast, 1 (5 to 6 pounds)

Cotija cheese, 1 ounce

Shaved Parmesan cheese, 1 ounce (¼ cup)

Sour cream, full-fat, 4 ounces (½ cup)

PANTRY

Avocado oil, 2 tablespoons

Balsamic vinegar, 2 tablespoons

Canned chipotle pepper in adobo sauce, 1, plus 2 tablespoons sauce from the can

Chicken broth, 32 fluid ounces (1 quart)

Crushed tomatoes, 1 (28-ounce) can

Extra-virgin olive oil, 2 tablespoons plus ½ teaspoon

Polenta meal or corn grits, 9 ounces (1½ cups)

Red wine, 12 fluid ounces (1½ cups)

SEASONINGS

Ancho chili powder, 1 teaspoon

Bay leaves, 2

Dried basil, 2 teaspoons

Dried oregano leaves, 2 teaspoons

Dried thyme leaves, 1½ teaspoons

Garlic powder, ½ teaspoon

Ground cumin, 1 teaspoon

Onion powder, ½ teaspoon

Ingredient Subs

To make this week DAIRY-FREE:

· Substitute ¼ cup plus 2 tablespoons ghee or oil of choice for the butter.

· Omit the cheeses.

· Use avocado oil mayonnaise (or vegan mayo for egg-free) in place of the sour cream.

Bonus Dinner Options

Dinner 1

Paprika Lime Chicken Breasts (page 347)

Roasted Asparagus (page 360)

Baked Acorn Squash (page 364)

Bonus Dinner Ingredients

Acorn squash, 1

Asparagus, fresh, 1 pound

Chicken breasts, boneless, skinless, 1½ pounds

Extra-virgin olive oil, 2 tablespoons plus 1 teaspoon

Lime, 1

Paprika, 1 tablespoon

Bonus Dinner Ingredient Subs

To make this meal LOW-CARB:

Omit the squash.

Dinner 2

Honey Mustard Pork Tenderloin (page 351)

Roasted Broccoli (page 357)

Basic Quinoa (page 369)

Bonus Dinner Ingredients

Broccoli, 2 medium to large heads

Dijon mustard, 2 tablespoons

Extra-virgin olive oil, 3 tablespoons

Garlic powder, ½ teaspoon

Honey, 1 tablespoon

Pork tenderloin, 1 (1¼ pounds)

Quinoa, 6 ounces (1 cup)

Bonus Dinner Ingredient Subs

To make this meal LOW-CARB, PALEO, and/or GRAIN-FREE:

· Replace the quinoa with 1 large head cauliflower (about 3 pounds) or 18 ounces frozen riced cauliflower; make Basic Cauliflower Rice (page 363) instead of the Basic Quinoa.

· If low-carb, omit the honey.

Prep Day

Today you're going to get the bulk of the work out of the way for this week's dinners! I like to start by getting the beef in the Instant Pot (my chosen method for cooking shredded beef, though you do have other options). Right after that, I get the zucchini noodles salted and the onions on the stove so that they have a good amount of time to caramelize. Once the beef and onions are cooking, I pop the peppers in the oven, prep the kale, start on the red wine reduction, and then make the polenta. Because polenta is much easier to work with on the day you cook it, I like to assemble the casserole and stuff the roasted poblano peppers with the polenta (minus the beef) on prep day. Then, on the day you plan to enjoy your dinner, you just pop the casserole in the oven or finish stuffing the peppers and then bake them. Note that the order of tasks here is based on using a pressure cooker to cook the beef; if you're using the oven or a slow cooker for the beef, skip ahead to the last two tasks—making the tomato and chipotle cream sauces—while waiting for the beef to finish cooking. Then, about 30 minutes before the beef is done, make the polenta and complete the tasks of assembling the casserole and stuffing the poblanos.

note: *To save myself a step, I purchase preshaved Parmesan cheese; if you are using block cheese, add the step of shaving the Parmesan to the prep day tasks.*

Cook and shred the beef

Yield: about 10 cups shredded beef
Prep Time: 10 minutes
Cook Time: 1 to 8 hours, depending on method

1. If using the Instant Pot method, cut a 5- to 6-pound chuck roast into three or four equal pieces; otherwise, leave it whole. Season the meat with 1½ teaspoons of coarse sea salt.

2. Cook the roast using one of these three methods:

- **Oven Method** (Cook Time: 4 to 5 hours)
  Preheat the oven to 325°F. Place the seasoned roast in a Dutch oven or other large oven-safe pot with a lid along with 2 cups of water. Bake, covered, for 4 to 5 hours, until the meat pulls apart easily with a fork.

- **Instant Pot Method** (Cook Time: 1½ hours)
  Place the seasoned pieces of beef in a 6-quart Instant Pot along with ½ cup of water. Seal the lid and press the Meat/Stew button, then set the timer for 60 minutes. When the timer goes off, allow the pressure to release naturally (meaning, do not manually move the pressure release knob). This should take about 30 minutes; the lid will automatically unlock when the pressure is fully released.

- **Slow Cooker Method** (Cook Time: 4 to 8 hours)
Place the seasoned roast in a 6-quart slow cooker along with 1 cup of water. Cover and cook on low for 6 to 8 hours or on high for 4 hours, until the meat pulls apart easily.

3. Shred the beef with two forks. Set about 4 cups of the shredded beef aside for use later in the day (for assembling the polenta and beef casserole). Divide the remaining shredded beef evenly between two containers, putting about 3 cups in each. Label one container "Stuffed Peppers" and the other "Beef Ragu." Store in the refrigerator for use later in the week.

Prep the zucchini noodles

1. Using the flat blade of your spiral slicer, slice five large zucchini to make wide ribbons, then toss with 1½ teaspoons of coarse sea salt.

2. Line two rimmed baking sheets with tea towels or triple layers of paper towels, then spread the zucchini noodles across the towels.

3. Let sit for 30 to 60 minutes, then gather the zucchini noodles in the towels and wring them to squeeze out as much water as possible.

4. Line an airtight container with paper towels (the zucchini will continue to release water) and place the zucchini noodles in it, then store in the refrigerator for use later in the week.

Caramelize the onions

Prep Time: 10 minutes

Cook Time: 45 minutes

3 large yellow onions

2 tablespoons salted butter, ghee, or oil of choice

1 teaspoon coarse sea salt

1. Thinly slice the onions.

2. Melt the butter in a large heavy skillet (cast iron is a good choice) over medium-low heat. Add the onions and salt and stir. Cook for about 45 minutes, stirring occasionally, until the onions have reduced significantly in size and developed a deep caramel color. Set aside for use later in the prep day.

Roast the poblano peppers

Prep Time: 10 minutes

Cook Time: 10 minutes

6 poblano peppers

2 tablespoons avocado oil

1. Place an oven rack in the top position and preheat the broiler to high.

2. Place the peppers on a rimmed baking sheet and brush them with the oil. Set under the broiler for 10 minutes, turning the peppers every 3 minutes.

3. When charred and evenly blistered on all sides, remove the peppers from the oven, place in a bowl, and cover with foil or plastic wrap. When cool enough to handle, carefully peel the skin off of each pepper. Cut a 3-inch slit down the side of each pepper and scrape out the seeds and membranes.

4. Set the peppers aside for use later in the prep day.

Prepare the kale

Prep Time: 15 minutes

Cook Time: 4 minutes

2 bunches Lacinato (aka dinosaur) kale

1½ teaspoons extra-virgin olive oil

Juice of ½ lemon

Pinch of coarse sea salt

1. Wash and dry both bunches of kale, keeping them separate.

2. Wilt one bunch of kale:

- Destem the bunch of kale and coarsely chop it.

- Heat the olive oil in a skillet with a lid over medium heat. Once hot, add the kale and toss it in the oil.

- Place the lid on the pan and allow the kale to wilt, 3 to 4 minutes. Once completely wilted, remove the lid and stir in the lemon juice and salt.

- Set aside for use later in the prep day.

3. Prepare the second bunch of kale:

- Destem the second bunch of kale, then cut it into ½-inch-thick strips. Store in the refrigerator for use later in the week.

Make the red wine reduction

Prep Time: 2 minutes

Cook Time: 10 minutes

1 cup red wine

2 tablespoons balsamic vinegar

1 teaspoon coarse sea salt

½ teaspoon dried thyme leaves

Place the wine, vinegar, salt, and thyme in a medium-sized saucepan over medium-high heat. Bring to a boil, then reduce the heat to medium and simmer for 7 to 10 minutes, until reduced by half. Set aside.

Make the polenta

Yield: about 6 cups

Prep Time: 5 minutes

Cook Time: 30 minutes

1 quart chicken broth

1½ to 2 teaspoons coarse sea salt, divided

1½ cups polenta meal or corn grits

¼ cup (½ stick) salted butter, ghee, or oil of choice

½ teaspoon ground black pepper

½ teaspoon garlic powder

1. In a large saucepan, bring the broth and 1 teaspoon of the salt to a boil over high heat.

2. Reduce the heat to low, then whisk in the polenta meal and bring back up to a boil.

3. Cover and cook for 10 minutes, then whisk the polenta again, making sure to scrape everything up from the bottom of the pan. Place the lid back on the pan and cook for 15 more minutes.

4. Stir in the butter, pepper, garlic powder, and another ½ teaspoon of salt. Taste for seasoning and add up to ½ teaspoon more salt, if needed. Reduce the heat to the lowest setting to keep the polenta from cooling and hardening while you assemble the casserole and poblanos.

Assemble the casserole

4 cups shredded beef *(from earlier in prep day)*

Red wine reduction *(from earlier in prep day)*

4 cups cooked polenta *(from earlier in prep day)*

Wilted kale *(from earlier in prep day)*

Caramelized onions *(from earlier in prep day)*

1. Place the beef and red wine reduction in a large bowl and toss to coat.

2. Spread the polenta in a 3-quart casserole dish, then layer the kale over the top. Spread the beef over the kale, then top with the caramelized onions.

3. Cover the dish either with the lid or with aluminum foil and store in the refrigerator for use later in the week.

Stuff the poblano peppers with polenta

6 roasted poblano peppers *(from earlier in prep day)*

2 cups cooked polenta *(from earlier in prep day)*

1. Place the roasted poblano peppers on a rimmed baking sheet. Stuff each pepper with about ⅓ cup of the prepared polenta.

2. Once all of the peppers are stuffed, cover the baking sheet with aluminum foil or plastic wrap and store in the refrigerator for use later in the week.

Make the tomato sauce

Prep Time: 5 minutes

Cook Time: 12 minutes

1 tablespoon extra-virgin olive oil

½ yellow onion, diced

3 cloves garlic, minced

1 (28-ounce) can crushed tomatoes

2 teaspoons dried basil

1 teaspoon dried oregano leaves

1 teaspoon dried thyme leaves

2 bay leaves

½ teaspoon coarse sea salt

¼ teaspoon ground black pepper

½ cup red wine

1. Place the olive oil in a pot over medium heat. Once hot, add the onion and sauté for 3 to 4 minutes, until the onion is translucent. Add the garlic to the pot and sauté for 1 minute, until fragrant.

2. Add the remaining ingredients to the pot and stir to combine. Reduce the heat to medium-low and cook, stirring occasionally, for 5 to 7 minutes, until the sauce is bubbling and slightly reduced.

3. Store in the refrigerator for use later in the week.

Make the chipotle cream sauce

½ cup full-fat sour cream or avocado oil mayonnaise

Juice of 1 lime

1 chipotle pepper in adobo sauce

2 tablespoons adobo sauce (from the can of chipotle peppers)

1. Place all of the ingredients in a blender and blend until smooth.

2. Store in the refrigerator for use later in the week.

Rustic Polenta and Beef Casserole

Yield: 5 servings   Prep Time: 2 minutes   Cook Time: 30 minutes

Pre-assembled Rustic Polenta and Beef Casserole (see tip below) ✓

2 tablespoons chopped fresh flat-leaf parsley, for garnish (optional)

1. Preheat the oven to 350°F.

2. Bake the casserole for 30 minutes, until the beef is slightly browned and the casserole is fully warmed through. Let cool slightly, garnish with the parsley, and serve!

tip: *About 15 minutes before preheating the oven, remove the casserole from the refrigerator and set it on the counter to take the chill off (to avoid putting a chilled glass or ceramic dish directly into a hot oven, which could cause it to shatter).*

Barbacoa-Stuffed Poblanos

Yield: 6 servings   Prep Time: 5 minutes   Cook Time: 20 minutes

FOR THE BARBACOA:

3 cups shredded beef ✓

½ teaspoon coarse sea salt

1 teaspoon ancho chili powder

1 teaspoon ground cumin

1 teaspoon dried oregano leaves

½ teaspoon garlic powder

½ teaspoon onion powder

¼ teaspoon ground black pepper

Juice of 1 lime

6 polenta-stuffed roasted poblano peppers ✓

Chipotle cream sauce ✓

1 ounce Cotija cheese, crumbled, for garnish (omit for dairy-free)

2 tablespoons chopped fresh cilantro, for garnish

6 lime wedges, for serving

1. Preheat the oven to 375°F.

2. To make the barbacoa, place the shredded beef, salt, spices, and lime juice in a large bowl and toss to coat. Place equal amounts of the beef mixture on top of the polenta-stuffed peppers.

3. Bake the stuffed peppers for 20 minutes, until the beef is slightly browned and crisp on top.

4. Remove the stuffed peppers from the oven. Drizzle the chipotle cream sauce over the peppers and sprinkle with the cheese and cilantro. Serve with lime wedges.

Beef Ragu

Yield: 5 servings   Prep Time: 2 minutes   Cook Time: 13 minutes

FOR THE RAGU:

Tomato sauce ✓

3 cups shredded beef ✓

Coarse sea salt

1 bunch Lacinato (aka dinosaur) kale, sliced ✓

FOR THE ZUCCHINI NOODLES:

2 teaspoons extra-virgin olive oil

Zucchini noodles from 5 large zucchini ✓

¼ cup shaved Parmesan cheese, for garnish (omit for Paleo/dairy-free)

Freshly ground black pepper, for garnish (optional)

1. Make the ragu: Bring the tomato sauce to a simmer in a large pot over medium heat, 3 to 4 minutes.

2. Add the shredded beef to the sauce and stir to combine, then reduce the heat to medium-low and cook for 5 to 7 minutes, until the meat is warmed through. Taste the sauce and season with salt, if needed.

3. While the ragu is cooking, make the noodles: Heat the oil in a large skillet over medium heat. Once hot, add the zucchini noodles and sauté for 4 to 5 minutes, until the zucchini is reduced in volume and cooked through. Drain off any excess water.

4. Stir the sliced kale into the ragu and cook for 1 to 2 minutes, until the kale is wilted and turns bright green.

5. Serve the ragu with the zucchini noodles, garnished with the shaved Parmesan and some freshly ground pepper.

GROUND BEEF, SPINACH, and SPAGHETTI SQUASH

This is one of those weeks that just makes a lot of sense! These recipes transform ground beef, spinach, and spaghetti squash into classic comfort foods, but with a twist. This week features a Bolognese Casserole as a spin on the classic spaghetti Bolognese, a Mediterranean Skillet as a spin on the all-American ground beef skillet dinner, and Spinach Pesto Spaghetti Squash Boats as a spin on traditional meatball hoagies. These dishes deliver a lot of flavor and ease! This week is also ready-made for low-carb eaters: there are no substitutions needed. If you'd like to supplement this week's three main dinner recipes with two additional meals, see the suggested "Bonus Dinner Options" on the next page.

Weekly Ingredients

FRESH PRODUCE

Basil, 1 bunch (about 2 ounces)

Flat-leaf parsley, 16 sprigs

Garlic, 5 cloves

Grape tomatoes, 5 ounces (about ½ pint or 1 cup)

Lemons, 3

Onion, red, 1 small

Onion, white, 1

Spaghetti squash, 2 (about 4½ pounds each)

Spinach, 1 pound

FROZEN FOODS

Artichoke hearts, quartered, 16 ounces

MEAT/DAIRY

Feta cheese, 1 ounce (¼ cup crumbled)

Ground beef, 5 pounds

Shaved or shredded Parmesan cheese, 1 ounce (¼ cup)

Shredded Parmesan cheese, 2½ ounces (½ cup plus 2 tablespoons)

PANTRY

Crushed tomatoes, 1 (28-ounce) can

Extra-virgin olive oil, 6 fluid ounces (¾ cup)

Kalamata olives, pitted, 3 ounces (½ cup)

Red wine or beef broth, 4 fluid ounces (½ cup)

Walnut halves, raw, 2 ounces (½ cup)

SEASONINGS

Dried basil, 2 tablespoons

Dried dill weed, 1 teaspoon

Dried oregano leaves, 2 tablespoons

Dried parsley, 2½ teaspoons

Garlic powder, 1½ teaspoons

Ingredient Subs

To make this week PALEO and/or DAIRY-FREE:

· *Omit the cheeses.*

Bonus Dinner Options

Dinner 1

Seared Chicken Breasts
(page 346)

Crispy Brussels Sprouts
(page 356)

Roasted Butternut Squash
Cubes
(page 366)

Bonus Dinner Ingredients

Brussels sprouts, 12 ounces

Butternut squash, 1 medium
(about 2 pounds)

Chicken breasts, boneless,
skinless, 1½ pounds

Extra-virgin olive oil,
3 tablespoons

Lemon, 1

Texas Grill Rub, 2 tablespoons
(see page 374 for ingredients)

Bonus Dinner Ingredient Subs

To make this meal LOW-CARB:

*Replace the butternut squash
with 1 large head cauliflower
(about 3 pounds) or 18 ounces
frozen riced cauliflower; make
Basic Cauliflower Rice (page
363) instead of the Roasted
Butternut Squash Cubes.*

Dinner 2

Crispy Curried Chicken
Thighs   (page 348)

Roasted Broccoli
(page 357)

Basic White Rice
(page 368)

Bonus Dinner Ingredients

Broccoli, 2 medium to large
heads

Chicken thighs, bone-in,
skin-on, 2 pounds

Curry powder, 1 tablespoon

Extra-virgin olive oil,
2 tablespoons

Garlic powder, ½ teaspoon

Lime, 1

White rice, 6½ ounces (1 cup)

Bonus Dinner Ingredient Subs

**To make this meal LOW-CARB,
PALEO, and/or GRAIN-FREE:**

*Replace the white rice with
1 large head cauliflower (about
3 pounds) or 18 ounces frozen
riced cauliflower; make Basic
Cauliflower Rice (page 363)
instead of the Basic White Rice.*

Prep Day

Today we're going to switch things up a bit! Instead of cooking the protein first, I like to get the spaghetti squash into the oven right away. Once the squash is baking, I turn my attention to the pesto because it's needed for the meatballs a little later in the day. When the pesto is finished, I start on the beef. I get a portion browning on the stove and then use the rest to make the meatballs, which are then baked.

note: *To save myself a step, I purchase Parmesan cheese already shaved or shredded; if you are using block cheese, add the step of shaving and/or shredding the Parmesan to this week's prep day tasks.*

Bake the squash and remove the strands from one

Prep Time: 5 minutes
Cook Time: 1 hour

Preheat the oven to 400°F. Cut two spaghetti squash in half lengthwise, scoop out the seeds and stringy membranes with a spoon, and place the halves cut side up on two rimmed baking sheets. Bake for 45 to 60 minutes, until the strands of the squash easily pull away from the shells with a fork.

Once cool enough to handle, set aside two squash halves, cover, and store in the refrigerator for use later in the week. Remove the squash strands from the other two halves with a fork, discard the shells, and store the strands in the refrigerator for use later in the week.

Make the spinach pesto

2 packed cups fresh spinach

1 packed cup fresh basil leaves

½ cup raw walnut halves

½ cup shredded Parmesan cheese (omit for Paleo/dairy-free)

½ teaspoon garlic powder

Pinch of coarse sea salt

Pinch of ground black pepper

2 tablespoons fresh lemon juice (about 1 lemon)

½ cup extra-virgin olive oil

1. Place the spinach, basil, walnuts, Parmesan, garlic powder, salt, and pepper in a food processor. Pulse until the mixture has a coarse, sandlike texture.

2. Add the lemon juice to the food processor, then turn it to high speed and slowly drizzle in the olive oil. Keep the food processor running for an additional minute, until the pesto has a smooth consistency.

3. Set aside ⅓ cup of the pesto for use in the meatballs later in the prep day, then transfer the rest to a container and store in the refrigerator for use later in the week.

tip: *To prevent browning, cover the pesto with plastic wrap and press the plastic down onto the surface of the pesto, then place the lid on the storage container.*

Brown some of the ground beef

Yield: 8 scant cups

Cook Time: 15 minutes

1. Place 3½ pounds of ground beef and 1 teaspoon of coarse sea salt in a large skillet over medium heat. (You will add more seasoning later.) Cook for 10 to 15 minutes, crumbling the meat as it cooks, until fully browned. Let cool completely.

2. Once cool, drain the fat. Set half of the browned meat, about 3¾ cups, aside for use in the Bolognese sauce later in the prep day. Put the remaining browned meat in a storage container, label it "Med Skillet," and store in the refrigerator for use later in the week.

Make the meatballs

Prep Time: 15 minutes

Cook Time: 18 minutes

1½ pounds ground beef

⅓ cup spinach pesto *(from earlier in prep day)*

½ teaspoon garlic powder

½ teaspoon coarse sea salt

¼ teaspoon ground black pepper

1. Preheat the oven to 400°F.

2. In a large bowl, combine all of the ingredients with your hands.

3. Shape the meat mixture into ½-inch balls with your hands or a ½-tablespoon scoop and place the meatballs on a rimmed baking sheet.

4. Bake for 18 minutes, until browned.

5. Store in the refrigerator for use later in the week.

Dice the onions

Dice a white onion. Store in the refrigerator for use later in the week.

Dice a small red onion and set aside for use in the Bolognese sauce later in the prep day.

Mince the garlic

Mince two cloves of garlic and put in a small container. Store in the refrigerator for use later in the week. Mince the remaining three cloves of garlic and set aside for use in the Bolognese sauce, which you'll make next.

Make the Bolognese sauce

Prep Time: 5 minutes

Cook Time: 12 minutes

1 tablespoon extra-virgin olive oil

1 small red onion, diced *(from earlier in prep day)*

3 cloves garlic, minced *(from earlier in prep day)*

1 (28-ounce) can crushed tomatoes

1 tablespoon dried basil

1 tablespoon dried oregano leaves

1½ teaspoons dried parsley

½ teaspoon coarse sea salt

¼ teaspoon ground black pepper

½ cup red wine or beef broth

3¾ cups cooked ground beef *(from earlier in prep day)*

1. Heat the oil in a large sauté pan or pot over medium-high heat. Once hot, add the onion and garlic. Sauté for 4 to 5 minutes, until the onion is slightly browned.

2. Add the tomatoes and seasonings and stir. Cook until the sauce begins to bubble, then stir in the red wine.

3. Add the ground beef, then reduce the heat to medium, cover, and cook for an additional 3 to 4 minutes, until the meat is warmed through. Remove from the heat.

4. Store in the refrigerator for use later in the week.

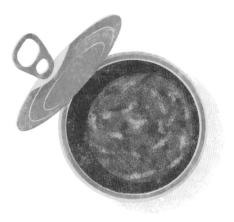

Halve the olives

Slice ½ cup of pitted Kalamata olives in half, then store in the refrigerator for use later in the week.

Bolognese Casserole

Yield: 5 servings   Prep Time: 10 minutes   Cook Time: 20 minutes

Strands scraped from 2 baked spaghetti squash halves ✓

1 tablespoon extra-virgin olive oil

1 teaspoon dried parsley

½ teaspoon garlic powder

½ teaspoon coarse sea salt

Bolognese sauce ✓

8 sprigs fresh flat-leaf parsley, for garnish

¼ cup shaved or shredded Parmesan cheese, for garnish (omit for Paleo/dairy-free)

1. Preheat the oven to 350°F.

2. Toss the squash strands with the olive oil, parsley, garlic powder, and salt, then place in a 3-quart baking dish.

3. Top the squash mixture with the Bolognese sauce, then bake for 20 minutes, until the top is slightly browned and bubbling.

4. Meanwhile, chop the parsley and set aside.

5. Garnish the casserole with the parsley and Parmesan cheese and serve!

Mediterranean Skillet

Yield: 5 servings   Prep Time: 10 minutes   Cook Time: 12 minutes

2 tablespoons extra-virgin olive oil, divided

1 white onion, diced ✓

2 cloves garlic, minced ✓

1 pound frozen quartered artichoke hearts, thawed

1 cup grape tomatoes

2 lemons

6 cups fresh spinach

3¾ cups cooked ground beef ✓

½ teaspoon coarse sea salt

1 tablespoon dried basil

1 tablespoon dried oregano leaves

1 teaspoon dried dill weed

¼ teaspoon ground black pepper

FOR GARNISH:

Halved Kalamata olives ✓

¼ cup crumbled feta cheese (omit for Paleo/dairy-free)

8 sprigs fresh flat-leaf parsley

1. Heat 1 tablespoon of the oil in a large cast-iron skillet or sauté pan over medium heat. Add the onion and garlic and cook for 3 to 4 minutes, until the onion is translucent.

2. Add the artichoke hearts and tomatoes and cook, stirring occasionally, for an additional 3 to 4 minutes, until slightly browned.

3. Meanwhile, juice the lemons until you have about ¼ cup of juice. Set aside.

4. Add the remaining tablespoon of oil to the pan with the tomatoes and artichokes, then stir in the spinach and cook for about 1 minute, until the spinach is wilted. Mix in the beef.

5. Add the lemon juice, salt, and seasonings and toss to combine. Cook for 1 to 2 minutes to let the flavors combine.

6. Meanwhile, chop the parsley.

7. Garnish the mixture in the skillet with the olives, feta, and chopped parsley and serve!

Spinach Pesto Spaghetti Squash Boats

Yield: 4 servings   Prep Time: 10 minutes   Cook Time: 15 minutes

2 baked spaghetti squash halves ✓

Spinach pesto ✓

½ teaspoon coarse sea salt

Pesto meatballs ✓

2 tablespoons shredded Parmesan cheese, for garnish (omit for Paleo/dairy-free)

1. Preheat the oven to 350°F.

2. Use a fork to scrape the squash strands from the shells, reserving the shells. In a large bowl, toss the squash strands with the spinach pesto and salt. Stuff the mixture back into the shells and top with the meatballs.

3. Bake for 15 minutes or until fully warmed through, then garnish with the Parmesan cheese and serve!

SHREDDED PORK, KALE, and PLANTAINS

This week is obviously going to be delicious because it starts with shredded pork, kale, and plantains! Pork shoulder yields a lot of prepared protein, and you'll make good use of it by transforming the components into epic Al Pastor Pizzas, a Green Pork Chili (a big bowl of comfort right there), and Caribbean Plantain Bowls (one of my personal favorites). If you live in an area where plantains are hard to find, bookmark this week so that you can hop right to it when you do find them! You won't regret it. If you'd like to supplement this week's three main dinner recipes with two additional meals, see the suggested "Bonus Dinner Options" on the next page.

Weekly Ingredients

FRESH PRODUCE

Cilantro, ½ bunch

Garlic, 2 cloves

Lacinato (aka dinosaur) kale, 2 bunches

Lemon, ½

Limes, 3

Onion, red, ¼

Pineapple tidbits, 8 ounces (1 cup) (or use frozen or canned in juice)

Plantains, 2 ripe (yellow with some brown spots) and 4 green

MEAT/DAIRY

Pork shoulder, boneless, 1 (5 pounds)

Sour cream, 6 ounces (¾ cup)

PANTRY

Avocado oil, 3 fluid ounces (¼ cup plus 2 tablespoons)

Avocado oil mayonnaise, store-bought or homemade (page 372), 8 fluid ounces (1 cup)

Canned chipotle peppers in adobo sauce, 2

Chicken broth, 16 fluid ounces (2 cups)

Coconut oil, 3 ounces (¼ cup plus 2 tablespoons)

Extra-virgin olive oil, 1½ teaspoons

Salsa verde, 1 (16-ounce) jar

SEASONINGS

Dried oregano leaves, 1 teaspoon

Ground cumin, 1 teaspoon

Ingredient Subs

To make this week PALEO and/or DAIRY-FREE:

· Replace ½ cup of the sour cream with the cream from 1 (13½-ounce) can of full-fat coconut milk. Omit the remaining ¼ cup.

To make this week EGG-FREE:

· Use vegan mayo instead of egg-based mayonnaise.

Bonus Dinner Options

Dinner 1

Crispy Curried Chicken Thighs   (page 348)

Steamed Green Beans
(page 361)

Basic White Rice
(page 368)

Bonus Dinner Ingredients

Chicken thighs, bone-in, skin-on, 2 pounds

Curry powder, 1 tablespoon

Extra-virgin olive oil, 1 tablespoon plus 2 teaspoons

Green beans, fresh, 1 pound

Lime, 1

White rice, 6½ ounces (1 cup)

Bonus Dinner Ingredient Subs

To make this meal PALEO and/or GRAIN-FREE:

Replace the white rice with 1 large head cauliflower (about 3 pounds) or 18 ounces frozen riced cauliflower; make Basic Cauliflower Rice (page 363) instead of the Basic White Rice.

Dinner 2

Pan-Seared White Fish
(page 353)

Simple Roasted Cauliflower (page 357)

Basic Quinoa
(page 369)

Bonus Dinner Ingredients

Cauliflower, 1 large head (2½ to 3 pounds)

Extra-virgin olive oil, 2 fluid ounces (¼ cup)

Garlic powder, ½ teaspoon

Lemon, 1

Quinoa, 6 ounces (1 cup)

White fish fillets (such as snapper), 4 (6 ounces each)

Bonus Dinner Ingredient Subs

To make this meal PALEO and/or GRAIN-FREE:

Replace the quinoa with 1 large head cauliflower (about 3 pounds) or 18 ounces frozen riced cauliflower; make Basic Cauliflower Rice (page 363) instead of the Basic Quinoa.

Prep Day

You're in for another fun day in the kitchen! I like to get the pork shoulder going first. After seasoning the pork, I cook it using the Instant Pot method because it saves me so much time, but you can use the oven or a slow cooker if you prefer. While the pork cooks, I prepare the plantains, frying the ripe ones and transforming the green ones into pizza crusts. Once the plantains are cooking, I whip up the sauces, prep the kale (wilting half of it), and then chop the rest of the veggies. When the pork is finished, it gets shredded. Then everything is packaged and stored in the refrigerator.

note: *If you're planning to make homemade mayonnaise rather than use store-bought, I recommend that you add it to your prep day tasks so that it's ready for use in the adobo and garlic sauces later in the day.*

Cook and shred the pork

Yield: 9 cups shredded pork

Prep Time: 10 minutes

Cook Time: 1½ to 10 hours, depending on method

1 (5-pound) boneless pork shoulder

1½ teaspoons coarse sea salt

1 tablespoon avocado oil (for oven and Instant Pot methods)

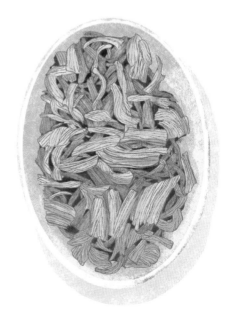

1. If using the Instant Pot method, cut the pork shoulder into four or five equal pieces; otherwise, leave it whole. Season the meat with the salt.

2. Cook the pork using one of these three methods:

- **Oven Method** (Cook Time: 3½ to 4½ hours)
  Preheat the oven to 325°F. Heat the oil in a Dutch oven or enameled cast-iron pot with a lid over medium-high heat. Add the seasoned pork to the pot and sear for 3 to 4 minutes per side, until browned. Once browned, pour 1½ cups of water into the pot, then cover with the lid and transfer to the oven. Cook for 3½ to 4½ hours, until the pork shreds easily.

- **Instant Pot Method** (Cook Time: 1½ hours)
  Set a 6-quart Instant Pot to Sauté mode and heat the oil in the pot. Working in batches, add the seasoned pieces of pork and sear for 2 to 3 minutes per side. (If you are short on time, you can skip this step, but it gives the pork more flavor!) Once seared, return all of the pork to the pot, along with ½ cup of water. Seal the lid onto the Instant Pot, press Pressure Cook or Manual, and set the timer for 90 minutes. Once the cooking is finished, release the pressure manually by slowly turning the pressure valve to "venting."

- **Slow Cooker Method** (Cook Time: 8 to 10 hours)
  Place the seasoned pork in a 6-quart slow cooker. Cook on low for 8 to 10 hours, until the pork shreds easily.

3. Shred the meat with two forks, removing the excess fat. Place 2 cups in a container labeled "Pizzas," 4 cups in a container labeled "Chili," and 3 cups in a container labeled "Bowls." Store in the refrigerator for use later in the week.

Fry the yellow plantains

Prep Time: 5 minutes

Cook Time: 10 minutes

2 ripe plantains (yellow with some brown spots)

2 tablespoons avocado oil

1 teaspoon coarse sea salt

1. To peel the plantains, slice off the ends, then, with a small paring knife, score the peel of each plantain lengthwise four times, along the seams. Carefully separate the peels from the plantains, then slice the plantains crosswise at a slight angle into ½-inch-thick ovals.

2. Heat the oil in a large skillet over medium heat. Once hot, add the plantains. If the plantains don't all fit in the pan at once without crowding, work in batches.

3. Fry the plantains for 3 to 4 minutes, then flip and fry on the other side for an additional 3 to 4 minutes, until golden brown on both sides.

4. Remove from the pan and sprinkle the plantains with the salt. Store in the refrigerator for use later in the week.

Use the green plantains to make the pizza crusts

Yield: two 8-inch crusts

Prep Time: 15 minutes

Cook Time: 30 minutes

4 green plantains

¼ cup plus 2 tablespoons coconut oil

½ teaspoon coarse sea salt

1. Preheat the oven to 375°F.

2. To peel the plantains, slice off the ends, then, with a small paring knife, score the peel of each plantain lengthwise four times, along the seams. Carefully separate the peels from the plantains, then cut each plantain into thirds. Put the plantains in a food processor or blender.

3. To the food processor or blender with the plantains, add the coconut oil and salt and blend until smooth.

4. Line a cookie sheet with parchment paper or a silicone baking mat and spread the plantain mixture into two 8-inch circles, making the thickness as even as possible.

5. Bake for 25 to 30 minutes, until the crusts are browned and no longer sticky.

6. Let cool on the cookie sheet for at least 10 minutes before removing. Wrap the crusts in foil and store in the refrigerator for use later in the week.

Prepare the kale

Prep Time: 10 minutes

Cook Time: 5 minutes

2 bunches Lacinato (aka dinosaur) kale

1½ teaspoons extra-virgin olive oil

Juice of ½ lemon

Pinch of coarse sea salt

1. Wash and dry both bunches of kale, then remove the stems and coarsely chop the leaves.

2. Place half of the chopped kale in an airtight container or resealable plastic bag with a paper towel to absorb the excess moisture, label the container "Chili," and store in the refrigerator for use later in the week.

3. To prepare the remaining half of the chopped kale, heat the oil in a large skillet with a lid over medium heat. Once hot, add the kale and toss it in the oil.

4. Place the lid on the pan and allow the kale to wilt, 3 to 4 minutes. Once completely wilted, remove the lid and stir in the lemon juice and salt. Transfer to a container labeled "Bowls" and store in the refrigerator for use later in the week.

Make the adobo sauce

½ cup avocado oil mayonnaise or vegan mayo

2 tablespoons fresh lime juice (about 1 lime)

2 chipotle peppers in adobo sauce

Place the mayonnaise, lime juice, and chipotles in a blender and blend until fully combined and smooth. Transfer to a container labeled "Pizzas" and store in the refrigerator for use later in the week.

Chop the cilantro

Wash one bunch of cilantro, then chop one-third of the bunch (leaves and stems), or enough to equal ¼ cup. Transfer to a container labeled "Pizzas." Place another four sprigs of cilantro in a separate container labeled "Chili." Store in the refrigerator for use later in the week.

Dice the red onion

Dice one-quarter of a red onion. Transfer to a container labeled "Pizzas" and refrigerate for use later in the week.

Make the garlic sauce

½ cup avocado oil mayonnaise or vegan mayo

2 cloves garlic, finely minced or grated

2 tablespoons fresh lime juice (about 1 lime)

Place all of the ingredients in a bowl and stir until fully combined. Transfer to a container labeled "Bowls" and store in the refrigerator for use later in the week.

Al Pastor Pizzas

Yield: 4 servings   Prep Time: 10 minutes   Cook Time: 50 minutes

2 cups shredded pork ✓

1 cup pineapple tidbits, drained

2 par-baked pizza crusts ✓

Adobo sauce ✓

¼ cup chopped fresh cilantro, for garnish ✓

¼ red onion, diced, for garnish ✓

1. Place an oven rack in the lower position. Preheat the oven to 375°F.

2. Spread the shredded pork and pineapple over the pizza crusts, then top with the adobo sauce.

3. Place the pizzas directly on the lower oven rack and bake for 15 minutes, until the pork is browned and the sauce is bubbling.

4. Garnish with the cilantro and red onion, then slice and serve!

Green Pork Chili

Yield: 5 servings   Prep Time: 5 minutes   Cook Time: 15 minutes

2 cups chicken broth

1 (16-ounce) jar salsa verde

½ cup sour cream or cream scooped from the top of 1 (13½-ounce) can chilled full-fat coconut milk

2 tablespoons fresh lime juice (about 1 lime)

1 teaspoon coarse sea salt

1 teaspoon ground cumin

1 teaspoon dried oregano leaves

½ teaspoon ground black pepper

4 cups shredded pork ✓

1 bunch Lacinato (aka dinosaur) kale, destemmed and chopped ✓

4 sprigs fresh cilantro, for garnish

¼ cup sour cream, for garnish (omit for dairy-free)

1. In a large pot over medium heat, whisk together the chicken broth, salsa, sour cream, lime juice, and seasonings, then stir in the shredded pork and kale.

2. Let the chili come to a slight simmer, then reduce the heat to medium-low and cook for 15 minutes.

3. Serve in bowls and garnish with the fresh cilantro and sour cream.

Caribbean Plantain Bowls

Yield: 4 servings   Cook Time: 15 minutes

2 tablespoons avocado oil, divided

Pan-fried plantains ✓

Wilted kale ✓

3 cups shredded pork ✓

Garlic sauce ✓

1. Heat 1 tablespoon of the oil in a large skillet over medium-high heat. Once hot, add the plantains and cook for 1 to 2 minutes per side, until warmed through. Remove from the pan and set aside.

2. Add the wilted kale to the skillet and cook for 1 to 2 minutes, until warmed through. Remove from the pan and set aside.

3. Add the remaining tablespoon of oil to the skillet and evenly spread the shredded pork over the pan. Cook for 3 to 4 minutes, until crisp on the bottom, then flip and cook for an additional 3 to 4 minutes, until crisp on the other side.

4. Assemble the bowls with the crispy pork, plantains, and kale. Drizzle with the garlic sauce and serve!

ROASTED CHICKEN, BRUSSELS SPROUTS, and PARSNIPS

This week is a classic example of how you can take basic ingredients, prepare them in simple ways, and then transform those components into the most interesting finished dishes! We make use of roasted whole chickens, parsnips (prepped in two ways), Brussels sprouts, and Yukon gold potatoes. The menu for this week includes a fabulous mash-up of chicken pot pie and shepherd's pie that tops the classic creamy chicken filling with a potato-parsnip mash, a truly delicious Buffalo chicken–themed sheet pan dinner, and a satisfying Cashew Chicken. If you'd like to supplement this week's three main dinner recipes with two additional meals, see the suggested "Bonus Dinner Options" on the next page.

Weekly Ingredients

FRESH PRODUCE

Bell peppers, red, 2

Broccoli, 1 medium head (or 8 ounces precut florets)

Brussels sprouts, 1 pound

Cilantro, 4 sprigs

Flat-leaf parsley, 4 sprigs

Garlic, 2 cloves

Green onions, 2

Onion, red, 1 small

Onion, yellow, 1 small

Parsnips, 2 pounds

Snow peas, 6 ounces

Yukon gold potatoes, 1 pound

FROZEN FOODS

Peas and carrots, 5 ounces (1 cup)

MEAT/DAIRY

Butter, salted, 6 ounces (1½ sticks)

Chickens, 2 whole (4 to 5 pounds each)

Heavy cream, 2 fluid ounces (¼ cup)

Whole milk, 4 fluid ounces (½ cup)

PANTRY

Arrowroot powder, 1 teaspoon

Avocado oil or ghee, 2 tablespoons

Cashews, raw, 7 ounces (1½ cups)

Chicken broth, 28 fluid ounces (3½ cups)

Coconut aminos, Coconut Secret brand, 4 fluid ounces (½ cup)

Extra-virgin olive oil, 3 tablespoons

Gluten-free flour blend, 1 tablespoon

Medium-hot hot sauce, such as Frank's RedHot, 3 fluid ounces (⅓ cup)

Ranch dressing, store-bought or homemade (page 372), 2 fluid ounces (¼ cup)

Toasted sesame oil, 1 teaspoon

Unseasoned rice wine vinegar, 1½ teaspoons

White rice, 10 ounces (1½ cups)

SEASONINGS

Dried rubbed sage, ½ teaspoon

Dried thyme leaves, ½ teaspoon

Ginger powder, ½ teaspoon

Red pepper flakes, ½ teaspoon

Sesame seeds, 1 tablespoon

Ingredient Subs

To make this week PALEO:

· Use the substitutions listed below for making the week grain-free and dairy-free.

To make this week GRAIN-FREE:

· Replace the gluten-free flour blend with arrowroot powder.

· Replace the white rice with 1 large head cauliflower (about 3 pounds) or 18 ounces frozen riced cauliflower.

To make this week DAIRY-FREE:

· Replace the butter with ghee or oil of choice.

· Replace the heavy cream and milk with 6 fluid ounces (¾ cup) canned full-fat coconut milk.

· Use a dairy-free ranch dressing.

To make this week EGG-FREE:

· Use an egg-free ranch dressing. If making homemade, use vegan mayo.

To make this week NUT-FREE:

· Omit the cashews.

Bonus Dinner Options

Dinner 1

Basic Pork Tenderloin
(page 350)

Simple Roasted
Cauliflower (page 357)

Pan-Fried Plantains
(page 368)

Bonus Dinner Ingredients

Cauliflower, 1 large head (2½ to 3 pounds)

Extra-virgin olive oil, 2 fluid ounces (¼ cup)

Garlic powder, ½ teaspoon

Plantains, yellow, 2 large (about 1 pound)

Pork tenderloin, 1 (1¼ pounds)

Texas Grill Rub, 2 tablespoons (see page 374 for ingredients)

Dinner 2

Easy Tuna Steak
(page 353)

Lemony Kale
(page 359)

Basic Quinoa
(page 369)

Bonus Dinner Ingredients

Extra-virgin olive oil, 2 fluid ounces (¼ cup)

Kale, 1 small bunch (about 1 pound)

Lemon, ½

Quinoa, 1 cup

Tuna steaks, 1 inch thick, 4 (6 to 8 ounces each)

Bonus Dinner Ingredient Subs

To make this meal GRAIN-FREE:

Replace the quinoa with 1 large head cauliflower or 18 ounces frozen riced cauliflower; make Basic Cauliflower Rice (page 363) instead of the Basic Quinoa.

Prep Day

Today you will be roasting the chickens, Brussels sprouts, and half of the parsnips and making a potato-parsnip mash using the remainder of the parsnips. I find it most efficient to get the chickens going first because they take the longest to cook, and then to get the Brussels and parsnips into the oven to roast on a rack below the chicken. The mash can be put together while the chickens and vegetables are roasting. You can do the raw vegetable prep while the chickens are cooling, which you can break down last.

note: *If you're planning to make homemade ranch dressing rather than use store-bought, I recommend that you add it to your prep day tasks so that it's ready for use later in the week.*

Roast and break down the chickens

Yield: 6 cups cubed breast meat, 4 quarters, 4 wings
Prep Time: 10 minutes
Cook Time: 1 hour 15 minutes

2 (4- to 5-pound) whole chickens

2 tablespoons extra-virgin olive oil

2 teaspoons coarse sea salt

½ teaspoon ground black pepper

1. If you are planning to roast the chickens and vegetables at the same time, position one oven rack in the middle of the oven (for the chickens) and position a second rack below the middle rack (for the Brussels sprouts and parsnips). Preheat the oven to 375°F.

2. Place the chickens on a rimmed baking sheet and pat dry with paper towels. Rub the chickens with the oil, then season with the salt and pepper.

3. Bake for 1 hour 15 minutes, or until a thermometer inserted into the thickest part of a chicken breast registers 165°F.

4. Let cool for at least 30 minutes, then break down the chickens: First, cut off the wings and leg quarters, leaving the legs and thighs connected. Next, separate the breasts from the bone and cut the breast meat into ½-inch cubes, discarding the skin.

5. Transfer the wings and leg quarters to an airtight container and put the cubed breast meat in another container. Store in the refrigerator for use later in the week.

Roast the Brussels sprouts and half of the parsnips

Prep Time: 10 minutes

Cook Time: 50 minutes

1 pound Brussels sprouts, trimmed and cut in half

1 pound parsnips, peeled, trimmed, and cut into 1-inch pieces

1 tablespoon extra-virgin olive oil

1 teaspoon coarse sea salt

½ teaspoon ground black pepper

1. Preheat the oven to 375°F. Line a rimmed baking sheet with parchment paper.

2. Toss the Brussels sprouts and parsnips with the olive oil, salt, and pepper, then spread the vegetables on the lined baking sheet.

3. Roast for 45 to 50 minutes, until both vegetables are browned and the parsnips are easily pierced with a fork.

4. Store in the refrigerator for use later in the week.

Make the potato-parsnip mash

Prep Time: 10 minutes

Cook Time: 30 minutes

1 pound Yukon gold potatoes, peeled and cut into 1-inch cubes

1 pound parsnips, peeled, trimmed, and cut into 1-inch pieces

2 teaspoons coarse sea salt, divided

½ cup whole milk or canned full-fat coconut milk

¼ cup (½ stick) salted butter, ghee, or oil of choice

¼ teaspoon ground black pepper

1. Place the potatoes and parsnips in a large pot. Cover with water and add 1½ teaspoons of the salt.

2. Bring to a boil over medium-high heat, then simmer for 15 to 20 minutes, until the potatoes and parsnips are easily pierced with a fork.

3. Drain the water, then return the potatoes and parsnips to the pot and mash with a potato masher. Stir in the milk, butter, pepper, and remaining ½ teaspoon of salt.

4. Store in the refrigerator for use later in the week.

Toast the cashews
(omit for nut-free)

Prep Time: 1 minute

Cook Time: 8 minutes

Preheat the oven to 350°F. Spread 1½ cups of raw cashews evenly on a rimmed baking sheet. Bake for 5 minutes, then remove from the oven, stir, and return to the oven to toast for an additional 3 minutes, until lightly browned and fragrant. Store in the refrigerator for use later in the week.

Cook the rice

Yield: 4½ cups

Prep Time: 2 minutes

Cook Time: about 20 minutes

Cook 1½ cups of white rice according to the package instructions. Store in the refrigerator for use later in the week.

 **PALEO/GRAIN-FREE RICE SUBSTITUTE**
Make a double batch of Basic Cauliflower Rice (page 363), then follow the storage instructions for the white rice above.

Prepare the onions

1. Dice a small yellow onion, then transfer to a container labeled "Pot Pie." Store in the refrigerator for use later in the week.

2. Thinly slice 1 small red onion, then place in a container labeled "Sheet Pan Dinner." Store in the refrigerator for use later in the week.

Mince the garlic

Mince three cloves of garlic, or enough to equal 3 teaspoons. Store in the refrigerator for use later in the week.

Make the stir-fry sauce

Prep time: 2 minutes

Cook time: 6 minutes

½ cup coconut aminos

½ cup chicken broth

1 teaspoon toasted sesame oil

1½ teaspoons unseasoned rice wine vinegar

½ teaspoon ginger powder

½ teaspoon red pepper flakes

¼ teaspoon coarse sea salt

1 teaspoon arrowroot powder

1. In a small saucepan over medium heat, combine all of the ingredients except the arrowroot powder. Bring to a simmer and cook for 5 minutes, until the sauce is slightly reduced in volume.

2. In a small bowl, whisk the arrowroot powder with 1 tablespoon of water to make a slurry, then whisk the slurry into the sauce. Bring the sauce to a boil, stir, and cook for an additional minute, until thickened.

3. Store in the refrigerator for use later in the week.

Prepare the stir-fry veggies

1. Cut the florets off of a medium-sized head of broccoli (unless you purchased precut florets).

2. Thinly slice two red bell peppers.

3. Thinly slice two green onions, or enough to equal ¼ cup.

4. Store the stir-fry veggies in separate containers in the refrigerator for use later in the week.

Mashed Potato and Parsnip–Crusted Chicken Pot Pie

Yield: 6 servings   Prep Time: 15 minutes   Cook Time: 30 minutes

2 tablespoons salted butter, ghee, or oil of choice

1 small yellow onion, diced ✓

2 teaspoons minced garlic ✓

1 tablespoon gluten-free flour blend (see note below)

3 cups chicken broth

¼ cup heavy cream or coconut cream

½ teaspoon dried rubbed sage

½ teaspoon dried thyme leaves

½ teaspoon coarse sea salt

½ teaspoon ground black pepper

Half of the cubed roasted chicken breasts (about 3 cups) ✓

1 cup frozen peas and carrots

Potato-parsnip mash ✓

1 tablespoon chopped fresh flat-leaf parsley, for garnish

1. Preheat the oven to 350°F.

2. Melt the butter in a Dutch oven or other heavy-bottomed pot over medium heat, then add the onion and garlic. Sauté for 4 to 5 minutes, until the onion is translucent.

3. Sprinkle the flour over the onion mixture and whisk to combine.

4. Pour in the broth 1 cup at a time, whisking constantly, then add the cream, sage, thyme, salt, and pepper, continuing to whisk until the mixture is smooth.

5. Stir in the chicken and the peas and carrots. Simmer for 5 minutes.

6. While the chicken mixture is simmering, rewarm the potato-parsnip mash in the microwave for 3 minutes or in a covered saucepan on the stovetop over medium heat for 3 to 5 minutes. It should have a spreadable consistency.

7. Transfer the chicken mixture to a 4-quart casserole dish or deep-sided ovenproof sauté pan, then top with the potato-parsnip mash. Bake for 30 minutes, until browned and bubbly on top.

8. Remove from the oven and let cool slightly, then garnish with the parsley and serve!

note: *If using arrowroot powder instead of the gluten-free flour blend, skip Step 3 and pick up with Step 4. When the broth begins to bubble in Step 5, whisk 2 teaspoons arrowroot powder with 2 tablespoons water to make a slurry, then pour the slurry into the chicken mixture, whisking constantly, and return it to a simmer. Continue to cook for 1 minute, until thickened.*

Buffalo Chicken Sheet Pan Dinner

Yield: 4 servings   Prep Time: 5 minutes   Cook Time: 20 minutes

⅓ cup salted butter, ghee, or oil of choice

⅓ cup medium-hot hot sauce

4 roasted chicken leg quarters and 4 roasted chicken wings ✓

Roasted Brussels sprouts and parsnips ✓

1 small red onion, sliced ✓

¼ cup ranch dressing, for drizzling

Leaves from 4 stems fresh cilantro, chopped, for garnish

1. Preheat the oven to 375°F.

2. To make the Buffalo sauce, melt the butter in the microwave or in a small saucepan over medium heat, then pour it into a large bowl. Add the hot sauce and whisk to combine.

3. Dunk the chicken pieces in the Buffalo sauce, then place on a rimmed baking sheet. Place the roasted Brussels sprouts and parsnips and the sliced onion on the baking sheet alongside the chicken.

4. Bake for 20 minutes, or until the chicken is warmed through and slightly crisp. Drizzle with the ranch dressing and sprinkle with the cilantro, then serve!

Cashew Chicken

Yield: 4 servings   Prep Time: 5 minutes   Cook Time: 12 minutes

2 tablespoons avocado oil or ghee, divided

2 red bell peppers, sliced into thin strips ✓

Florets from 1 head broccoli (or 8 ounces precut fresh florets) ✓

6 ounces snow peas

Half of the cubed roasted chicken breast (about 3 cups) ✓

2 green onions, thinly sliced ✓

Toasted cashews ✓

Stir-fry sauce ✓

4½ cups cooked white rice or cauli-rice ✓

1 tablespoon sesame seeds, for garnish

1. Preheat a large wok or skillet over medium-high heat. Once hot, add 1 tablespoon of the avocado oil and swirl it around the pan. Add the bell pepper strips and cook for 2 to 3 minutes, stirring occasionally, until slightly browned.

2. Add the broccoli florets and snow peas to the pan. Cook for 2 to 3 minutes, stirring occasionally, until the vegetables begin to soften.

3. Add the remaining tablespoon of oil to the pan, then add the chicken, green onions, and toasted cashews. Cook for 1 to 2 minutes, until the chicken is warmed through, then pour the stir-fry sauce over the chicken mixture and toss to coat.

4. To reheat the rice, place it in a medium-sized saucepan over low heat, covered, for 5 minutes or microwave for 2 minutes, or until hot.

5. Garnish with the sesame seeds and serve with the rice.

BAKED TURKEY BREAST, KALE, and BUTTERNUT SQUASH

This week tackles the task of transforming a turkey breast, kale, and butternut squash into three fabulous dinners. This is a budget-friendly week for sure, especially if you make it in the cooler months when all of the ingredients are in peak season. You'll be making a Twice-Baked Loaded Butternut Squash, a Tuscan Turkey Kale Soup, and a Harvest Casserole. If you'd like to supplement this week's three main dinner recipes with two additional meals, see the suggested "Bonus Dinner Options" on the next page.

Weekly Ingredients

FRESH PRODUCE

Butternut squash, 2 medium (about 2 pounds each)

Carrots, 4 medium (about 5 ounces)

Chives, 4 (optional)

Lacinato (aka dinosaur) kale, 2 bunches

Lemons, 1½

Pomegranate, ½ medium (or 3 ounces/½ cup fresh or frozen pomegranate seeds)

Sage leaves, 12 (or 1 teaspoon dried rubbed sage)

MEAT/DAIRY

Bacon, 5 strips

Butter, salted, 2 ounces (¼ cup)

Greek yogurt, plain, full-fat, 4 ounces (½ cup)

Turkey breast, bone-in, skin-on, 1 (5 to 6 pounds)

PANTRY

Chicken broth, 48 fluid ounces (6 cups)

Diced tomatoes, 1 (14½-ounce) can

Extra-virgin olive oil, 1½ tablespoons

Honey, 1 tablespoon

Pecans, raw, 5¼ ounces (1⅓ cups)

SEASONINGS

Garlic powder, 1½ teaspoons

Ground cinnamon, ¼ teaspoon

Italian seasoning, 1 tablespoon

Rosemary leaves, ½ teaspoon

Thyme leaves, 1 teaspoon

Ingredient Subs

To make this week PALEO and/or DAIRY-FREE:

· *Substitute ghee or another fat for the butter.*

· *Use plain, unsweetened dairy-free Greek-style yogurt in place of the Greek yogurt.*

To make this week NUT-FREE:

· *Make the casserole without the pecan topping: omit the pecans, honey, and cinnamon and reduce the amount of butter for the week to 2 tablespoons.*

Bonus Dinner Options

Dinner 1

Basic Pork Tenderloin
(page 350)

Italian Side Salad
(page 362)

Green Peas
(page 367)

Bonus Dinner Ingredients

Artichoke hearts, marinated and quartered,
1 (6-ounce) jar

Dried dill weed, 1 teaspoon

Extra-virgin olive oil, 2 fluid ounces (¼ cup)

Lemon, 1 small

Lettuce, mixed, 8 ounces (about 6 cups chopped)

Olives, assorted pitted, 3 ounces (½ cup)

Peas, frozen, 1 (10-ounce) package

Pork tenderloin, 1 (1¼ pounds)

Red wine vinegar, 2 tablespoons

Texas Grill Rub, 2 tablespoons (see page 374 for
ingredients)

Dinner 2

Ranch Chicken Thighs
(page 349)

Wilted Spinach
(page 358)

Baked Russet Potatoes
(page 366)

Bonus Dinner Ingredients

Chicken thighs, boneless,
skinless, 1½ pounds

Extra-virgin olive oil,
1 tablespoon

Lemon, ½

Ranch dressing, store-bought
or homemade (page 372),
2 fluid ounces (¼ cup)

Russet potatoes, 4 small to
medium (about 1 pound)

Spinach, fresh, 1 pound

Bonus Dinner Ingredient Subs

**To make this meal DAIRY-FREE
and/or EGG-FREE:**

*Use a dairy-free and/or egg-free
ranch dressing. If egg-free and
making homemade dressing,
use vegan mayo.*

Prep Day

Today's meal prep work is pretty minimal. You're going to roast the turkey breast, prep the kale (some is stored raw, and the rest will be cooked today), cook the bacon, roast the squash, slice the carrots, and seed a pomegranate. I find it most efficient to get the turkey in the oven first. While the turkey roasts, I prep the kale, which includes wilting one bunch. I also cook and then slice or crumble the bacon, slice the carrots, and seed the pomegranate. Once the turkey is finished roasting, I pull it out, crank up the oven temperature to 375°F, and then pop the squash in to roast. Once the turkey is cool enough to handle, I separate the meat from the bone, chop two-thirds of the meat, shred the rest, and store it in separate containers for later.

Roast the turkey breast

Prep Time: 15 minutes

Cook Time: 1 hour 30 minutes

1 (5- to 6-pound) bone-in, skin-on turkey breast

1 tablespoon extra-virgin olive oil

2 teaspoons coarse sea salt

1. Preheat the oven to 300°F. Have on hand a roasting pan, or line a rimmed baking sheet with parchment paper.

2. Brush the turkey breast with the olive oil and sprinkle with the salt, then place skin side up on the roasting pan or lined baking sheet. Roast for 75 to 90 minutes, until a thermometer inserted in the thickest part of the breast reads 165°F.

3. Let cool, then separate the meat from the bone. Cut two-thirds of the turkey breast into 1-inch cubes, then shred the remainder. You should have about 6 cups cubed turkey and 3 cups shredded. Divide the cubed turkey equally between two containers; label one "Loaded Squash" and the other "Harvest Casserole." Put the shredded turkey in a third container labeled "Tuscan Soup." Store in the refrigerator for use later in the week.

Prepare the kale

Prep Time: 15 minutes

Cook Time: 5 minutes

2 bunches Lacinato (aka dinosaur) kale

1½ teaspoons extra-virgin olive oil

Juice of ½ lemon

Pinch of coarse sea salt

1. Wash, dry, and destem both bunches of kale.

2. Chop one bunch, then place it in a container labeled "Tuscan Soup." Store in the refrigerator for use later in the week.

3. Coarsely chop the second bunch, then wilt it as follows:

- Place the olive oil in a skillet with a lid over medium heat. Once hot, add the chopped kale and toss it in the oil.

- Place the lid on the pan and allow the kale to wilt, 3 to 4 minutes. Once completely wilted, remove the lid and stir in the lemon juice and salt.

- Place in a container labeled "Harvest Casserole" and store in the refrigerator for use later in the week.

Cook and slice or crumble the bacon

Prep Time: 3 minutes

Cook Time: 6 minutes

1. In a medium-sized skillet over medium heat, cook five strips of bacon until crisp, about 6 minutes. Transfer the bacon to a paper towel–lined plate and let cool.

2. When the bacon is cool enough to handle, slice or crumble it into ½-inch pieces. (If you used thick-cut bacon, slicing it will be easier; if you used regular bacon, crumbling it will be easier.) Store in the refrigerator for use later in the week.

Slice the carrots

Peel four medium-sized carrots, then slice them into ¼-inch-thick coins. Store in the refrigerator for use later in the week.

Seed the half pomegranate

If you purchased fresh or frozen pomegranate seeds (aka arils), you can skip this task. Otherwise, remove the seeds from half of a pomegranate. To seed the half pomegranate, cut it in half around the smooth circumference, leaving the stems untouched on each half. From there, turn your pomegranate half cut side down over a bowl. Using a sturdy wooden spoon, firmly hit the pomegranate until all of the seeds pop out into the bowl. Alternatively, you can manually break the half pomegranate apart with your fingers under water. You should get about ½ cup of pomegranate seeds. Store in the refrigerator for use later in the week.

Roast the squash

Prep Time: 10 minutes
Cook Time: 1 hour

1. Preheat the oven to 375°F. Line a rimmed baking sheet with parchment paper.

2. Cut two medium-sized butternut squash in half lengthwise and scoop out the seeds and stringy membranes with a spoon.

3. Lay the halves cut side down on the lined baking sheet and roast for 45 to 60 minutes, until tender.

4. Place two of the squash halves in a large container labeled "Loaded Squash." Scoop the pulp out of the remaining two halves into another container, discarding the skins, and label the second container "Harvest Casserole." Store in the refrigerator for use later in the week.

Twice-Baked Loaded Butternut Squash

Yield: 4 servings   Prep Time: 10 minutes   Cook Time: 25 minutes

2 roasted butternut squash halves ✓

½ cup plain full-fat Greek yogurt or dairy-free Greek-style yogurt

1 teaspoon coarse sea salt

1 teaspoon garlic powder

1 teaspoon dried thyme leaves

½ teaspoon dried rosemary leaves

5 strips bacon, cooked and sliced or crumbled ✓

Half of the cubed roasted turkey breast (about 3 cups) ✓

4 fresh chives, for garnish (optional)

1. Preheat the oven to 375°F.

2. Place the squash halves on a rimmed baking sheet, then scoop the pulp out of the shells into a medium-sized bowl, leaving a ½-inch-thick wall of squash in the shells.

3. To the squash pulp, add the yogurt, salt, garlic powder, thyme, and rosemary. Mash with a potato masher or blend with an immersion blender until fully incorporated, then stir in the bacon. Taste for seasoning and add more salt, if needed.

4. Spoon the squash mixture back into the shells and top with the cubed turkey.

5. Bake for 25 minutes, until warmed through and slightly browned on top.

6. To serve, cut the squash halves in half to create four portions. Divide among four plates and snip the chives over the top, if using.

Tuscan Turkey Kale Soup

Yield: 4 servings   Prep Time: 15 minutes   Cook Time: 20 minutes

Shredded roasted turkey breast (about 3 cups) ✓

4 medium carrots, peeled and sliced into ¼-inch-thick coins ✓

1 (14½-ounce) can diced tomatoes, drained

1 tablespoon Italian seasoning

½ teaspoon garlic powder

½ to 1 teaspoon coarse sea salt

¼ teaspoon ground black pepper

6 cups chicken broth

1 bunch Lacinato (aka dinosaur) kale, destemmed and chopped ✓

2 tablespoons fresh lemon juice (about 1 small lemon)

1. Place the shredded turkey, carrots, tomatoes, Italian seasoning, garlic powder, ½ teaspoon of salt, and pepper in a large soup pot with a lid. Pour in the broth and stir to combine.

2. Bring to a low boil over medium-high heat, then reduce the heat to medium-low and cover. Simmer for 15 minutes, until the carrots are soft.

3. Stir the kale into the soup, then cover and cook for another 2 to 3 minutes, until the kale is bright green and wilted.

4. Remove from the heat and stir in the lemon juice. Taste for seasoning, add up to ½ teaspoon more salt as needed, and serve!

Harvest Casserole

Yield: 5 servings   Prep Time: 15 minutes   Cook Time: 20 minutes

Pulp from 2 roasted butternut squash halves ✓

2 tablespoons salted butter or ghee, melted

1 tablespoon chopped fresh sage, or 1 teaspoon dried rubbed sage

½ to 1 teaspoon coarse sea salt

¼ teaspoon ground black pepper

Wilted kale ✓

Half of the cubed roasted turkey breast (about 3 cups) ✓

FOR THE CINNAMON-PECAN TOPPING (omit for nut-free):

2 tablespoons salted butter or ghee, melted

1 tablespoon honey

¼ teaspoon ground cinnamon

Pinch of coarse sea salt

1 cup coarsely chopped raw pecans

½ cup pomegranate seeds, for garnish ✓

1. Preheat the oven to 375°F.

2. Place the butternut squash pulp, butter, sage, ½ teaspoon of salt, and pepper in a large bowl and mash with a potato masher or blend with an immersion blender. Taste for seasoning and add up to ½ teaspoon more salt, if needed.

3. Spread the squash mixture in an 8-inch baking dish or similar-sized enameled cast-iron pan, then top with the wilted kale. Next, layer on the cubed turkey.

4. To make the topping, whisk together the butter, honey, cinnamon, and salt in a small bowl, then add the pecans and toss to coat. Sprinkle the pecans on top of the casserole.

5. Bake for 20 minutes, until the casserole is warmed through and the pecans are toasted. Top with the pomegranate seeds and serve!

PORK SHOULDER, BRUSSELS SPROUTS, and SWEET POTATOES

This week, you'll be transforming pork shoulder, Brussels sprouts, and sweet potatoes into three craveable dishes that my family eats regularly. Crispy pork shoulder and sweet potatoes are already a match made in heaven, which is why the Smashed Sweet Potato and Pork Bowls is one of my favorite dishes in the book. Next up is an incredibly easy but flavorful Harvest Sheet Pan Dinner. We round out the week with Southwestern Stuffed Sweet Potatoes, which are bursting with flavor. If you'd like to supplement this week's three main dinner recipes with two additional meals, see the suggested "Bonus Dinner Options" on the next page.

Weekly Ingredients

FRESH PRODUCE

Apple, red, 1 large

Bell pepper, red, 1

Brussels sprouts, 1 pound

Cilantro, 10 sprigs

Garlic, 2 cloves

Lemon, ½ small

Lime, 1

Onion, white, 1 large

Sweet potatoes, small to medium, 3 pounds

Thyme, 8 sprigs

FROZEN FOODS

Yellow corn, 5 ounces (1 cup)

MEAT/DAIRY

Butter, salted, 1 tablespoon

Pork shoulder, boneless, 1 (5 to 6 pounds)

Shredded Mexican cheese blend, 4 ounces (½ cup)

PANTRY

Avocado oil, 3 tablespoons

Avocado oil mayonnaise, store-bought or homemade (page 372), 4 fluid ounces (½ cup)

Balsamic vinegar, 2 tablespoons

Extra-virgin olive oil, 2½ fluid ounces (5 tablespoons)

SEASONINGS

Ancho chili powder, ½ teaspoon

Dried oregano leaves, 1 teaspoon

Dried thyme leaves, 1 teaspoon

Garlic powder, 1½ teaspoons

Ground cumin, 1 teaspoon

Paprika, 1 teaspoon

Ingredient Subs

To make this week PALEO:

· *Use the substitutions listed below for making the week grain-free and dairy-free.*

To make this week GRAIN-FREE:

· *Omit the corn.*

To make this week DAIRY-FREE:

· *Substitute ghee or another fat for the butter.*

· *Omit the cheese.*

To make this week EGG-FREE:

· *Substitute vegan mayo for the avocado oil mayonnaise.*

Bonus Dinner Options

Dinner 1

Balsamic Chicken Thighs
(page 348)

Braised Collards
(page 358)

Perfect Parsnips
(page 365)

Bonus Dinner Ingredients

Balsamic vinegar, 2 tablespoons

Chicken thighs, boneless, skinless, 1½ pounds

Collard greens, 1 small bunch (about 1 pound)

Extra-virgin olive oil, 2 tablespoons

Lemon, ½

Parsnips, 2 pounds

Dinner 2

Honey Mustard Pork
Tenderloin (page 351)

Simple Roasted
Cauliflower (page 357)

Roasted Butternut Squash
Cubes (page 366)

Bonus Dinner Ingredients

Butternut squash, 1 medium (about 2 pounds)

Cauliflower, 1 large head (2½ to 3 pounds)

Dijon mustard, 2 tablespoons

Extra-virgin olive oil, 3 tablespoons

Garlic powder, ½ teaspoon

Honey, 1 tablespoon

Pork tenderloin, 1 (1¼ pounds)

Prep Day

Today you're going to cook the pork, bake the sweet potatoes, roast the Brussels sprouts, chop a few veggies, and make a quick sauce. It's a pretty easy day in the kitchen! To start off, I get the pork in my Instant Pot. (That's my chosen method because it's the quickest, but you can cook the pork in the oven or in a slow cooker if you prefer; just plan your time accordingly.) Once the pork is cooking, I put the sweet potatoes and Brussels in the oven; because they bake at the same temperature, they can cook at the same time, saving you time. The sweet potatoes will stay in about 20 minutes longer than the Brussels sprouts. While those two components are baking, I cut up the onion, dice the bell pepper, and then make the aioli. Once the pork is finished, I store one-third of it for slicing later (for the sheet pan dinner) and shred the remaining two-thirds.

note: *If you're planning to make homemade mayonnaise rather than use store-bought, you will need to add that to the prep day tasks so that it's ready to use for the aioli.*

Cook the pork shoulder

Yield: 7 cups shredded pork, plus about 1 pound cooked pork for slicing

Prep Time: 15 minutes

Cook Time: 1½ to 10 hours, depending on method

1 (5- to 6-pound) boneless pork shoulder

1½ teaspoons coarse sea salt

1 tablespoon avocado oil (for oven method)

1. If using the Instant Pot method, cut the pork shoulder into four or five equal pieces; otherwise, leave it whole. Season the meat with the salt.

2. Cook the pork using one of these three methods:

   - **Oven Method** (Cook Time: 3½ to 4½ hours)
     Preheat the oven to 325°F. Heat the oil in a Dutch oven or enameled cast-iron pot with a lid over medium-high heat. Add the seasoned pork shoulder to the pot and sear for 3 to 4 minutes per side, until browned. Pour 1½ cups of water into the pot, then cover with the lid and transfer to the oven. Cook for 3½ to 4½ hours, until the pork shreds easily.

   - **Instant Pot Method** (Cook Time: 1½ hours)
     Place the seasoned pork pieces in a 6-quart Instant Pot along with ½ cup of water. Seal the lid onto the Instant Pot, press the Pressure Cook or Manual button, and set the timer for 90 minutes. Once the cooking is finished, release the pressure manually by slowly turning the pressure valve to "venting."

   - **Slow Cooker Method** (Cook Time: 8 to 10 hours)
     Place the seasoned pork shoulder in a 6-quart slow cooker. Cover and cook on low for 8 to 10 hours, until the pork shreds easily.

3. Remove the pork from the pot. Place one-third of it in a container labeled "Harvest Dinner." Shred the remaining two-thirds of the meat with two forks, removing the excess fat. Transfer 4 cups of the shredded pork to a container labeled "Bowls" and the remaining 3 cups to another container labeled "Stuffed Potatoes." Store the containers of pork in the refrigerator for use later in the week.

Bake the sweet potatoes

Prep Time: 5 minutes

Cook Time: 1 hour

1. If you plan to put the sweet potatoes and Brussels sprouts in the oven at the same time (my suggestion!), place one oven rack in the upper third of the oven and another rack in the lower third of the oven.

2. Preheat the oven to 400°F. Line a rimmed baking sheet with parchment paper.

3. Wash and dry 3 pounds of sweet potatoes and poke each potato with a fork four or five times. Coat the potatoes with 1 tablespoon of extra-virgin olive oil and place on the lined baking sheet.

4. Bake for 50 to 60 minutes, until the sweet potatoes are easily pierced with a fork.

5. Store in the refrigerator for use later in the week.

Roast the Brussels sprouts alongside the sweet potatoes

Prep Time: 15 minutes
Cook Time: 40 minutes

1 pound Brussels sprouts

1 tablespoon extra-virgin olive oil

1 teaspoon coarse sea salt

1. Preheat the oven to 400°F. (*Note:* This preheating step is not needed if you're cooking the Brussels and sweet potatoes at the same time, as I suggest above.) Line a rimmed baking sheet with parchment paper.

2. Cut the stem ends off the Brussels sprouts and halve them, then toss with the olive oil and salt.

3. Spread the Brussels sprouts out on the lined baking sheet and bake for 35 to 40 minutes, until browned and crisp.

4. Store in the refrigerator for use later in the week.

Cut the onion into wedges

Cut a large white onion in half lengthwise, then cut each half into five wedges through the core (to make a total of ten wedges). Store in the refrigerator for use later in the week.

Dice the bell pepper

Dice a red bell pepper and store in the refrigerator for use later in the week.

Make the aioli

½ cup avocado oil mayonnaise or vegan mayo

2 cloves garlic, minced

1 tablespoon fresh lemon juice (about ½ small lemon)

Pinch of fine sea salt

Place all of the ingredients in a bowl and whisk until the mixture is smooth. Store in the refrigerator for use later in the week.

Smashed Sweet Potato and Pork Bowls

Yield: 5 servings   Prep Time: 5 minutes   Cook Time: 15 minutes

Half of the baked sweet potatoes ✓

1 tablespoon salted butter, ghee, or other fat of choice, melted

2 teaspoons coarse sea salt, divided

2 tablespoons avocado oil

4 cups shredded pork ✓

1 teaspoon dried oregano leaves

¼ teaspoon ground black pepper

Half of the roasted Brussels sprouts ✓

Aioli ✓

1. Preheat the oven to 425°F. Line a rimmed baking sheet with parchment paper.

2. Cut the sweet potatoes crosswise into 1-inch-thick rounds and place on the lined baking sheet, then smash the potatoes with a metal spatula to a ¼-inch thickness.

3. Brush the sweet potatoes with the melted butter and sprinkle with 1 teaspoon of the salt. Bake for 15 minutes, until slightly browned and crisp on top.

4. While the potatoes are cooking, place the oil in a large sauté pan over medium-high heat. Once hot, add the shredded pork, oregano, pepper, and remaining teaspoon of salt to the pan. Cook for 3 to 4 minutes, until the pork is crisp, then flip and cook for an additional 2 to 3 minutes, until it is browned and crisp on the other side.

5. Remove the pork from the pan and set aside. Add the Brussels sprouts and cook, stirring occasionally, for 4 to 5 minutes, until heated through, then remove the pan from the heat.

6. Assemble the bowls: Place two or three sweet potato rounds in each bowl and divide the pork and Brussels sprouts evenly among the bowls. Drizzle with the aioli before serving.

Harvest Sheet Pan Dinner

Yield: 4 servings   Prep Time: 10 minutes   Cook Time: 30 minutes

1 large red apple

1 white onion, cut into 10 wedges ✓

3 tablespoons extra-virgin olive oil, divided

1 teaspoon dried thyme leaves

One-third of the cooked pork shoulder ✓

2 tablespoons balsamic vinegar

½ teaspoon garlic powder

Half of the roasted Brussels sprouts ✓

1 teaspoon coarse sea salt

8 sprigs fresh thyme

1. Preheat the oven to 400°F.

2. Cut the apple into ½-inch wedges, discarding the core.

3. In a medium-sized bowl, toss the apple and onion wedges in 1 tablespoon of the olive oil and the thyme, then spread out on the lined baking sheet and bake for 15 minutes, until softened.

4. While the apple and onion are cooking, cut the pork shoulder into 1-inch slices. Then whisk together the remaining 2 tablespoons of oil, the balsamic vinegar, and garlic powder in a large bowl and toss the pork and Brussels sprouts in this mixture.

5. Lay the pork and Brussels sprouts on the baking sheet with the apple and onion, sprinkle the salt over the pork, lay the thyme sprigs on top, and bake for an additional 15 minutes, until the pork is browned. Let cool slightly, then serve!

Southwestern Stuffed Sweet Potatoes

Yield: 4 servings   Prep Time: 12 minutes   Cook Time: 25 minutes

Half of the baked sweet potatoes ✓

1 teaspoon coarse sea salt

1 teaspoon garlic powder

1 teaspoon ground cumin

1 teaspoon paprika

½ teaspoon ancho chili powder

¼ teaspoon ground black pepper

3 cups shredded pork ✓

1 red bell pepper, diced ✓

1 cup frozen yellow corn (omit for Paleo and grain-free)

2 tablespoons fresh lime juice (about 1 lime)

Leaves from 10 sprigs fresh cilantro, for garnish

½ cup shredded Mexican cheese blend (omit for Paleo and dairy-free)

1. Preheat the oven to 400°F.

2. Cut the sweet potatoes in half lengthwise and scoop the flesh into a large bowl, reserving the skins. Add the salt and spices and stir to combine, then add the shredded pork, bell pepper, corn, and lime juice and stir until evenly incorporated.

3. Scoop the mixture into the sweet potato skins and bake for 15 minutes. While the sweet potatoes bake, chop the cilantro and set aside.

4. After 15 minutes, remove the stuffed sweet potatoes from the oven, top with the cheese, and bake for an additional 10 minutes, until the cheese is browned and bubbly.

5. Garnish with the chopped cilantro and serve!

BAKED CHICKEN BREAST, COLLARD GREENS, and SWEET POTATOES

This week, you're going to use three classic healthy ingredients to make some delicious family-friendly eats! Baked chicken breast, collard greens, and sweet potatoes are transformed into a dreamy Chipotle Chicken Casserole, Buffalo Chicken–Stuffed Sweet Potatoes, and a decadent Chicken Florentine Lasagna. If you'd like to supplement this week's three main dinner recipes with two additional meals, see the suggested "Bonus Dinner Options" on the next page.

Weekly Ingredients

FRESH PRODUCE

Cilantro, ½ bunch

Collard greens, 2 bunches

Garlic, 3 cloves

Green onions, 2

Lemon, ½ small

Lime, 1

Onion, white, 1 medium

Sliced baby bella (aka cremini) mushrooms, 8 ounces

Sweet potatoes, medium, 8 (about 3 pounds)

MEAT/DAIRY

Butter, salted, 2 ounces (¼ cup)

Chicken breasts, boneless, skinless, 5 pounds

Heavy cream, 2 tablespoons

Shredded Parmesan cheese, 3 ounces (1 cup)

PANTRY

Avocado oil mayonnaise, store-bought or homemade (page 372), 2 fluid ounces (¼ cup)

Chicken broth, 6 fluid ounces (¾ cup)

Extra-virgin olive oil, 4 fluid ounces (½ cup)

Lasagna noodles, no-boil, gluten-free, 8

Medium-hot hot sauce, such as Frank's RedHot, 4 fluid ounces (½ cup)

Sun-dried tomatoes, dry packed, 3 ounces (1 cup)

White wine, 4 fluid ounces (½ cup)

SEASONINGS

Chipotle chili powder, ½ teaspoon

Garlic powder, ½ teaspoon

Onion powder, ½ teaspoon

Paprika, 1 tablespoon

Ingredient Subs

To make this week DAIRY-FREE:

· *Substitute ghee or avocado oil for the butter.*

· *Use full-fat coconut milk in place of the heavy cream.*

· *Omit the Parmesan cheese.*

To make this week EGG-FREE:

· *Replace the mayonnaise with 2 tablespoons extra-virgin olive oil and 1 tablespoon fresh lime juice.*

Bonus Dinner Options

Dinner 1

Jerk Pork Tenderloin
(page 351)

Sautéed Bell Peppers
(page 361)

Basic Cauliflower Rice
(page 363)

Bonus Dinner Ingredients

Bell peppers, red, 1 pound

Cauliflower, 1 large head (about 3 pounds), or 18 ounces frozen riced cauliflower

Extra-virgin olive oil, 3 tablespoons plus 2 teaspoons

Jerk Seasoning, 1 tablespoon (see page 375 for ingredients)

Pork tenderloin, 1 (1¼ pounds)

Dinner 2

Salmon Bake
(page 354)

Crispy Brussels Sprouts
(page 356)

Baked Russet Potatoes
(page 366)

Bonus Dinner Ingredients

Brussels sprouts, 12 ounces

Extra-virgin olive oil, 1 tablespoon

Lemon, 1

Ranch dressing, store-bought or homemade (page 372), 2 ounces (¼ cup)

Russet potatoes, 4 small to medium (about 1 pound)

Salmon fillet, 1 (1½ pounds)

Prep Day

This week's prep day is really straightforward! You're going to cook the chicken, sweet potatoes (whole and cubed), and collard greens; make an easy blender sauce; and prep a few fresh veggies. To get things rolling, I like to get the chicken in the oven first. While the chicken bakes, I cook the collards and make the cilantro-lime sauce. Then I prep the sweet potatoes to get them ready for the oven. As soon as the chicken comes out of the oven, I increase the temperature and pop in the sweet potatoes. While the potatoes bake, I dice the white onion, slice the green onions, and mince the garlic. Lastly, once the chicken is cool to the touch, I cut it into cubes.

note: *If you're planning to make homemade mayonnaise rather than use store-bought, I recommend that you add it to your prep day tasks so that it's ready for use later in the week. To save myself a couple of steps, I purchase presliced mushrooms and preshredded Parmesan cheese; if you are using whole mushrooms and/ or block cheese, add the steps of cleaning and slicing the mushrooms and shredding the Parmesan to the prep day tasks.*

Bake and cube the chicken

Yield: 10 cups

Prep Time: 10 minutes

Cook Time: 40 minutes

5 pounds boneless, skinless chicken breasts

1 tablespoon extra-virgin olive oil

1 teaspoon coarse sea salt

½ teaspoon ground black pepper

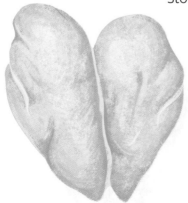

1. Preheat the oven to 375°F. Line a rimmed baking sheet with parchment paper.

2. Place the chicken on the lined baking sheet. Brush with the olive oil and season with the salt and pepper.

3. Bake for 40 minutes, until the chicken reaches an internal temperature of 165°F.

4. Let cool, then cut the chicken into ½-inch cubes.

5. Place 3 cups of the cubed chicken in a container labeled "Casserole," 3 cups in a container labeled "Stuffed Potatoes," and the remaining 4 cups in a container labeled "Lasagna." Store in the refrigerator for use later in the week.

Wilt the collard greens

Prep Time: 15 minutes

Cook Time: 4 minutes

2 bunches collard greens

1 tablespoon extra-virgin olive oil

¼ teaspoon coarse sea salt

1. Wash and destem the collard greens, then coarsely chop them. Heat the olive oil in a large skillet (with a lid) over medium heat. Once hot, add the collards and toss to coat them in the oil.

2. Cover and allow the collard greens to wilt, 3 to 4 minutes. Once completely wilted, remove the lid and stir in the salt. Place half of the collards in a container labeled "Casserole" and the other half in a container labeled "Lasagna" and store in the refrigerator for use later in the week.

Make the cilantro-lime sauce

½ cup fresh cilantro (leaves and stems)

3 tablespoons extra-virgin olive oil

2 tablespoons fresh lime juice (about 1 lime)

Place all of the ingredients in a blender and blend until smooth. Store in the refrigerator for use later in the week.

Bake the sweet potatoes

Prep Time: 20 minutes

Cook Time: 1 hour

8 medium sweet potatoes (about 3 pounds)

2 tablespoons extra-virgin olive oil, divided

1 teaspoon coarse sea salt

1. Place an oven rack in the upper third of the oven and another rack in the lower third of the oven. Preheat the oven to 400°F. Line two rimmed baking sheets with parchment paper.

2. Wash and dry each sweet potato and poke with a fork four or five times. Rub four of the potatoes with 1 tablespoon of the olive oil and put them on one of the lined baking sheets.

3. Bake the whole sweet potatoes on the lower rack for 45 to 60 minutes, depending on the size of the potatoes, until they are easily pierced with a fork.

4. Peel the remaining four sweet potatoes, then cut them into 1-inch cubes. Toss with the remaining tablespoon of oil and the salt.

5. Spread the cubed sweet potatoes on the second lined baking sheet and place on the upper rack of the oven, above the whole potatoes. Bake for 40 to 50 minutes, until browned and easily pierced with a fork.

6. Place the whole potatoes in one container and the cubed potatoes in another container. Store in the refrigerator for use later in the week.

Prep the onions

Dice a medium-sized white onion. Slice two green onions, or enough to equal 2 tablespoons. Store the white and green onions in separate containers in the refrigerator for use later in the week.

Mince the garlic

Peel and mince three cloves of garlic. Store in the refrigerator for use later in the week.

Slice the sun-dried tomatoes

Thinly slice 1 cup (3 ounces) of dry-packed sun-dried tomatoes. Store in a container at room temperature for use later in the week.

Chipotle Chicken Casserole

Yield: 5 servings   Prep Time: 10 minutes   Cook Time: 30 minutes

1 tablespoon paprika

½ teaspoon chipotle chili powder

½ teaspoon garlic powder

½ teaspoon onion powder

½ teaspoon fine sea salt

¼ cup avocado oil mayonnaise (omit for egg-free; see note below)

3 cups cubed baked chicken breast ✓

Cubed roasted sweet potatoes ✓

Half of the wilted collard greens ✓

Cilantro-lime sauce ✓

2 tablespoons chopped fresh cilantro, for garnish (optional)

1. Preheat the oven to 350°F.

2. Place the paprika, chili powder, garlic powder, onion powder, salt, and mayonnaise in a medium-sized bowl and whisk until smooth. Add the chicken and toss to coat.

3. Place the cubed sweet potatoes in a deep 8-inch square casserole dish, then layer the collard greens on top and cover with the chicken mixture.

4. Bake for 30 minutes, until the top is slightly browned and the casserole is warmed through.

5. Remove from the oven, drizzle with the cilantro-lime sauce, garnish with the chopped cilantro, if using, and serve!

note: *To make this dish egg-free, omit the mayo and whisk together the paprika, chili powder, garlic powder, onion powder, and salt with 2 tablespoons extra-virgin olive oil and 1 tablespoon fresh lime juice.*

Buffalo Chicken–Stuffed Sweet Potatoes

Yield: 4 servings   Prep Time: 5 minutes   Cook Time: 20 minutes

½ cup medium-hot hot sauce

¼ cup (½ stick) salted butter, ghee, or avocado oil

3 cups cubed baked chicken breast ✓

4 baked sweet potatoes ✓

2 tablespoons sliced green onions, for garnish ✓

1. Preheat the oven to 350°F. Line a rimmed baking sheet with parchment paper.

2. To make the Buffalo chicken, heat the hot sauce and butter in a medium-sized saucepan over medium heat until melted and bubbling, then toss the chicken in the sauce. Remove from the heat.

3. Place the baked sweet potatoes on the lined baking sheet, then cut a slit in each potato. Stuff the potatoes with the Buffalo chicken.

4. Bake for 15 minutes, until the potatoes are warmed through and the tops are slightly browned.

5. Remove from the oven, garnish with the green onions, and serve!

Chicken Florentine Lasagna

Yield: 6 servings   Prep Time: 25 minutes   Cook Time: 40 minutes

1 tablespoon extra-virgin olive oil

1 white onion, diced ✓

3 cloves garlic, minced ✓

8 ounces sliced baby bella (aka cremini) mushrooms

Half of the wilted collard greens ✓

Sliced sun-dried tomatoes ✓

½ cup white wine

¾ cup chicken broth

2 tablespoons heavy cream or full-fat coconut milk

1 tablespoon fresh lemon juice (about ½ small lemon)

½ teaspoon coarse sea salt

8 no-boil gluten-free lasagna noodles

4 cups cubed baked chicken breast ✓

1 cup shredded Parmesan cheese (about 3 ounces), for topping (omit for dairy-free)

1. Preheat the oven to 350°F.

2. Heat the olive oil in a large sauté pan over medium-high heat. Once hot, add the onion, garlic, and mushrooms. Cook for 5 to 6 minutes, until the onion and mushrooms are beginning to brown and the garlic is fragrant.

3. Add the collard greens and sun-dried tomatoes, then pour in the wine, broth, heavy cream, and lemon juice. Season with the salt. Stir to combine, then simmer for 3 to 5 minutes, until the liquid has reduced slightly.

4. Place ½ cup of the collard green mixture in a 2-quart rectangular casserole dish, then layer half of the lasagna noodles on top.

5. Layer half of the remaining collard green mixture on top of the noodles, followed by half of the chicken, then repeat the layers.

6. Bake for 15 minutes, then top with the Parmesan cheese and return the casserole to the oven to bake for another 15 minutes, until the sauce is bubbly around the edges and the cheese is browned.

7. Remove from the oven and let cool slightly, then cut and serve!

GROUND BEEF, CABBAGE, and CARROTS

What a fun week this is! You are going to transform the wonderfully affordable ground beef, cabbage, and carrots into three fantastic dinners that your family will love. On the menu for this week: Italian Wedding Soup (so delicious), Texas Beef Chili (the fastest chili you've ever made), and Asian Beef Lettuce Cups. If you'd like to supplement this week's three main dinner recipes with two additional meals, see the suggested "Bonus Dinner Options" on the next page.

Weekly Ingredients

FRESH PRODUCE

Butter lettuce, 1 head

Carrots, 6 medium (about 1 pound)

Escarole, ½ head (or one 6-ounce bag prewashed baby spinach)

Flat-leaf parsley, ¼ bunch

Garlic, 6 cloves

Green onions, 3

Jalapeño pepper, 1

Lacinato (aka dinosaur) kale, 1 bunch

Lemon, 1 small

Napa cabbage, 1 small head

Onion, white, 1

MEAT/EGGS/DAIRY

Butter, salted, 1 tablespoon

Eggs, 2 large

Ground beef, 5 pounds

Ground pork, 1 pound

Shredded Parmesan cheese, 2 tablespoons

Sour cream, full-fat, 2 ounces (¼ cup)

PANTRY

Chicken broth, 76 fluid ounces (2 quarts plus 1½ cups)

Coconut aminos, Coconut Secret brand, 1 (8-ounce) bottle

Extra-virgin olive oil, 1 tablespoon

Fish sauce, ¼ teaspoon

Ghee or avocado oil, 1 tablespoon

Strained tomatoes or tomato puree, 24 ounces

Toasted sesame oil, 2 teaspoons

Unseasoned rice wine vinegar, 1 tablespoon

Water chestnuts, whole, 1 (8-ounce) can

White rice, 16½ ounces (2½ cups)

SEASONINGS

Chili powder, 1 ounce (¼ cup)

Dried parsley, 1 tablespoon

Garlic powder, 1½ teaspoons

Ginger powder, 1 teaspoon

Ground cumin, 2 tablespoons

Onion powder, ½ teaspoon

Sesame seeds, 1 teaspoon

Ingredient Subs

To make this week LOW-CARB:

· Make the Low-Carb Teriyaki Sauce on page 373.

· Replace the white rice with 2 medium to large heads cauliflower (4½ to 5 pounds total) or 28 ounces frozen riced cauliflower.

To make this week PALEO:

· Use the substitutions listed below for making the week grain-free and dairy-free.

To make this week GRAIN-FREE:

· Replace the white rice with 2 medium to large heads cauliflower (4½ to 5 pounds total) or 28 ounces frozen riced cauliflower.

To make this week DAIRY-FREE:

· Replace the butter with ghee or oil of choice.

· Omit the Parmesan cheese and sour cream.

To make this week EGG-FREE:

· Omit the eggs.

Bonus Dinner Options

Dinner 1

Lemon Pepper Chicken Breasts (page 347)

Sautéed Squash
(page 356)

Baked Okra
(page 359)

Bonus Dinner Ingredients

Chicken breasts, boneless, skinless, 1½ pounds

Extra-virgin olive oil, 2 tablespoons plus 1 teaspoon

Lemon, 1

Okra, fresh, 1 pound

Zucchini or yellow squash, 4

Dinner 2

Ranch Chicken Thighs
(page 349)

Roasted Broccoli
(page 357)

Basic Cauliflower Rice
(page 363)

Bonus Dinner Ingredients

Broccoli, 2 medium to large heads

Cauliflower, 1 large head (about 3 pounds)

Chicken thighs, boneless, skinless, 1½ pounds

Extra-virgin olive oil, 2 tablespoons

Garlic powder, ½ teaspoon

Ranch dressing, store-bought or homemade (page 372), 2 fluid ounces (¼ cup)

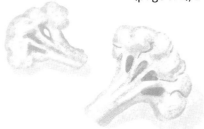

Prep Day

The bulk of today's prep work revolves around chopping fresh ingredients. Your tasks are limited to browning some of the ground beef, then using the rest of the beef, along with the ground pork, to make mini meatballs (which will go into the soup); making the Teriyaki Sauce; and cooking the rice. Because ground beef cooks so quickly, I like to get that task out of the way first. I get the beef started on the stovetop and then turn my attention to the meatballs. Once those are in the oven, I start on the sauce and rice. Then I busy myself slicing the cabbage, shredding the carrots, slicing and dicing the onions, mincing the garlic, chopping the escarole, parsley, cilantro, and water chestnuts, cleaning the lettuce, and slicing the jalapeño. Lastly, I make the spice blend and then call it a day!

note: *To save myself a step, I purchase preshredded Parmesan cheese; if you are using block cheese, add the step of shredding the Parmesan to this week's prep day tasks.*

Brown most of the ground beef

Yield: 9 scant cups
Prep Time: 1 minute
Cook Time: 15 minutes

Place 4 pounds of ground beef and 1 teaspoon of coarse sea salt in a large skillet over medium heat. (You will add more seasoning later.) Cook for 10 to 15 minutes, crumbling the meat as it cooks, until fully browned. Let cool completely. Once cool, drain the fat. Divide the browned meat evenly between two containers, putting about 4½ scant cups in each. Label one container "Chili" and the other "Lettuce Cups." Store in the refrigerator for use later in the week.

Make the mini meatballs

Prep Time: 15 minutes
Cook Time: 15 minutes

1 pound ground beef

1 pound ground pork

1 tablespoon dried parsley

1 teaspoon garlic powder

½ teaspoon onion powder

1 teaspoon coarse sea salt

½ teaspoon ground black pepper

1. Preheat the oven to 400°F. Line a rimmed baking sheet with parchment paper.

2. Place all of the ingredients in a large bowl and mix with your hands until the meats and seasonings are evenly distributed.

3. Shape the meat mixture into 1-inch balls and place on the lined baking sheet, ensuring that they are evenly spaced.

4. Bake for 15 minutes, until browned. Store in the refrigerator for use later in the week.

Make the Teriyaki Sauce

Follow the recipe on page 373 to make a full batch of Teriyaki Sauce (or Low-Carb Teriyaki Sauce for low-carb).

Cook the rice

Yield: 7½ cups

Prep Time: 2 minutes

Cook Time: about 20 minutes

Cook 2½ cups of white rice according to the package instructions, then store in the refrigerator for use later in the week.

 **LOW-CARB/PALEO/GRAIN-FREE RICE SUBSTITUTE**

Make 1½ batches of Basic Cauliflower Rice (page 363), then follow the storage instructions for the white rice above.

Slice the cabbage

Slice a small head of napa cabbage crosswise into ½-inch strips to equal 2 cups, then store in the refrigerator for use later in the week.

Peel, slice, and shred the carrots

Peel eight medium-sized carrots. Slice six of the carrots into ¼-inch-thick coins and place in a container labeled "Wedding Soup." Shred the remaining two carrots either with a cheese grater or with the shredder attachment of a food processor to equal ½ cup of shredded carrots and place in a container labeled "Lettuce Cups." Store in the refrigerator for use later in the week.

Slice the green onions

Thinly slice three green onions, or enough to make ¼ cup of sliced onions. Store in the refrigerator for use later in the week.

Dice the white onion

Dice a white onion and divide it evenly between two containers. Label one container "Wedding Soup" and the other "Chili." Store in the refrigerator for use later in the week.

Mince the garlic

Mince two cloves of garlic, to equal 2 teaspoons, then place in a container and label it "Wedding Soup." Mince an additional four cloves of garlic, to equal 4 teaspoons, then place in a container and label it "Chili." Store in the refrigerator for use later in the week.

Chop the escarole

Trim off the root end from half of a head of escarole and separate the leaves. Wash and dry the leaves, then coarsely chop them. Store in the refrigerator for use later in the week.

Chop the parsley

Wash and dry one-quarter bunch of parsley, then finely chop it. Store in the refrigerator for use later in the week.

Chop the water chestnuts

Drain an 8-ounce can of water chestnuts, then coarsely chop them. Store in the refrigerator for use later in the week.

Wash and dry the lettuce leaves

Remove the leaves from a head of butter lettuce, then wash and dry them. Store in the refrigerator for use later in the week.

Slice the jalapeño pepper

Thinly slice a jalapeño pepper, then store in the refrigerator for use later in the week.

Make the Texas Chili Spice Blend

Make a half batch of the Texas Chili Spice Blend following the recipe on page 374.

Italian Wedding Soup

Yield: 6 servings   Prep Time: 12 minutes   Cook Time: 10 minutes

1 tablespoon extra-virgin olive oil

½ white onion, diced ✓

2 teaspoons minced garlic ✓

6 carrots, sliced into ¼-inch-thick coins ✓

2 quarts chicken broth

Baked mini meatballs ✓

½ teaspoon coarse sea salt

¼ teaspoon ground black pepper

2 cups coarsely chopped escarole leaves ✓, or 6 ounces baby spinach

1 cup shredded napa cabbage ✓

¼ cup chopped fresh parsley ✓

2 large eggs (omit for egg-free)

2 tablespoons shredded Parmesan cheese (omit for dairy-free)

2 tablespoons fresh lemon juice (about 1 small lemon)

1. Heat the olive oil in a soup pot that has a lid over medium-high heat. Once hot, add the onion, garlic, and carrots. Sauté for 3 to 4 minutes, until the onion is translucent and the carrots are slightly browned.

2. Add the broth, meatballs, salt, pepper, escarole, cabbage, and parsley to the pot. Cover with the lid and cook for 5 minutes, until the escarole and cabbage are tender.

3. Place the eggs and Parmesan cheese in a small bowl and whisk together. While stirring the simmering soup, slowly pour in the egg mixture until thin strands of eggs form, about 1 minute.

4. Stir in the lemon juice, then taste for seasoning and add more salt, if needed. Remove from the heat and serve!

Texas Beef Chili

Yield: 4 servings   Prep Time: 5 minutes   Cook Time: 20 minutes

1 tablespoon salted butter, ghee, or oil of choice

½ white onion, diced ✓

4 teaspoons minced garlic ✓

4½ scant cups cooked ground beef ✓

¼ cup plus 2 tablespoons Texas Chili Spice Blend ✓

24 ounces strained tomatoes or tomato puree

1½ cups chicken broth

3½ cups cooked white rice or cauli-rice ✓

FOR GARNISH:

¼ cup full-fat sour cream (omit for dairy-free)

1 jalapeño pepper, sliced ✓

1. Melt the butter in a soup pot over medium-high heat. Once melted, add the onion and sauté for 3 to 4 minutes, until the onion is translucent. Then add the garlic and continue cooking for 2 to 3 minutes, until the onion starts to develop a light brown color and the garlic is fragrant.

2. Add the ground beef and stir to combine. Then add the spice blend and cook for an additional 2 minutes, or until the spices become fragrant.

3. Add the strained tomatoes and broth, stir to combine, and simmer over medium heat for 10 minutes, or until some of the liquid has evaporated.

4. While the chili is simmering, reheat the rice either by placing it in a medium-sized saucepan, covered, over low heat for 5 minutes or by microwaving it for about 2 minutes, until hot.

5. Serve the chili over the warmed rice and garnish with the sour cream and jalapeño slices.

Asian Beef Lettuce Cups

Yield: 4 servings   Prep Time: 15 minutes   Cook Time: 12 minutes

1 tablespoon ghee or avocado oil

1 cup shredded napa cabbage ✓

½ cup shredded carrots ✓

4½ scant cups cooked ground beef ✓

1 (8-ounce) can water chestnuts, drained and chopped ✓

¼ cup sliced green onions ✓

½ teaspoon ginger powder

½ teaspoon coarse sea salt

¼ teaspoon ground black pepper

Teriyaki Sauce ✓

4 cups cooked white rice or cauli-rice ✓

Leaves from 1 head butter lettuce ✓

1 teaspoon sesame seeds, for garnish

1. Melt the ghee in a large skillet or wok over medium-high heat. Once melted, add the cabbage and carrots. Cook for 4 to 5 minutes, until the vegetables are reduced in size and slightly browned.

2. Add the ground beef, water chestnuts, green onions, ginger, salt, and pepper to the pan and cook for 3 to 4 minutes, until the beef is warmed through.

3. Pour the sauce over the beef mixture and cook for an additional 1 to 2 minutes to let the flavors meld, then remove from the heat.

4. Meanwhile, reheat the rice either by placing it in a medium-sized saucepan, covered, over low heat for 5 minutes or by microwaving it for about 2 minutes, until hot.

5. Serve the beef mixture in the lettuce leaves, garnished with sesame seeds, with the rice on the side.

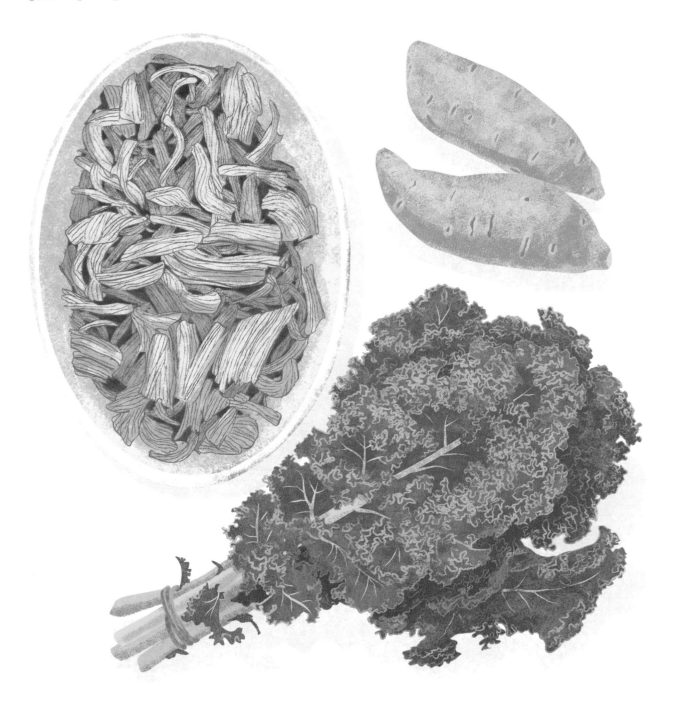

SHREDDED PORK, KALE, and SWEET POTATOES

This week, three of my favorite components morph into three all-star dinners! Pork shoulder, kale, and sweet potato are such a natural pairing. You will use them to make Jerk Pork–Stuffed Sweet Potatoes with Mango Kale Slaw (nom nom), a Honey Garlic Pork Skillet (I can't even begin to tell you how tasty this is), and a Sweet Potato Tamale Pie (the easiest tamale you've ever made!). If you'd like to supplement this week's three main dinner recipes with two additional meals, see the suggested "Bonus Dinner Options" on the next page.

Weekly Ingredients

FRESH PRODUCE

Avocado, 1 small

Cilantro, ⅓ bunch

Curly or Lacinato (aka dinosaur) kale, 2 bunches

Garlic, 4 large cloves

Jalapeño pepper, 1

Lemon, ½

Limes, 2½

Mango, 1 medium

Sweet potatoes, medium, 4 pounds

MEAT/DAIRY

Butter, salted, 2 ounces (¼ cup)

Pork shoulder, boneless, 1 (5 to 6 pounds)

Sour cream, full-fat, 2 ounces (¼ cup)

PANTRY

Apple cider vinegar, 3 tablespoons

Coconut aminos, Coconut Secret brand, 3 tablespoons

Coconut sugar, 1 tablespoon

Extra-virgin olive oil, 3½ fluid ounces (7 tablespoons)

Honey, 3 ounces (¼ cup)

Toasted sesame oil, 1 teaspoon

Tomato paste, 1 (6-ounce) can

White rice, 10 ounces (1½ cups)

SEASONINGS

Cayenne pepper, ½ teaspoon

Chili powder, 1 tablespoon plus 1 teaspoon

Dried oregano leaves, 2 teaspoons

Dried thyme leaves, 2 teaspoons

Garlic powder, 1 teaspoon

Ginger powder, 2 teaspoons

Ground allspice, 2 teaspoons

Ground cinnamon, ½ teaspoon

Ground cloves, ¼ teaspoon

Ground cumin, 1½ tablespoons

Ground nutmeg, ¼ teaspoon

Red pepper flakes, ¼ teaspoon

Ingredient Subs

To make this week PALEO:

· *Use the substitutions listed below for making the week grain-free and dairy-free.*

To make this week GRAIN-FREE:

· *Substitute 1 large head cauliflower (about 3 pounds) or 18 ounces frozen riced cauliflower for the white rice.*

To make this week DAIRY-FREE:

· *Use ghee in place of the butter.*

· *Omit the sour cream.*

Bonus Dinner Options

Dinner 1

Balsamic Chicken Thighs
(page 348)

Italian Side Salad
(page 362)

Perfect Parsnips
(page 365)

Bonus Dinner Ingredients

Artichoke hearts, marinated and quartered,
1 (6-ounce) jar

Balsamic vinegar, 2 tablespoons

Chicken thighs, boneless, skinless, 1½ pounds

Extra-virgin olive oil, 3 tablespoons

Lettuce, mixed, 8 ounces (about 6 cups
chopped)

Olives, assorted, 3 ounces (½ cup)

Parsnips, 2 pounds

Red wine vinegar, 2 tablespoons

Dinner 2

Pan-Seared Steak
(page 352)

Roasted Cherry Tomatoes
(page 360)

Pan-Fried Plantains
(page 368)

Bonus Dinner Ingredients

Cherry tomatoes, 2 pints

Extra-virgin olive oil, 2⅓ fluid ounces (¼ cup
plus 2 teaspoons)

Plantains, yellow, 2 large (about 1 pound)

Sirloin or rib-eye steaks, boneless, about 1 inch
thick, 4 (4 to 6 ounces each)

Texas Grill Rub, 2 tablespoons (see page 374 for
ingredients)

Prep Day

The list of prep tasks for today is really straightforward! You will cook and then shred the pork, bake the sweet potatoes, prep the kale (storing half raw and cooking the other half), cook the rice (either traditional or grain-free), make a sweet potato mash for topping the tamale pie, prep a few fresh ingredients, and whip up a quick jerk seasoning mix. I find it easiest to start by getting the pork into my Instant Pot. Once that is programmed, I pop the sweet potatoes in the oven. From there, I prepare the kale and cook the rice. While the sweet potatoes and pork continue to cook, I cube the mango, chop the jalapeño and cilantro, and mince the garlic. I also quickly mix up the seasoning mixture and make the honey sauce. When the pork and potatoes are done, I shred the meat and make the sweet potato mash.

Note that for cooking the protein, you have the choice to use the oven, an Instant Pot, or a slow cooker, as usual, but I highly recommend using either an Instant Pot or a slow cooker here if you have one. This will allow you to get the sweet potatoes into the oven immediately rather than having to wait for the pork to finish up, and it will save you a lot of time in the kitchen!

Cook and shred the pork

Yield: 10 cups

Prep Time: 15 minutes

Cook Time: 1½ to 10 hours, depending on method

1 (5- to 6-pound) boneless pork shoulder

1½ teaspoons coarse sea salt

1 tablespoon extra-virgin olive oil (for oven and Instant Pot methods)

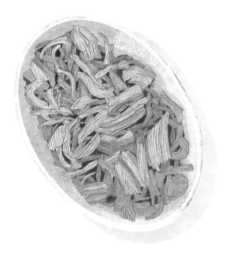

1. If using the Instant Pot method, cut the pork shoulder into four or five equal pieces; otherwise, leave it whole. Season the meat with the salt.

2. Cook the pork using one of these three methods:

- **Oven Method** (Cook Time: 4½ hours)
Preheat the oven to 325°F. Heat the oil in a Dutch oven or enameled cast-iron pot with a lid over medium-high heat. Add the seasoned pork to the pot and sear for 3 to 4 minutes per side, until browned. Once browned, pour 1½ cups of water into the pot, then cover with the lid and transfer to the oven. Cook for 3½ to 4½ hours, until the meat shreds easily.

- **Instant Pot Method** (Cook Time: 90 minutes)
Set a 6-quart Instant Pot to the Sauté mode and heat the oil in the pot. Working in batches, sear the seasoned pork pieces for 2 to 3 minutes per side. Return all of the seared pork to the pot, along with ½ cup of water. Seal the lid onto the Instant Pot, press the Pressure Cook or Manual button, and set the timer for 90 minutes. Once the cooking is finished, release the pressure manually by slowly turning the pressure valve to "venting."

- **Slow Cooker Method** (Cook Time: 8 to 10 hours)
Place the seasoned pork in the slow cooker. Cover and cook on low for 8 to 10 hours, until the pork shreds easily.

3. Remove the pork from the pot. Shred the meat with two forks, removing the excess fat. Place 2 cups in a container labeled "Stuffed Potatoes," 4 cups in a container labeled "Skillet," and 4 cups in a container labeled "Tamale Pie." Store in the refrigerator for use later in the week.

Bake the sweet potatoes

Prep Time: 5 minutes

Cook Time: 1 hour

4 pounds sweet potatoes

1 tablespoon extra-virgin olive oil

1. Preheat the oven to 400°F. Line a rimmed baking sheet with parchment paper.

2. Wash and dry each sweet potato and poke with a fork four or five times. Coat the potatoes with the olive oil and place on the lined baking sheet.

3. Bake for 50 to 60 minutes, until the potatoes are easily pierced with a fork.

4. Store four of the largest sweet potatoes in the refrigerator for use later in the week. Remove the skins from the remaining sweet potatoes and set aside for making the sweet potato mash later in the prep day.

Prepare the kale

Yield: 1 bunch wilted kale, 1 bunch sliced kale

Prep Time: 15 minutes

Cook Time: 4 minutes

2 bunches kale

1½ teaspoons extra-virgin olive oil

Juice of ½ lemon

Pinch of coarse sea salt

1. Wash and dry both bunches of kale, then destem them, keeping the two bunches separate.

2. Wilt one bunch of kale:

- Coarsely chop the bunch of kale.

- Heat the olive oil in a skillet with a lid over medium heat. Once hot, add the kale and toss it in the oil.

- Place the lid on the pan and allow the kale to wilt, 3 to 4 minutes. Once completely wilted, remove the lid and stir in the lemon juice and salt.

3. Prepare the second bunch of kale: Thinly slice the kale into ¼-inch-thick strips.

4. Store the wilted and sliced kale in the refrigerator for use later in the week.

Cook the rice

Yield: 4½ cups

Prep Time: 2 minutes

Cook Time: 20 minutes

Cook 1½ cups of white rice according to the package instructions, then store in the refrigerator for use later in the week.

  PALEO/GRAIN-FREE RICE SUBSTITUTE
Make a batch of Basic Cauliflower Rice (page 363), then follow the storage instructions for the white rice above.

Make the sweet potato mash

Skinned baked sweet potatoes *(from earlier in prep day)*

2 tablespoons salted butter or ghee, melted

1 tablespoon fresh lime juice (about ½ lime)

1 teaspoon coarse sea salt

½ teaspoon ground cumin

1. Place the skinned potatoes in a large bowl. Using a potato masher, mash them to a smooth consistency.

2. Add the butter, lime juice, salt, and cumin to the mashed sweet potatoes and stir to combine.

3. Store in the refrigerator for use later in the week.

Cube the mango

Peel and chop a medium-sized mango into ½-inch cubes. Store in the refrigerator for use later in the week.

Chop the jalapeño pepper

Seed and finely chop a jalapeño pepper. Store in the refrigerator for use later in the week.

Chop the cilantro

Wash and dry one-third bunch of cilantro. Set aside one or two sprigs to garnish the tamale pie and coarsely chop the rest, or enough to equal ¼ cup. Store the chopped cilantro and cilantro sprigs in the refrigerator for use later in the week.

Mince the garlic

Peel and mince four large cloves of garlic. Store in the refrigerator for use later in the week.

Mix the Jerk Seasoning

Make a half batch of Jerk Seasoning following the recipe on page 375. Note that you will have some left over for later use.

Make the honey sauce

¼ cup honey

3 tablespoons apple cider vinegar

3 tablespoons coconut aminos

1 teaspoon toasted sesame oil

¼ teaspoon red pepper flakes

Place all of the ingredients in a small bowl and whisk until fully combined, then store in the refrigerator for later use.

Jerk Pork–Stuffed Sweet Potatoes with Mango Kale Slaw

Yield: 4 servings   Prep Time: 10 minutes   Cook Time: 10 minutes

4 baked sweet potatoes ✓

FOR THE SLAW:

¼ cup extra-virgin olive oil

2 tablespoons fresh lime juice (about 1 lime)

Pinch of fine sea salt

1 bunch kale, thinly sliced into ¼-inch strips ✓

1 medium mango, cubed ✓

1 jalapeño pepper, seeded and finely chopped ✓

¼ cup coarsely chopped fresh cilantro ✓

FOR THE JERK PORK:

2 cups shredded pork ✓

1½ tablespoons Jerk Seasoning ✓

1 tablespoon extra-virgin olive oil

1. Preheat the oven to 350°F. Line a rimmed baking sheet with parchment paper.

2. Place the sweet potatoes on the lined baking sheet and bake for 10 minutes, until warmed through.

3. Meanwhile, make the slaw: Put the olive oil, lime juice, and salt in a medium-sized bowl and whisk together until combined and thickened. Add the kale to the dressing and massage the dressing into the kale with your hands. Add the mango, jalapeño, and cilantro to the bowl and toss to coat, then set aside.

4. To make the jerk pork, place the shredded pork and Jerk Seasoning in a medium-sized bowl and mix to evenly coat the meat in the seasoning.

5. Pour the olive oil into a large heavy skillet over medium-high heat. Once hot, add the seasoned pork. Cook, undisturbed, for 2 to 3 minutes, then flip and cook for an additional 2 to 3 minutes, until golden brown. Remove from the heat.

6. Cut a slit in each sweet potato, then stuff with the pork and top with the slaw. Serve!

Honey Garlic Pork Skillet

Yield: 5 servings   Prep Time: 2 minutes   Cook Time: 10 minutes

1 tablespoon salted butter or ghee

4 large cloves garlic, minced ✓

4 cups shredded pork ✓

½ teaspoon coarse sea salt

Honey sauce ✓

4½ cups cooked white rice or cauli-rice ✓

1. Place the butter in a large skillet over medium-high heat. Once hot, add the garlic and cook for 30 seconds or until fragrant. Remove the garlic from the pan and set aside.

2. Spread the pork evenly across the pan and sprinkle with the salt. Cook for 2 to 3 minutes, until the pork starts to brown, then flip and cook for an additional 1 to 2 minutes, until browned on the other side.

3. Pour the honey sauce and cooked garlic over the browned pork and stir to combine. Cook for 2 to 3 minutes, until the sauce bubbles and begins to reduce.

4. Reheat the rice either by placing it in a medium-sized saucepan, covered, over low heat for 5 minutes or by microwaving it for about 2 minutes, until hot.

5. Serve the pork mixture over the rice. Enjoy!

Sweet Potato Tamale Pie

Yield: 5 servings   Prep Time: 8 minutes   Cook Time: 30 minutes

FOR THE FILLING:

4 cups shredded pork ✓

1 bunch Lacinato (aka dinosaur) kale, wilted ✓

1 (6-ounce) can tomato paste

2 tablespoons fresh lime juice (about 1 lime)

1 tablespoon plus 1 teaspoon chili powder

1 tablespoon plus 1 teaspoon ground cumin

2 teaspoons dried oregano leaves

½ teaspoon coarse sea salt

Sweet potato mash ✓

1 small avocado, for garnish

¼ cup full-fat sour cream, for garnish (omit for dairy-free)

1 or 2 sprigs fresh cilantro, for garnish

1. Preheat the oven to 350°F.

2. To make the filling, place the pork, kale, tomato paste, lime juice, chili powder, cumin, oregano, and salt in a large bowl and stir until fully combined.

3. Spread the filling in a 3-quart casserole dish or a 10-inch cast-iron skillet, then layer the sweet potato mash over the top.

4. Bake for 30 minutes, until the pie is warmed through and the sweet potato topping is slightly browned.

5. Just before the pie is done, thinly slice the avocado and set it aside.

6. Garnish the pie with the sour cream, sliced avocado, and cilantro and serve!

GROUND PORK, CABBAGE, and RED POTATOES

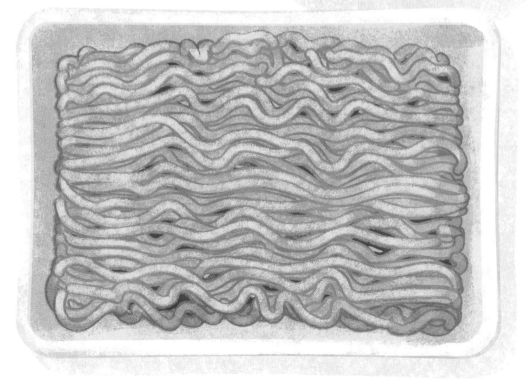

Boy howdy are you in for some tasty dinners this week! Though these ingredients may seem plain and simple, I'm going to show you how to transform ground pork, cabbage, and red potatoes into three diverse, delicious dinners that your family is sure to love. First up is a fun taco night with Chorizo and Potato Tacos, then a Chinese food night with Egg Roll in a Bowl, and finally some classic comfort food with Swedish Meatballs Over Mashed Potatoes! If you'd like to supplement this week's three main dinner recipes with two additional meals, see the suggested "Bonus Dinner Options" on the next page.

Weekly Ingredients

FRESH PRODUCE

Carrots, 4 medium (or 5 ounces preshredded carrots)

Cilantro, 1 small bunch

Flat-leaf parsley, 8 sprigs

Garlic, 4 cloves

Ginger, 1 (1-inch) piece

Green cabbage, 1 small head

Green onions, 1 small bunch (about 5 onions)

Limes, 2

Onion, yellow, 1 small

Purple cabbage, 1 small head

Red potatoes, 3 pounds

MEAT/DAIRY

Butter, salted, 3 ounces (6 tablespoons)

Cotija cheese, 3 ounces

Ground pork, 5 pounds

Heavy cream, 4 fluid ounces (½ cup)

PANTRY

Apple cider vinegar, 2 fluid ounces (¼ cup)

Avocado oil, 2½ fluid ounces (5 tablespoons)

Avocado oil mayonnaise, store-bought or homemade (page 372), 4 fluid ounces (½ cup)

Chicken broth, 16 fluid ounces (2 cups)

Coconut aminos, Coconut Secret brand, 4 fluid ounces (½ cup)

Coconut milk, full-fat, 2 tablespoons

Corn tortillas (about 6 inches in diameter), 10

Extra-virgin olive oil, 1 tablespoon

Gluten-free flour blend, 2 tablespoons

Toasted sesame oil, 1 teaspoon

Unseasoned rice wine vinegar, 2 tablespoons

SEASONINGS

Chili powder, 1 tablespoon

Dried oregano leaves, 1 teaspoon

Dried parsley, 1 tablespoon

Dried rubbed sage, 1 teaspoon

Garlic powder, 1 teaspoon

Ground allspice, ⅛ teaspoon

Ground cinnamon, ¼ teaspoon

Ground cloves, ⅛ teaspoon

Ground cumin, 1 teaspoon

Onion powder, ½ teaspoon

Paprika, 2 teaspoons

Red pepper flakes, ½ teaspoon

Sesame seeds, 1 teaspoon

Ingredient Subs

To make this week PALEO:

· *Use the substitutions listed below for making the week grain-free and dairy-free.*

To make this week GRAIN-FREE:

· *Use grain-free tortillas in place of the corn tortillas.*

· *Replace the gluten-free flour blend with arrowroot powder.*

To make this week DAIRY-FREE:

· *Replace the butter with ghee or oil of choice.*

· *Omit the cheese.*

· *Replace the heavy cream with full-fat coconut milk.*

To make this week EGG-FREE:

· *Use avocado oil in place of the mayonnaise.*

Bonus Dinner Options

Dinner 1

Ranch Chicken Thighs
(page 349)

Baked Okra
(page 359)

Basic White Rice
(page 368)

Bonus Dinner Ingredients

Chicken thighs, boneless, skinless, 1½ pounds

Extra-virgin olive oil, 1 tablespoon plus 2 teaspoons

Okra, fresh, 1 pound

Ranch dressing, store-bought or homemade (page 372), 2 fluid ounces (¼ cup)

White rice, 6½ ounces (1 cup)

Bonus Dinner Ingredient Subs

To make this meal PALEO:

Use the substitutions listed below for making the week grain-free and dairy-free.

To make this meal GRAIN-FREE:

Replace the white rice with 1 large head cauliflower (about 3 pounds) or 18 ounces frozen riced cauliflower; make Basic Cauliflower Rice (page 363) instead of the Basic White Rice.

To make this meal DAIRY-FREE:

Use a dairy-free ranch dressing.

To make this meal EGG-FREE:

Use an egg-free ranch dressing.

Dinner 2

Lemon-Garlic Shrimp
(page 354)

Roasted Asparagus
(page 360)

Basic Quinoa
(page 369)

Bonus Dinner Ingredients

Asparagus, fresh, 1 pound

Extra-virgin olive oil, 1 tablespoon plus 2 teaspoons

Garlic powder, ½ teaspoon

Lemon, 1

Quinoa, 6 ounces (1 cup)

Shrimp, large, 1½ pounds, peeled and deveined

Bonus Dinner Ingredient Subs

To make this meal PALEO and/ or GRAIN-FREE:

Replace the quinoa with 1 large head cauliflower (about 3 pounds) or 18 ounces frozen riced cauliflower; make Basic Cauliflower Rice (page 363) instead of the Basic Quinoa.

Prep Day

Today you'll be digging your hands into some strategic prep work that will make dinnertime much easier in the days ahead. To start, divide the potatoes into thirds. One-third will head into the oven while the other two-thirds are boiled and then mashed. While the potatoes cook, you'll brown some of the ground pork on the stovetop and use the rest to make meatballs. While the meatballs bake, I suggest turning your attention to the fresh veggies: slice, shred, grate, mince, dice, and chop while the other components cook. It all gets packaged up and stored in the refrigerator for when you're ready to get dinner on the table!

note: *If you're planning to make homemade mayonnaise rather than use store-bought, I recommend that you add it to your prep day tasks so that it's ready to use for the cilantro-lime dressing.*

Bake a third of the potatoes

Prep Time: 5 minutes

Cook Time: 1 hour 15 minutes

1 pound red potatoes

1 tablespoon extra-virgin olive oil

Preheat the oven to 375°F. Rub the potatoes with the olive oil, then place on a rimmed baking sheet. Bake for 60 to 75 minutes, until the potatoes are easily pierced with a fork. Once the potatoes are cool to the touch, remove the peels and cut the potatoes into 1-inch cubes. Store in the refrigerator for use later in the week.

Make the mashed potatoes

Prep Time: 15 minutes

Cook Time: 20 minutes

2 pounds red potatoes, cut into 1-inch cubes

¼ cup (½ stick) salted butter, ghee, or oil of choice

¼ cup heavy cream or full-fat coconut milk

1 teaspoon coarse sea salt

½ teaspoon ground black pepper

½ teaspoon garlic powder

1. Place the potatoes in a large pot and cover with water. Bring to a boil over high heat, then reduce the heat and simmer for 15 to 20 minutes, until the potatoes are easily pierced with a fork.

2. Place the cooked potatoes in a large bowl with the butter, cream, salt, pepper, and garlic powder. Using a potato masher, mash until the ingredients are well incorporated and the potatoes are mashed to your desired consistency.

3. Store in the refrigerator for use later in the week.

Brown some of the ground pork

Yield: about 8 cups

Prep Time: 1 minute

Cook Time: 10 minutes

Place a large skillet over medium heat. Put 3½ pounds of ground pork in the pan along with 1 teaspoon of coarse sea salt. Cook, crumbling the meat as it cooks, until slightly browned and fully cooked through, 8 to 10 minutes. Divide the browned meat evenly between two containers, putting about 4 cups in each. Label one container "Tacos" and the other "Egg Roll in a Bowl." Store in the refrigerator for use later in the week.

Make the meatballs

Prep Time: 15 minutes

Cook Time: 18 minutes

1½ pounds ground pork

1 tablespoon dried parsley

1 teaspoon dried rubbed sage

½ teaspoon coarse sea salt

½ teaspoon ground black pepper

½ teaspoon garlic powder

½ teaspoon onion powder

¼ teaspoon ground cinnamon

⅛ teaspoon ground allspice

⅛ teaspoon ground cloves

1. Preheat the oven to 400°F. Line a rimmed baking sheet with parchment paper.

2. Place all of the ingredients in a large mixing bowl. Work the seasonings into the meat with your hands until the mixture has an even consistency.

3. Form the meat mixture into 1-inch balls using your hands or a 1-tablespoon scoop. Place the meatballs on the lined baking sheet.

4. Bake for 18 minutes, or until slightly browned.

5. Store in the refrigerator for use later in the week.

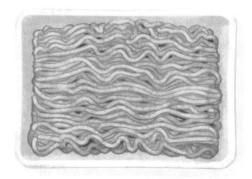

Make the cilantro-lime dressing

½ cup avocado oil mayonnaise or avocado oil

⅓ cup fresh cilantro (leaves and stems)

2 tablespoons full-fat coconut milk

2 tablespoons fresh lime juice (about 1 lime)

1 tablespoon sliced green onions

Place all of the ingredients in a blender and blend until smooth. Store in the refrigerator for use later in the week.

Prep the cabbage

Cut a small head of green cabbage and a small head of purple cabbage in half.

Coarsely chop half of a head of green cabbage and half of a head of purple cabbage into rectangular pieces, about ½ inch wide by 1 inch long, until you have 6 cups of chopped cabbage.

Shred the remaining half heads of cabbage until you have 2 cups of shredded green cabbage and 2 cups of shredded purple cabbage.

Place the chopped cabbage in a container labeled "Stir-Fry" and the shredded cabbage in a container labeled "Tacos." Store in the refrigerator for use later in the week.

Dice an onion and mince the garlic

Dice a small yellow onion, then mince four cloves of garlic. Place them in the same container and store in the refrigerator for use later in the week.

Grate the ginger

Grate a 1-inch piece of ginger until you have enough to equal 1 teaspoon. Store in the refrigerator for use later in the week.

Shred the carrots and slice the green onions

Peel and shred four medium-sized carrots, or enough to equal 1 cup.

Thinly slice five green onions, or enough to equal ½ cup.

Place the carrots and green onions in the same container and store in the refrigerator for use later in the week.

Chorizo and Potato Tacos with Cilantro-Lime Slaw

Yield: 5 servings   Prep Time: 5 minutes   Cook Time: 20 minutes

FOR THE CHORIZO-POTATO FILLING:

¼ cup avocado oil

1 pound baked and cubed red potatoes ✓

4 cups cooked ground pork ✓

1 teaspoon coarse sea salt

1 tablespoon chili powder

2 teaspoons paprika

1 teaspoon ground cumin

1 teaspoon dried oregano leaves

½ teaspoon ground black pepper

¼ cup apple cider vinegar

FOR THE CILANTRO-LIME SLAW:

4 cups shredded green and purple cabbage ✓

Cilantro-lime dressing ✓

Coarse sea salt

10 corn or grain-free tortillas

2 tablespoons chopped fresh cilantro, for garnish

3 ounces Cotija cheese, crumbled, for garnish (omit for Paleo/dairy-free)

1 lime, cut into wedges, for serving

1. To make the filling, heat the oil in a large skillet over medium-high heat. Once hot, add the potatoes. Fry for 3 to 4 minutes, then flip and cook for an additional 3 minutes, until browned and crispy. Remove the potatoes from the pan and set aside.

2. Drain all but 1 tablespoon of oil from the pan, then add the pork, salt, spices, and vinegar. Cook, stirring occasionally, for 4 to 5 minutes, until the pork is crispy.

3. Return the potatoes to the pan and stir them into the pork, then remove the pan from the heat.

4. To make the slaw, toss the shredded cabbage with the cilantro-lime dressing. Season to taste with salt.

5. Place a small skillet over medium-high heat. Once hot, put a tortilla in the pan and warm for 30 seconds per side, until the tortilla is pliable and begins to brown slightly. Repeat with the remaining tortillas. To keep them warm while you heat the remaining tortillas, you can wrap them in a kitchen towel.

6. To assemble the tacos, fill each warmed tortilla with the chorizo-potato filling, top with the slaw, and then garnish with the cilantro and cheese. Serve with lime wedges.

Egg Roll in a Bowl

Yield: 4 servings   Prep Time: 5 minutes   Cook Time: 10 minutes

1 tablespoon avocado oil

1 small yellow onion, diced ✓

4 cloves garlic, minced ✓

1 teaspoon grated fresh ginger ✓

4 cups cooked ground pork ✓

½ cup coconut aminos

2 tablespoons unseasoned rice wine vinegar

1 teaspoon toasted sesame oil

½ teaspoon red pepper flakes

½ teaspoon coarse sea salt

6 cups chopped green and purple cabbage ✓

1 cup shredded carrots ✓

½ cup sliced green onions ✓

1 teaspoon sesame seeds, for garnish

1. Heat the avocado oil in a large skillet over medium-high heat. Once hot, add the onion and garlic and sauté for 2 to 3 minutes, until the onion is translucent.

2. Stir in the ginger, then add the pork, coconut aminos, vinegar, sesame oil, red pepper flakes, and salt. Stir to combine and cook for 2 minutes, until the sauce begins to bubble.

3. Add the cabbage, carrots, and green onions to the pan and toss to coat in the sauce. Cook for 3 to 4 minutes, stirring occasionally, until the cabbage and carrots are wilted, then serve!

Swedish Meatballs Over Mashed Potatoes

Yield: 4 servings   Prep Time: 5 minutes   Cook Time: 15 minutes

2 tablespoons salted butter, ghee, or oil of choice (omit if using arrowroot powder)

2 tablespoons gluten-free flour blend, or 1 tablespoon arrowroot powder (see note below)

2 cups chicken broth

¼ cup heavy cream or full-fat coconut milk

¼ teaspoon coarse sea salt

¼ teaspoon ground black pepper

Cooked meatballs ✓

Mashed potatoes, for serving ✓

2 tablespoons chopped fresh flat-leaf parsley, for garnish

1. Melt the butter in a large skillet over medium heat. Once melted, sprinkle in the flour and whisk until smooth.

2. Pour in the chicken broth ½ cup at a time, whisking constantly to smooth out any lumps. Bring the mixture to a low boil, then reduce the heat to medium-low and whisk in the cream, salt, and pepper.

3. Add the meatballs to the pan and stir to coat, then cover and cook for 5 minutes, until heated through. Before serving, taste the sauce for seasoning and add more salt, if desired.

4. While the meatballs are warming, reheat the mashed potatoes either by microwaving for 3 minutes, stirring halfway through, or by placing in a small saucepan over medium heat and cooking, covered, for 5 minutes, stirring occasionally.

5. Serve the meatballs and sauce over the mashed potatoes and garnish with the parsley.

note: *If using arrowroot powder, bring the broth to a boil in a large skillet. Meanwhile, stir the arrowroot powder and 2 tablespoons of water together in a small bowl to form a slurry. Once the broth is boiling, whisk in the slurry. Boil for 1 minute, until the broth begins to thicken. Reduce the heat to medium-low and whisk in the cream, salt, and pepper, then proceed to Step 3.*

ROASTED CHICKEN, MUSHROOMS, and SPAGHETTI SQUASH

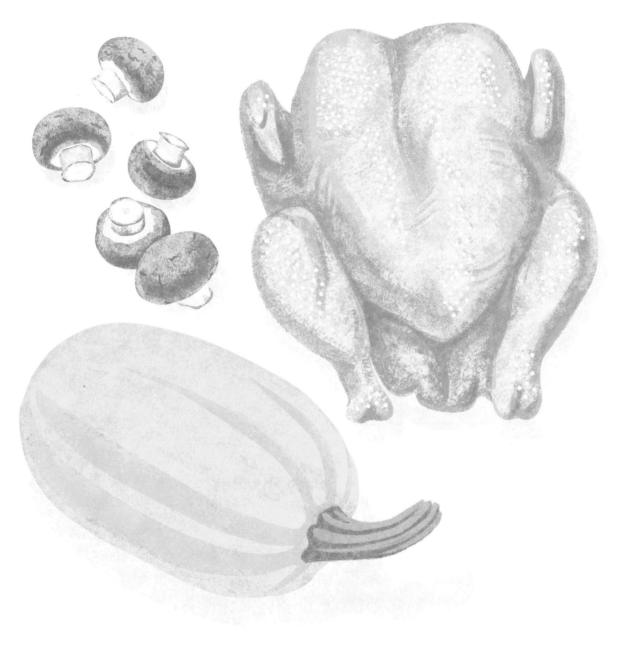

This week is comfort food central! Because spaghetti squash can be found around most of the United States during the fall and winter months, I wanted to make sure that the three dinners for this week are warming. You'll transform roasted chicken, mushrooms, and squash into a fabulous Chicken Marsala Casserole, a really delicious Spaghetti Squash Chicken Chow Mein, and a comforting Creamy Chicken and Mushroom Soup. This is a great week to choose when the weather is cool, and it is perfect for those following a low-carb diet. If you'd like to supplement this week's three main dinner recipes with two additional meals, see the suggested "Bonus Dinner Options" on the next page.

Weekly Ingredients

FRESH PRODUCE

Baby bella (aka cremini) mushrooms, 16 ounces (8 ounces whole and 8 ounces sliced)

Celery, 2 stalks

Flat-leaf parsley, 8 sprigs

Garlic, 9 cloves

Green onions, 6

Lemon, ½

Onions, yellow, 2 medium

Purple or green cabbage, ½ head

Spaghetti squash, 2 (about 4½ pounds each)

Thyme, 9 sprigs

MEAT/DAIRY

Butter, salted, 3 tablespoons

Chickens, 2 whole (4 to 5 pounds each)

Heavy cream, 6 fluid ounces (¾ cup)

Prosciutto, 4 thin slices

PANTRY

Avocado oil, 2 fluid ounces (¼ cup)

Chicken broth, 26 ounces (3¼ cups)

Coconut aminos, Coconut Secret brand, 1 (8-ounce) bottle

Extra-virgin olive oil, 1 tablespoon plus 2 teaspoons

Fish sauce, ½ teaspoon

Gluten-free flour blend, 2 tablespoons

Marsala wine, 6 fluid ounces (¾ cup)

Spicy brown mustard, 2 tablespoons

Toasted sesame oil, 2 teaspoons

Unseasoned rice wine vinegar, 1 tablespoon

SEASONINGS

Dried parsley, 1 teaspoon

Garlic powder, ½ teaspoon

Sesame seeds, 1 teaspoon

Ingredient Subs

To make this week PALEO:

· *Use the substitutions listed below for making the week grain-free and dairy-free.*

To make this week GRAIN-FREE:

· *Substitute arrowroot powder for the gluten-free flour blend.*

To make this week DAIRY-FREE:

· *Substitute ghee or oil of choice for the butter.*

· *Substitute full-fat coconut milk for the heavy cream.*

Bonus Dinner Options

Dinner 1

Honey Mustard Pork Tenderloin (page 351)

Italian Side Salad (page 362)

Baked Acorn Squash (page 364)

Bonus Dinner Ingredients

Acorn squash, 1

Artichoke hearts, marinated and quartered, 1 (6-ounce) jar

Dijon mustard, 2 tablespoons

Extra-virgin olive oil, 3 tablespoons plus 2 teaspoons

Honey, 1 tablespoon

Lettuce, such as romaine or iceberg, and/or purple cabbage, 8 ounces (6 cups chopped)

Olives, assorted pitted, 3 ounces (about ½ cup)

Pork tenderloin, 1 (1¼ pounds)

Red wine vinegar, 2 tablespoons

Bonus Dinner Ingredient Subs

To make this meal LOW-CARB:

Omit the honey.

Skip the acorn squash.

Dinner 2

Pan-Seared Salmon (page 355)

Basic Cauliflower Rice (page 363)

Roasted Carrots (page 364)

Bonus Dinner Ingredients

Carrots, slender, 2 bunches (about 1 pound)

Cauliflower, 1 large head (about 3 pounds), or 18 ounces frozen riced cauliflower

Extra-virgin olive oil, 2 tablespoons plus 2 teaspoons

Lemon, ½

Salmon fillets, 4 (6 ounces each)

Prep Day

For your prep work today, you're going to get a couple of components into the oven, sauté a few things on the stove, make a sauce, and chop some veggies. First, I like to get the chickens in the oven to start roasting. The spaghetti squash heads into the oven next. After that, you can prep the mushrooms and then turn your attention to the stove. You're going to crisp the prosciutto and then, using the same pan, cook the onion, garlic, and mushroom mixture for the casserole. Lastly, you'll start the easy chow mein sauce (it's pretty hands-off) and chop the veggies! Everything gets labeled and stored in the refrigerator, ready to use for dinners during the week.

Roast and break down the chickens

Yield: 3 cups cubed white meat, 6 cups shredded dark meat

Prep Time: 10 minutes

Cook Time: 1 hour 15 minutes

2 (4- to 5-pound) whole chickens

2 tablespoons avocado oil or other fat of choice

2 teaspoons coarse sea salt

1 teaspoon ground black pepper

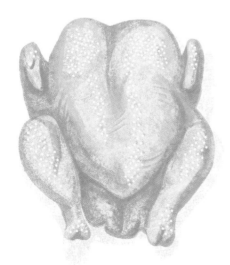

1. Preheat the oven to 375°F.

2. Place the chickens on a rimmed baking sheet and pat dry with paper towels.

3. Rub the chickens with the oil, then season with the salt and pepper.

4. Bake for 1 hour 15 minutes, until a thermometer inserted into the thickest part of a chicken breast registers 165°F.

5. Let the chickens cool for at least 30 minutes, then separate the breasts from the bone and cut two of the breasts into ½-inch cubes, discarding the skin. You should get about 3 cups. Place in a container.

6. Shred the rest of the chicken, discarding the skin. Divide the shredded chicken between two containers, putting about 3 cups in each; label one "Chow Mein" and the other "Soup."

7. Store the containers of chicken in the refrigerator for use later in the week.

Bake the squash and remove the strands

Yield: 10 cups "noodles"
Prep Time: 5 minutes
Cook Time: 1 hour

1. Preheat the oven to 400°F. Cut two spaghetti squash in half lengthwise, scoop out the seeds with a spoon, and place the halves cut side up on two rimmed baking sheets. Bake for 45 to 60 minutes, until the strands of squash easily pull away from the shells with a fork.

2. Once cool enough to handle, use the fork to remove the squash strands from the shells. Divide the strands evenly between two containers, putting about 5 cups in each; label one container "Chow Mein" and the other "Marsala." Store in the refrigerator for use later in the week.

Prep the whole mushrooms

Clean 8 ounces of whole mushrooms, then dice them. Store in the refrigerator for use later in the week.

Note: If you opted to buy 16 ounces of whole mushrooms for the week instead of buying half whole and half presliced, clean and slice the rest of the whole mushrooms and set them aside for use later in the prep day.

Crisp the prosciutto

Prep Time: 1 minute
Cook Time: 3 minutes

1 teaspoon extra-virgin olive oil

4 thin slices prosciutto

Heat the olive oil in a medium-sized skillet over medium heat. Meanwhile, coarsely chop the prosciutto, then add it to the pan. Cook for 2 to 3 minutes, stirring occasionally, until the prosciutto is crisp. Transfer to a container and store in the refrigerator for use later in the week. Do not wash the skillet; you will use it again momentarily.

Cook the onion, garlic, and mushroom mixture

Prep Time: 5 minutes
Cook Time: 6 minutes

1 medium yellow onion

3 cloves garlic

1 teaspoon extra-virgin olive oil

8 ounces sliced baby bella (aka cremini) mushrooms

1. Dice the onion and mince the garlic.

2. Put the olive oil in the same skillet you used to crisp the prosciutto and place it over medium heat. Once hot, add the onion, garlic, and sliced mushrooms.

3. Cook, stirring occasionally, for 5 to 6 minutes, until the onion is translucent and the mushrooms have started to brown slightly. Store in the refrigerator for use later in the week.

Make the chow mein sauce

Prep Time: 5 minutes

Cook Time: 6 minutes

1 (8-ounce) bottle coconut aminos

1 tablespoon unseasoned rice wine vinegar

2 teaspoons toasted sesame oil

½ teaspoon fish sauce

Pour the coconut aminos into a large skillet over medium heat. Simmer for 10 to 15 minutes, until it thickens enough to coat the back of a spoon. Whisk in the vinegar, sesame oil, and fish sauce. Store in the refrigerator for use later in the week.

Slice the celery

Cut two stalks of celery crosswise into ¼-inch slices, to equal 1 cup. Store in the refrigerator for use later in the week.

Chop the cabbage

Cut half of a head of purple or green cabbage in half down the middle, through the core, then remove the tough center core from each wedge. Place the flat side of a wedge on the cutting board so it's stable, then thinly slice the cabbage. Cut the sliced wedge crosswise into 2-inch sections until you end up with ¼- to ½-inch by 2-inch strips. Repeat with the other wedge. Store in the refrigerator for use later in the week.

Dice a yellow onion

Dice a medium-sized yellow onion, then divide the diced onions evenly between two storage containers, labeling one "Chow Mein" and the other "Soup." Store in the refrigerator for use later in the week.

Mince the garlic

Mince six cloves of garlic, or until you have 6 teaspoons. Store in the refrigerator for use later in the week.

Cut the green onions

Cut six green onions into 1-inch pieces, then store in the refrigerator for use later in the week.

Chicken Marsala Casserole

Yield: 6 servings   Prep Time: 10 minutes   Cook Time: 25 minutes

2 tablespoons extra-virgin olive oil, divided

Cooked onion, garlic, and mushroom mixture ✓

¾ cup Marsala wine

¼ cup chicken broth

¼ cup heavy cream or coconut milk

1 tablespoon salted butter, ghee, or oil of choice

1 teaspoon dried parsley

1 teaspoon coarse sea salt, divided

½ teaspoon ground black pepper, divided

4 thin slices prosciutto, crisped ✓

5 cups strands scraped from 1 roasted spaghetti squash ✓

½ teaspoon garlic powder

3 cups cubed cooked chicken breast ✓

2 tablespoons chopped fresh flat-leaf parsley, for garnish

1. Preheat the oven to 350°F.

2. Heat 1 tablespoon of the olive oil in a saucepan over medium heat. Once hot, add the cooked onion, garlic, and mushroom mixture and sauté for 1 to 2 minutes, until warmed through.

3. Pour in the wine and broth and boil for 1 minute to cook off the alcohol, then whisk in the cream, butter, dried parsley, ½ teaspoon of the salt, and ¼ teaspoon of the pepper. Stir in the prosciutto, then slide the pan off the heat.

4. Place the squash strands in an 8-inch round casserole dish and toss with the remaining tablespoon of oil, the garlic powder, remaining ½ teaspoon of salt, and remaining ¼ teaspoon of pepper.

5. Spread the chicken on top of the squash, then pour the mushroom sauce over the chicken.

6. Bake for 20 minutes to warm the casserole through. Garnish with the fresh parsley and serve.

Spaghetti Squash Chicken Chow Mein

Yield: 4 servings   Prep Time: 2 minutes   Cook Time: 15 minutes

2 tablespoons avocado oil

½ yellow onion, diced ✓

½ head purple cabbage, cut into 2-inch strips ✓

1 cup sliced celery ✓

4 teaspoons minced garlic ✓

5 cups strands scraped from 1 roasted spaghetti squash ✓

3 cups cooked shredded chicken ✓

Chow mein sauce ✓

6 green onions, cut into 1-inch pieces ✓

1 teaspoon sesame seeds, for garnish

1. Heat the oil in a large sauté pan over medium heat. Add the onion and sauté for 3 to 4 minutes, until fragrant and translucent. Add the cabbage, celery, and garlic and cook for an additional 4 to 5 minutes, until the vegetables are slightly browned.

2. Stir in the squash strands, chicken, sauce, and green onions. Toss to combine, then cook for an additional 3 to 4 minutes, until the squash is warmed through and the sauce has started to bubble. Garnish with the sesame seeds and serve!

Creamy Chicken and Mushroom Soup

Yield: 4 servings   Prep Time: 10 minutes   Cook Time: 12 minutes

2 tablespoons salted butter, ghee, or oil of choice

½ yellow onion, diced ✓

8 ounces mushrooms, diced ✓

2 teaspoons minced garlic ✓

2 tablespoons gluten-free flour blend or arrowroot powder (see note below)

3 cups chicken broth

½ cup heavy cream or coconut cream

2 tablespoons spicy brown mustard

1 tablespoon fresh lemon juice (about ½ small lemon)

1 tablespoon chopped fresh thyme

½ teaspoon coarse sea salt

¼ teaspoon ground black pepper

3 cups shredded, cooked chicken ✓

1. Melt the butter in a soup pot over medium heat, then add the onion, mushrooms, and garlic. Cook, stirring occasionally, for 4 to 5 minutes, until the onion and mushrooms are slightly browned.

2. Sprinkle the flour blend into the pot and whisk until it has been absorbed into the mushroom mixture. Pour in the broth 1 cup at a time, whisking constantly to smooth out any lumps.

3. To the pot, add the cream, mustard, lemon juice, thyme, salt, pepper, and chicken. Give the soup a stir and cook for about 5 minutes, until the chicken is warmed through, then serve.

note: *If using arrowroot powder, complete Step 1, then add all of the chicken broth to the pot, cover, and bring to a boil over medium-high heat. Meanwhile, whisk together the arrowroot powder and ¼ cup water, then stir the slurry into the boiling broth. Simmer for 1 to 2 minutes, until thickened, then reduce the heat to medium and proceed to Step 3.*

BRISKET,
BRUSSELS SPROUTS,
and RICE

This week involves a little kitchen wizardry, showing you how brisket, Brussels sprouts, and rice can be magically renewed into three delicious dinners. You're going to use these basic components to make BBQ Brisket Bowls (so comforting), Chipotle Brisket Tacos with the tastiest Green Apple Slaw, and Brisket Fried Rice (it's as good as it sounds). If you'd like to supplement this week's three main dinner recipes with two additional meals, see the suggested "Bonus Dinner Options" on the next page.

Weekly Ingredients

FRESH PRODUCE

Apple, green, 1 small

Brussels sprouts, 1 pound

Carrots, 2 medium

Cilantro, ½ bunch

Garlic, 4 cloves

Ginger, 1 (1-inch) piece

Green onions, 5

Lemon, 1 small

Lime, ½

Onion, red, ½ medium

MEAT/EGGS

Brisket, 1 (6 to 7 pounds)

Eggs, 2 large

PANTRY

Avocado oil, 1 tablespoon

Avocado oil mayonnaise, store-bought or homemade (page 372), 2⅔ fluid ounces (⅓ cup)

BBQ sauce, store-bought or homemade (page 373), 4 fluid ounces (½ cup)

Beef broth, 8 to 16 fluid ounces (1 to 2 cups, depending on brisket cooking method)

Coconut aminos, Coconut Secret brand, 2 fluid ounces (¼ cup)

Coconut sugar, 1 tablespoon

Corn tortillas (about 6 inches in diameter), 8

Dill pickle spears, 10

Extra-virgin olive oil, 3 tablespoons

Ghee or avocado oil, 3 tablespoons plus 1 teaspoon

Honey, 1 tablespoon

Toasted sesame oil, 2 teaspoons

White rice, 16½ ounces (2½ cups)

SEASONINGS

Ancho chili powder, 1 teaspoon

Chipotle chili powder, 1 teaspoon

Dried oregano leaves, 1 teaspoon

Garlic powder, ½ teaspoon

Ground cumin, 1 teaspoon

Paprika, 2 tablespoons plus ½ teaspoon

Red pepper flakes, ¼ teaspoon

Ingredient Subs

To make this week LOW-CARB:

· *Use a low-carb BBQ sauce.*

· *Omit the tortillas and eat the taco fillings in a bowl, or use butter lettuce leaves as wraps.*

· *Substitute 2 medium to large heads cauliflower (4½ to 5 pounds total) or 28 ounces frozen riced cauliflower for the white rice.*

· *Omit the coconut sugar from the BBQ Spice Rub.*

· *Omit the honey from the slaw.*

To make this week PALEO and/ or GRAIN-FREE:

· *Use grain-free tortillas in place of the corn tortillas.*

· *Substitute 2 medium to large heads cauliflower (4½ to 5 pounds total) or 28 ounces frozen riced cauliflower for the white rice.*

To make this week EGG-FREE:

· *Omit the eggs.*

· *Substitute vegan mayo for the avocado oil mayonnaise.*

Bonus Dinner Options

Dinner 1

Crispy Curried Chicken Thighs (page 348)

Lemony Kale
(page 359)

Roasted Carrots
(page 364)

Bonus Dinner Ingredients

Carrots, slender, 2 bunches (about 1 pound)

Chicken thighs, bone-in, skin-on, 2 pounds

Curry powder, 1 tablespoon

Extra-virgin olive oil, 1 tablespoon plus 2 teaspoons

Kale, 1 small bunch (about 1 pound)

Lemon, 1

Lime, 1

Dinner 2

Southwestern Pork Chops
(page 350)

Sautéed Bell Peppers
(page 361)

Green Peas
(page 367)

Bonus Dinner Ingredients

Bell peppers, red, 1 pound

Dried dill weed, 1 teaspoon

Extra-virgin olive oil, 2 tablespoons plus 2 teaspoons

Lemon, 1 small

Peas, frozen, 1 (10-ounce) package

Pork chops, boneless, about 1 inch thick, 1½ pounds

Texas Chili Spice Blend, 2 tablespoons (see page 374 for ingredients)

Prep Day

For today's meal prep efforts, you're going to cook the brisket and rice, shred the Brussels, make the spice rub, and prep the remaining fresh produce components. It's an easy day for sure! To start off, I find it most efficient to get the brisket into the Instant Pot (my chosen method, although you can use the oven or a slow cooker if you prefer). Unlike other weeks, you don't need to chop or shred the cooked protein on prep day. Brisket is much easier to slice when chilled, so after cooking, it gets packaged up as is and stored right away. While the brisket cooks, I shred the Brussels sprouts (a food processor is the quickest tool for this task) and cook the rice. Once the Brussels are finished and the rice is cooking, I make the spice rub and then chop the cilantro, grate the ginger, mince the garlic, slice the red and green onions, and shred the carrots.

note: *If you're planning to make homemade mayonnaise and/or BBQ sauce rather than use store-bought, I recommend that you add them to your prep day tasks so that they're ready for use later in the week.*

Cook the brisket

Yield: 3½ to 4 pounds cooked brisket

Prep Time: 15 minutes

Cook Time: 1 hour 10 minutes to 8 hours, depending on method

1 (6- to 7-pound) brisket

1½ teaspoons coarse sea salt

1 tablespoon avocado oil (Instant Pot method only)

1 to 2 cups beef broth (depending on method)

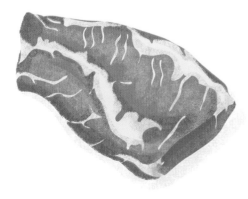

1. Take the brisket and trim off most of the excess fat, leaving a ¼-inch layer of fat. If using the Instant Pot method, cut the brisket into three equal pieces; otherwise, leave it whole. Season the meat with the salt.

2. Cook the brisket using one of these three methods:

- **Oven Method** (Cook Time: 4½ to 5 hours)
  Preheat the oven to 275°F. Place the seasoned brisket in a roasting pan or 9 by 13-inch baking dish. Pour in 1½ cups of beef broth, then cover the pan with a lid or aluminum foil. Bake for 4½ to 5 hours, until the brisket easily pulls apart with a fork.

- **Instant Pot Method** (Cook Time: 1 hour 25 minutes)
  Place the avocado oil in a 6-quart Instant Pot and set the cooker to the Sauté mode. Once hot, sear the seasoned brisket in two batches for 2 to 3 minutes per side, until browned. (If you're in a hurry, feel free to skip this step.) Once all of the brisket is seared, return all of the pieces to the pot and pour in 1 cup of beef broth. Seal the lid onto the Instant Pot, press the Meat/Stew button, and set the timer for 70 minutes. Once the cooking is finished, let the pressure release naturally until the lid opens easily, about 15 minutes.

- **Slow Cooker Method** (Cook Time: 4 or 8 hours)
  Place the seasoned brisket in a slow cooker and pour in 2 cups of beef broth. Cover and cook on low for 8 hours or high for 4 hours, until the brisket easily pulls apart with a fork.

3. Place the whole brisket in a container and refrigerate overnight to make it easier to slice later in the week.

Slice or shred the Brussels sprouts

Yield: about 7 cups
Prep Time: 10 to 20 minutes

Trim 1 pound of Brussels sprouts, then thinly slice them using a knife or shred them using the shredder attachment of a food processor. Place 4 cups in a container and label it "Tacos." Place the remaining 3 cups in another container and label it "Fried Rice." Store in the refrigerator for use later in the week.

Cook the rice

Yield: 7½ cups
Prep Time: 2 minutes
Cook Time: 20 minutes

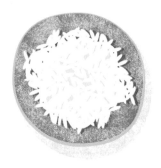

Cook 2½ cups of white rice according to the package instructions. Place 3½ cups of cooked rice in a container labeled "Bowls" and 4 cups in a container labeled "Fried Rice." Store in the refrigerator for use later in the week.

LOW-CARB/PALEO/GRAIN-FREE RICE SUBSTITUTE
Make 1½ batches of Basic Cauliflower Rice (page 363), then follow the storage instructions for the white rice above.

Make the BBQ Spice Rub

Make a half batch of the BBQ Spice Rub on page 374.

Prep the cilantro

Wash and dry one-third bunch of cilantro. Set 13 sprigs aside, then coarsely chop the remaining cilantro to equal ¼ cup plus 2 tablespoons. Store the sprigs and chopped cilantro in the refrigerator for use later in the week.

Grate the ginger

Peel and grate a 1-inch piece of ginger to equal 1 tablespoon. Store in the refrigerator for use later in the week.

Mince the garlic

Peel and mince four cloves of garlic to equal 4 teaspoons. Store in the refrigerator for use later in the week.

Slice the half red onion

Thinly slice half of a red onion, then store in the refrigerator for use later in the week.

Slice the green onions

Thinly slice five green onions, or enough to equal ¼ cup plus 2 tablespoons. Store in the refrigerator for use later in the week.

Shred the carrots

Peel and shred two medium-sized carrots using either a cheese grater or the shredder attachment of your food processor. Store in the refrigerator for use later in the week.

BBQ Brisket Bowls

Yield: 5 servings   Prep Time: 10 minutes   Cook Time: 6 minutes

One-third of the cooked brisket ✓

2 tablespoons BBQ Spice Rub ✓

2 tablespoons extra-virgin olive oil

3½ cups cooked white rice or cauli-rice ✓

10 dill pickle spears, for serving

½ red onion, thinly sliced, for serving ✓

½ cup BBQ sauce, for serving

2 tablespoons chopped fresh cilantro, for garnish ✓

1. Thinly slice the brisket, then put it in a medium-sized bowl along with the spice rub. Toss to coat the meat in the seasonings.

2. Heat the olive oil in a large skillet over medium-high heat. Once hot, add the seasoned brisket. Cook for 2 to 3 minutes, then flip each piece and cook for an additional 2 to 3 minutes, until browned on both sides.

3. Meanwhile, reheat the rice either by placing it in a medium-sized saucepan, covered, over low heat for 5 minutes or by microwaving for about 2 minutes, until hot.

4. Spoon the warmed rice into bowls and top with the brisket, pickles, onion slices, a drizzle of BBQ sauce, and a sprinkle of chopped cilantro. Enjoy!

Chipotle Brisket Tacos with Green Apple Slaw

Yield: 4 servings   Prep Time: 15 minutes   Cook Time: 15 minutes

FOR THE CHIPOTLE BRISKET:

1 teaspoon chipotle chili powder

1 teaspoon ground cumin

½ teaspoon garlic powder

½ teaspoon paprika

½ teaspoon coarse sea salt

¼ teaspoon ground black pepper

One-third of the cooked brisket ✓

1 tablespoon extra-virgin olive oil

FOR THE GREEN APPLE SLAW:

1 small green apple

⅓ cup avocado oil mayonnaise or vegan mayo

2 tablespoons fresh lemon juice (about 1 small lemon)

1 tablespoon honey

Pinch of fine sea salt

¼ teaspoon ground black pepper

4 cups shredded Brussels sprouts ✓

¼ cup chopped fresh cilantro ✓

8 corn tortillas or grain-free tortillas

8 sprigs fresh cilantro, for garnish ✓

1. Place the chili powder, cumin, garlic powder, paprika, salt, and pepper in a medium-sized bowl and whisk to combine.

2. Thinly slice the brisket and add it to the bowl with the seasonings. Toss the meat in the seasoning mixture until well coated.

3. Heat the olive oil in a large skillet over medium-high heat. Once hot, add the seasoned brisket and cook for 2 to 3 minutes, then flip and cook for an additional 2 to 3 minutes, until browned on both sides. Remove from the heat and set aside.

4. While the brisket is cooking, make the slaw: Cut the apple into ¼-inch-thick matchsticks, to equal 1 cup. Place the mayonnaise, lemon juice, honey, salt, and pepper in a large bowl and whisk until smooth. Stir in the apple, Brussels sprouts, and chopped cilantro.

5. To warm the tortillas, preheat a small skillet over medium-high heat. Once hot, put a tortilla in the pan and warm for 30 seconds per side, until the tortilla is pliable and begins to brown slightly. Repeat with the remaining tortillas. To keep them warm while you heat the remaining tortillas, you can wrap them in a kitchen towel.

6. Fill each tortilla with brisket and slaw, garnish with a cilantro sprig, and serve!

Brisket Fried Rice

Yield: 5 servings   Prep Time: 5 minutes   Cook Time: 18 minutes

2 large eggs

3 tablespoons plus 1 teaspoon ghee or avocado oil, divided

One-third of the cooked brisket ✓

1 tablespoon grated ginger ✓

4 teaspoons minced garlic ✓

3 cups shredded Brussels sprouts ✓

2 medium carrots, shredded ✓

¼ cup plus 2 tablespoons thinly sliced green onions ✓, divided

4 cups cooked white rice or cauli-rice ✓

¼ cup coconut aminos

1 tablespoon fresh lime juice (about ½ lime)

2 teaspoons toasted sesame oil

¼ teaspoon red pepper flakes

¼ teaspoon coarse sea salt

5 sprigs fresh cilantro, or 1 tablespoon chopped fresh cilantro, for garnish

1. In a small bowl, whisk the eggs.

2. Place 1 teaspoon of the ghee in a small skillet over medium-high heat. Once melted, add the eggs and spread evenly across the pan. Cook for 2 minutes, then flip and cook for an additional minute, until fully heated through.

3. Transfer the eggs to a cutting board and cut into ½-inch squares, then set aside.

4. Cut the brisket into ½-inch cubes.

5. Heat 1½ tablespoons of the ghee in a large sauté pan or wok over medium-high heat. Once hot, add the brisket. Cook for 3 to 4 minutes, until browned.

6. Add the ginger and garlic to the pan with the brisket and cook for 30 seconds, until fragrant.

7. Add the Brussels sprouts and carrots to the pan with the brisket. Cook for 3 to 4 minutes, until the carrots and Brussels sprouts are slightly browned, then stir in ¼ cup of the green onions.

8. Add the remaining 1½ tablespoons of ghee to the pan and stir it into the meat and vegetable mixture. Add the rice and toss to combine it with the rest of the ingredients.

9. Add the eggs, coconut aminos, lime juice, sesame oil, and red pepper flakes to the rice mixture and stir to combine. Add the salt, then taste for seasoning and add more salt, if needed.

10. Let the rice cook, untouched, for 2 minutes. Then stir the rice, scraping any browned bits off of the bottom of the pan. Cook for an additional 1 to 2 minutes, until the rice is slightly browned and crisp. Remove from the heat.

11. Garnish with the remaining 2 tablespoons of green onions and the cilantro and enjoy!

SHREDDED PORK, CABBAGE, and RED POTATOES

If you crave comfort food after a long day of work, chasing kids, or both, this week is for you. Here I transform highly versatile shredded pork, cabbage, and red-skinned potatoes into three incredibly comforting recipes. Get ready for a flavor-packed Honey Mustard Sheet Pan Dinner, a hearty Enchilada Verde Casserole, and some reminiscent-of-childhood Sloppy Joe–Stuffed Potatoes. If you'd like to supplement this week's three main dinner recipes with two additional meals, see the suggested "Bonus Dinner Options" on the next page.

Weekly Ingredients

FRESH PRODUCE

Avocado, 1

Cilantro, ½ bunch

Flat-leaf parsley, 8 sprigs

Green cabbage, ½ medium head

Jalapeño pepper, 1

Lime, 1

Onion, red, 1 medium

Purple cabbage, 1 medium head

Red potatoes, 5 pounds

MEAT/DAIRY

Pork shoulder, boneless, 1
(5 to 6 pounds)

Shredded white cheddar or
Monterey Jack cheese, 3 ounces
(¾ cup)

PANTRY

Apple cider vinegar, 1 tablespoon

Avocado oil, 3 tablespoons

Balsamic vinegar, 1 tablespoon

Corn tortillas (about 6 inches in
diameter), 6

Dijon mustard, 2 ounces (¼ cup)

Extra-virgin olive oil, 5 fluid
ounces (½ cup plus
3 tablespoons)

Honey, 4½ ounces (¼ cup plus
2 tablespoons)

Ketchup, 4½ ounces (½ cup)

Prepared yellow mustard,
2 tablespoons

Salsa verde, 2 (16-ounce) jars
(3 cups)

SEASONINGS

Chili powder, 1½ teaspoons

Dried oregano leaves,
1½ teaspoons

Garlic powder, 1 teaspoon

Ground cumin, 1½ teaspoons

Onion powder, ½ teaspoon

Paprika, ½ teaspoon

Ingredient Subs

To make this week PALEO:

· *Use grain-free tortillas and omit
the cheese.*

To make this week GRAIN-FREE:

· *Use grain-free tortillas.*

To make this week DAIRY-FREE:

· *Omit the cheese.*

Bonus Dinner Options

Dinner 1

Balsamic Chicken Thighs
(page 348)

Braised Collards
(page 358)

Perfect Parsnips
(page 365)

Bonus Dinner Ingredients

Balsamic vinegar, 2 tablespoons

Chicken thighs, boneless, skinless, 1½ pounds

Collard greens, 1 small bunch (about 1 pound)

Extra-virgin olive oil, 2 tablespoons

Lemon, ½

Parsnips, 2 pounds

Dinner 2

Mocha Coffee Steak
(page 352)

Italian Side Salad
(page 362)

Baked Russet Potatoes
(page 366)

Bonus Dinner Ingredients

Artichoke hearts, marinated and quartered, 1 (6-ounce) jar

Cocoa powder, 1 teaspoon

Extra-virgin olive oil, 2 fluid ounces (¼ cup)

Instant coffee powder, 1 teaspoon

Lettuce, mixed, 8 ounces (about 6 cups chopped)

Olives, assorted pitted, 3 ounces (about ½ cup)

Red wine vinegar, 2 tablespoons

Russet potatoes, 4 small to medium (about 1 pound)

Sirloin or rib-eye steaks, boneless, about 1 inch thick, 4 (4 to 6 ounces each)

Prep Day

Because the prep work for today is pretty minimal, this is a great week to make when you're especially short on time! Per the usual, I recommend getting the protein started first; I usually opt for the Instant Pot method. Then I pop the potatoes in the oven. From there, I get started on the honey mustard dressing and the Sloppy Joe sauce. After that, I turn my attention to the slicing and dicing! By the time I'm done tending to the cabbage and other veggies, I have extra hands-off time to spare (to fold a load of laundry) while I wait for the pork to finish cooking.

note: *To save myself a step, I purchase preshredded cheese; if you are using block cheese, add the step of shredding the cheddar or Monterey Jack cheese to this week's prep day tasks.*

Cook and shred the pork

Yield: 10 cups

Prep Time: 15 minutes

Cook Time: 1½ hours to 10 hours, depending on method

1 (5- to 6-pound) boneless pork shoulder

1½ teaspoons coarse sea salt

1 tablespoon avocado oil (for oven method)

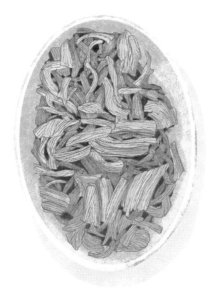

1. If using the Instant Pot method, cut the pork shoulder into four or five equal pieces; otherwise, leave it whole. Season the meat with the salt.

2. Cook the pork shoulder using one of these three methods:

- **Oven Method** (Cook Time: 4½ hours)
  Preheat the oven to 325°F. Heat the oil in a Dutch oven or enameled cast-iron pot with a lid over medium-high heat. Place the seasoned pork shoulder in the pot and sear for 3 to 4 minutes per side, until browned. Once browned, pour 1½ cups of water into the pot, then cover with the lid and transfer to the oven. Bake for 3½ to 4½ hours, until the pork shreds easily.

- **Instant Pot Method** (Cook Time: 1½ hours)
  Place the seasoned pork shoulder pieces in a 6-quart Instant Pot along with ½ cup of water. Seal the lid onto the Instant Pot, press the Pressure Cook or Manual button, and set the timer for 90 minutes. Once the cooking is finished, release the pressure manually by slowly turning the pressure valve to "venting."

- **Slow Cooker Method** (Cook Time: 8 to 10 hours)
  Place the seasoned pork shoulder in a 6-quart slow cooker. Cover and cook on low for 8 to 10 hours, until the pork shreds easily.

3. Remove the pork from the pot and shred the meat with two forks, discarding the excess fat. Place 3 cups in a container labeled "Sheet Pan Dinner," 4 cups in a container labeled "Casserole," and the remaining 3 cups in a container labeled "Stuffed Potatoes." Store in the refrigerator for use later in the week.

Roast the red potatoes

Prep Time: 5 minutes

Cook Time: 1 hour

5 pounds red potatoes

1 tablespoon extra-virgin olive oil

1 teaspoon coarse sea salt

1. Preheat the oven to 350°F.

2. Coat the potatoes with the olive oil and sprinkle with the salt.

3. Bake for 45 to 60 minutes, until the potatoes are easily pierced with a fork.

4. Store in the refrigerator for use later in the week.

Slice ½ head of purple cabbage

Cut a head of purple cabbage in half through the core. Set one half aside for use later in the prep day. Core the other half, then slice it crosswise into ½-inch-thick ribbons. Store in the refrigerator for use later in the week.

Roast the cabbage wedges

Prep Time: 5 minutes

Cook Time: 30 minutes

½ head purple cabbage

½ head green cabbage

1 tablespoon extra-virgin olive oil

1 teaspoon coarse sea salt

¼ teaspoon ground black pepper

1. Preheat the oven to 400°F. Line a rimmed baking sheet with parchment paper.

2. Leaving the cores intact, cut each half head of cabbage into four wedges, making a total of eight wedges. Place the cabbage wedges on the lined baking sheet.

3. Drizzle the cabbage with the olive oil, then season with the salt and pepper. Roast for 30 minutes, until slightly browned on top. Store in the refrigerator for use later in the week.

Make the honey mustard dressing

¼ cup honey

¼ cup Dijon mustard

1 tablespoon apple cider vinegar

½ cup extra-virgin olive oil

1. In a medium-sized bowl, whisk together the honey, mustard, and vinegar.

2. While constantly whisking the honey mixture, slowly pour in the olive oil. The slower you pour, the creamier the dressing will be. Store in the refrigerator for use later in the week.

Dice the onion

Dice a red onion, or until you have ½ cup plus 2 tablespoons of diced onions. Store in the refrigerator for use later in the week.

Chop the jalapeño

Seed and finely chop a jalapeño pepper, then store in the refrigerator for use later in the week.

Prep the cilantro

Wash and dry half of a bunch of cilantro. Refrigerate eight sprigs for use later in the week, then tear off enough leaves from the remaining cilantro (leaving a little stem is okay) to equal ¼ cup of leaves. Store the sprigs and leaves in the refrigerator for use later in the week.

Make the Sloppy Joe sauce

Prep Time: 2 minutes

Cook Time: 5 minutes

½ cup ketchup

2 tablespoons honey

2 tablespoons prepared yellow mustard

1 tablespoon balsamic vinegar

½ teaspoon garlic powder

½ teaspoon onion powder

½ teaspoon paprika

1. In a medium-sized saucepan, whisk together all of the ingredients for the sauce, along with ⅓ cup of water. Bring to a simmer over medium heat, then continue to simmer for 3 to 4 minutes. Remove from the heat.

2. Store in the refrigerator for use later in the week.

Honey Mustard Sheet Pan Dinner

Yield: 5 servings   Prep Time: 5 minutes   Cook Time: 15 minutes

3 cups shredded pork ✓

Honey mustard dressing, divided ✓

1½ teaspoons coarse sea salt, divided

4 roasted green cabbage wedges ✓

4 roasted purple cabbage wedges ✓

Half of the roasted red potatoes ✓

1 tablespoon extra-virgin olive oil

½ teaspoon ground black pepper

8 sprigs flat-leaf parsley, for garnish

1. Preheat the oven to 350°F.

2. Place the shredded pork, half of the honey mustard dressing, and ½ teaspoon of the salt in a medium-sized bowl and toss to coat.

3. Place the cabbage wedges and potatoes on a rimmed baking sheet. Drizzle with the olive oil, sprinkle with the pepper and remaining teaspoon of salt, and toss to coat.

4. Place clumps of the shredded pork mixture on the baking sheet in between the cabbage and potatoes.

5. Bake for 15 minutes, until the pork is browned and the potatoes and cabbage are warmed through.

6. Meanwhile, wash, dry, and chop the parsley.

7. Drizzle the remaining dressing over the potatoes and cabbage, garnish with the parsley, and serve.

Enchilada Verde Casserole with Avocado Slaw

Yield: 6 servings Prep Time: 15 minutes Cook Time: 30 minutes

FOR THE CASSEROLE:

4 cups shredded pork ✓

1½ teaspoons chili powder

1½ teaspoons ground cumin

1½ teaspoons dried oregano leaves

½ teaspoon garlic powder

½ teaspoon coarse sea salt

¼ teaspoon ground black pepper

4 cups salsa verde, divided

6 (6-inch) corn or grain-free tortillas

¾ cup shredded white cheddar or Monterey Jack cheese (omit for Paleo/dairy-free), divided

FOR THE AVOCADO SLAW:

2 tablespoons fresh lime juice (about 1 lime)

2 tablespoons avocado oil

½ cup diced red onions ✓

1 jalapeño pepper, finely chopped ✓

1 avocado, cut into ½-inch cubes

¼ cup fresh cilantro leaves ✓

Shredded purple cabbage ✓

1. Preheat the oven to 350°F.

2. Make the casserole: In a medium-sized bowl, toss the pork with the chili powder, cumin, oregano, garlic powder, salt, and pepper.

3. Spread 1 cup of the salsa in an 8-inch square baking dish, then cover with 2 tortillas: place a tortilla in one corner of the dish, then cut the second tortilla in half and use the halves to fill in the empty spaces along the side and bottom of the whole tortilla.

4. Spread one-third of the seasoned pork over the tortillas, then top with 1 cup of the salsa and ¼ cup of the cheese. Repeat for two more layers.

5. Bake the casserole, uncovered, for 30 minutes, until the cheese is bubbling.

6. Meanwhile, make the avocado slaw: In a medium-sized bowl, whisk together the lime juice and avocado oil. Add the onions, jalapeño, avocado, cilantro, and cabbage and toss to coat.

7. Place the slaw on top of the casserole and serve!

Mini Sloppy Joe–Stuffed Potatoes

Yield: 4 servings   Prep Time: 5 minutes   Cook Time: 20 minutes

Half of the roasted red potatoes ✓

Sloppy Joe sauce ✓

3 cups shredded pork ✓

2 tablespoons diced red onions, for garnish ✓

4 sprigs fresh cilantro, for garnish

1. Preheat the oven to 350°F.

2. Place the potatoes on a rimmed baking sheet and bake for 15 to 20 minutes, until warmed through.

3. While the potatoes are in the oven, reheat the Sloppy Joe sauce and shredded pork in a medium-sized saucepan over medium heat for 5 minutes, tossing the pork in the sauce to coat, until the sauce begins to bubble and the pork is warmed through.

4. Meanwhile, chop the leaves from the cilantro sprigs.

5. Cut a slit in each potato, fill with the pork mixture, and garnish with the red onions and cilantro. Serve!

part

2

SUPPLEMENTAL RECIPES

BONUS DINNER RECIPES

Gathered here are the recipes you can use to make bonus dinners, for when the three main weekly recipes just aren't enough! In each weekly meal plan, we suggest two bonus dinner options using recipes from this chapter. Each bonus dinner suggestion combines a protein, a veggie, and a starch. These bonus recipes yield four servings, so a combination of them (to make a meal) will provide dinner for a family of four or dinner plus leftovers for a family of two. You may use our bonus dinner suggestions or create your own, mixing and matching your choice of protein, veggie, and starch recipes from this chapter. If you decide to customize your bonus dinner options, just be sure to add the ingredients required to your weekly shopping list! (The ingredients needed for our suggested bonus dinners are already listed.)

The recipes in this chapter are designed to be very easy to make, adding minimal work to your weekly meal prep. You'll be happy to know that each of them has no more than five ingredients (save for salt and pepper) and five steps.

Proteins

Seared Chicken Breasts · 346
Lemon Pepper Chicken Breasts · 347
Paprika Lime Chicken Breasts · 347
Crispy Curried Chicken Thighs · 348
Balsamic Chicken Thighs · 348
Ranch Chicken Thighs · 349
Simple Seared Pork Chops · 349
Southwestern Pork Chops · 350
Basic Pork Tenderloin · 350
Honey Mustard Pork Tenderloin · 351
Jerk Pork Tenderloin · 351
Pan-Seared Steak · 352
Mocha Coffee Steak · 352
Easy Tuna Steak · 353
Pan-Seared White Fish · 353
Lemon-Garlic Shrimp · 354
Salmon Bake · 354
Pan-Seared Salmon · 355

Veggies

Crispy Brussels Sprouts · 356
Sautéed Squash · 356
Simple Roasted Cauliflower · 357
Roasted Broccoli · 357
Braised Collards · 358
Wilted Spinach · 358
Baked Okra · 359
Lemony Kale · 359
Roasted Asparagus · 360
Roasted Cherry Tomatoes · 360
Steamed Green Beans · 361
Sautéed Bell Peppers · 361
Italian Side Salad · 362
Spinach Salad · 362
Basic Cauliflower Rice · 363

Starches

Baked Acorn Squash · 364
Roasted Carrots · 364
Perfect Parsnips · 365
Baked Sweet Potatoes · 365
Baked Russet Potatoes · 366
Roasted Butternut Squash Cubes · 366
Easy Baked Beets · 367
Green Peas · 367
Pan-Fried Plantains · 368
Basic White Rice · 368
Basic Quinoa · 369
Basic Polenta · 369

PROTEINS

Seared Chicken Breasts

Yield: 4 servings   Prep Time: 5 minutes   Cook Time: 15 minutes

1½ pounds boneless, skinless chicken breast halves, rinsed and patted dry

2 tablespoons Texas Grill Rub (page 374)

1 tablespoon extra-virgin olive oil

1. Preheat the oven to 350°F.

2. Sprinkle the chicken on both sides with the rub.

3. Place a medium-sized ovenproof skillet over medium heat and pour in the olive oil. Once the oil thins from the heat, after about 30 seconds, add the chicken. Sear the chicken for about 3 minutes, until slightly golden on one side. Flip the chicken over and transfer to the oven to bake for 12 minutes, or until the juices run clear.

4. Let the chicken rest for 5 minutes before cutting.

Lemon Pepper Chicken Breasts

Yield: 4 servings   Prep Time: 5 minutes   Cook Time: 18 minutes

1½ pounds boneless, skinless chicken breast halves, rinsed and patted dry

Juice of 1 lemon

1 tablespoon extra-virgin olive oil

1 teaspoon coarse sea salt

½ teaspoon ground black pepper

1. Preheat the oven to 350°F. Line a rimmed baking sheet with parchment paper.

2. In a medium-sized bowl, whisk together the lemon juice and olive oil. Place the chicken in the bowl and toss to coat evenly.

3. Place the chicken on the lined baking sheet, then sprinkle both sides with the salt and pepper. Bake for 15 to 18 minutes, until the juices run clear.

4. Let the chicken rest for 5 minutes before cutting.

Paprika Lime Chicken Breasts

Yield: 4 servings   Prep Time: 5 minutes   Cook Time: 18 minutes

1½ pounds boneless, skinless chicken breast halves, rinsed and patted dry

Juice of 1 lime

1 tablespoon extra-virgin olive oil

1 tablespoon paprika

1 teaspoon coarse sea salt

½ teaspoon ground black pepper

1. Preheat the oven to 350°F. Line a rimmed baking sheet with parchment paper.

2. In a medium-sized bowl, whisk together the lime juice and olive oil. Place the chicken in the bowl and toss to coat evenly.

3. Place the chicken on the lined baking sheet, then sprinkle both sides with the paprika, salt, and pepper. Bake for 15 to 18 minutes, until the juices run clear.

4. Let the chicken rest for 5 minutes before cutting.

Crispy Curried Chicken Thighs

Yield: 4 servings   Prep Time: 5 minutes   Cook Time: 45 minutes

2 pounds bone-in, skin-on chicken thighs, rinsed and patted dry

Juice of 1 lime

1 tablespoon curry powder

1 teaspoon coarse sea salt

½ teaspoon ground black pepper

1. Preheat the oven to 400°F. Line a rimmed baking sheet with parchment paper.

2. In a medium-sized bowl, whisk together the lime juice and curry powder. Place the chicken in the bowl and toss to coat evenly.

3. Place the thighs, skin side up, on the lined baking sheet, then sprinkle both sides with the salt and pepper. Bake for 45 minutes, or until the juices run clear and the tops are browned.

4. Let the chicken rest for 5 minutes before cutting.

Balsamic Chicken Thighs

Yield: 4 servings   Prep Time: 5 minutes   Cook Time: 25 minutes

1½ pounds boneless, skinless chicken thighs, rinsed and patted dry

2 tablespoons balsamic vinegar

1 teaspoon coarse sea salt

½ teaspoon ground black pepper

1. Preheat the oven to 375°F. Line a rimmed baking sheet with parchment paper.

2. Pour the balsamic vinegar into a medium-sized bowl. Place the chicken in the bowl and toss to coat evenly.

3. Place the thighs on the lined baking sheet, then sprinkle with the salt and pepper. Bake for 25 minutes, or until the juices run clear and the tops are browned.

4. Let the chicken rest for 5 minutes before cutting.

Ranch Chicken Thighs

Yield: 4 servings   Prep Time: 5 minutes   Cook Time: 25 minutes

1½ pounds boneless, skinless chicken thighs, rinsed and patted dry

¼ cup ranch dressing, store-bought or homemade (page 372)

1 teaspoon coarse sea salt

½ teaspoon ground black pepper

1. Preheat the oven to 375°F. Line a rimmed baking sheet with parchment paper.

2. Pour the ranch dressing into a medium-sized bowl. Place the chicken in the bowl and toss to coat evenly.

3. Place the thighs on the lined baking sheet, then sprinkle both sides with the salt and pepper. Bake for 25 minutes, or until the juices run clear and the tops are browned.

4. Let the chicken rest for 5 minutes before cutting.

Simple Seared Pork Chops

Yield: 4 servings   Prep Time: 5 minutes   Cook Time: 15 minutes

1½ pounds boneless pork chops, about 1 inch thick

2 tablespoons Texas Grill Rub (page 374)

1 tablespoon extra-virgin olive oil

pro tip: If you want these pork chops to be extra juicy, let them sit in a refrigerated brine of 2 cups water plus 2 tablespoons sea salt and 2 tablespoons maple syrup for a minimum of 4 hours or a maximum of 24 hours. Pat dry and proceed with the cooking instructions above.

1. Preheat the oven to 350°F.

2. Sprinkle both sides of the pork chops with the rub.

3. Place a medium-sized ovenproof skillet over medium heat and pour in the olive oil. Once the oil thins from the heat, after about 30 seconds, add the pork chops. Sear the chops for about 3 minutes, or until slightly golden on one side. Flip the chops over and transfer to the oven to bake for 12 minutes, or until the juices run clear.

4. Let the chops rest for 5 minutes before cutting.

Southwestern Pork Chops

Yield: 4 servings   Prep Time: 5 minutes   Cook Time: 15 minutes

1½ pounds boneless pork chops, about 1 inch thick

2 tablespoons Texas Chili Spice Blend (page 374)

1 tablespoon extra-virgin olive oil

pro tip: *If you want these pork chops to be extra juicy, let them sit in a refrigerated brine of 2 cups water plus 2 tablespoons sea salt and 2 tablespoons maple syrup for a minimum of 4 hours or a maximum of 24 hours. Pat dry and proceed with the cooking instructions above.*

1. Preheat the oven to 350°F.

2. Sprinkle both sides of the pork chops with the spice blend.

3. Place a medium-sized ovenproof skillet over medium heat and pour in the olive oil. Once the oil thins from the heat, after about 30 seconds, add the pork chops. Sear the chops for about 3 minutes, or until slightly golden on one side. Flip the chops over and transfer to the oven to bake for 12 minutes, or until the juices run clear.

4. Let the chops rest for 5 minutes before cutting.

Basic Pork Tenderloin

Yield: 4 servings   Prep Time: 5 minutes   Cook Time: 35 minutes

1 tablespoon extra-virgin olive oil

1 (1¼-pound) pork tenderloin, trimmed

2 tablespoons Texas Grill Rub (page 374)

1. Preheat the oven to 375°F.

2. Heat the olive oil in a large cast-iron or other ovenproof skillet over high heat. While the oil heats, sprinkle all sides of the tenderloin with the rub.

3. Once the oil has thinned from the heat, sear the tenderloin on all sides for about 2 minutes per side, or until it develops a brown char. Transfer the skillet to the oven and bake for 25 minutes, or until the internal temperature of the pork reads 160°F.

4. Let the pork rest for 10 minutes before cutting.

Honey Mustard Pork Tenderloin

Yield: 4 servings   Prep Time: 5 minutes   Cook Time: 35 minutes

1 tablespoon extra-virgin olive oil

2 tablespoons Dijon mustard

1 tablespoon honey

1 teaspoon coarse sea salt

½ teaspoon ground black pepper

1 (1¼-pound) pork tenderloin, trimmed

1. Preheat the oven to 375°F.

2. Heat the olive oil in a large cast-iron or other ovenproof skillet over high heat. While the oil heats, whisk the mustard, honey, salt, and pepper together in a bowl. Spread the honey mustard evenly over the pork tenderloin.

3. Once the oil has thinned from the heat, sear the tenderloin on all sides for about 2 minutes per side, or until it develops a brown char. Transfer the skillet to the oven and bake for 25 minutes, or until the internal temperature of the pork reads 160°F.

4. Let the pork rest for 10 minutes before cutting.

Jerk Pork Tenderloin

Yield: 4 servings   Prep Time: 5 minutes   Cook Time: 35 minutes

2 tablespoons extra-virgin olive oil

1 (1¼-pound) pork tenderloin, trimmed

1 tablespoon Jerk Seasoning (page 375)

1. Preheat the oven to 375°F.

2. Heat the olive oil in a large cast-iron or other ovenproof skillet over high heat. While the oil heats, sprinkle all sides of the tenderloin with the seasoning.

3. Once the oil has thinned from the heat, sear the tenderloin on all sides for about 2 minutes per side, or until it develops a brown char. Transfer the skillet to the oven and bake for 25 minutes, or until the internal temperature of the pork reads 160°F.

4. Let the pork rest for 10 minutes before cutting.

Pan-Seared Steak

Yield: 4 servings   Prep Time: 5 minutes   Cook Time: 5 to 10 minutes

2 tablespoons extra-virgin olive oil

4 (4- to 6-ounce) boneless sirloin or rib-eye steaks, about 1 inch thick

2 tablespoons Texas Grill Rub (page 374)

1. Heat the olive oil in a large cast-iron or other ovenproof skillet over medium-high heat. Sprinkle both sides of the steaks with the rub.

2. Sear the steaks on each side for 2 minutes for rare, 3 minutes for medium-rare, or 4 minutes for well-done. Let rest for 5 minutes before serving.

Mocha Coffee Steak

Yield: 4 servings   Prep Time: 5 minutes   Cook Time: 5 to 10 minutes

2 tablespoons extra-virgin olive oil

4 (4- to 6-ounce) boneless sirloin or rib-eye steaks, about 1 inch thick

1 teaspoon coarse sea salt

1 teaspoon cocoa powder

1 teaspoon instant coffee powder

½ teaspoon ground black pepper

1. Heat the olive oil in a large cast-iron or other ovenproof skillet over medium-high heat. Mix the salt and spices together in a small bowl and sprinkle over both sides of the steaks.

2. Sear the steaks on each side for 2 minutes for rare, 3 minutes for medium-rare, or 4 minutes for well-done. Let rest for 5 minutes before serving.

Easy Tuna Steak

Yield: 4 servings   Prep Time: 5 minutes   Cook Time: 5 minutes

2 tablespoons extra-virgin olive oil

4 (6- to 8-ounce) tuna steaks, about 1 inch thick

1 teaspoon coarse sea salt

½ teaspoon ground black pepper

1. Heat the olive oil in a large skillet over medium-high heat. Sprinkle both sides of the tuna with the salt and pepper. Once the oil has thinned from the heat, sear the tuna for 2 minutes per side, or until a light brown crust develops on the outside and the inside is still pink. (This cook time results in medium-done tuna; if you like your tuna slightly more or less well-done, adjust the time accordingly.)

2. Let the tuna rest for 5 to 10 minutes before serving. Enjoy warm or chilled and sliced over a salad.

Pan-Seared White Fish

Yield: 4 servings   Prep Time: 5 minutes   Cook Time: 5 minutes

2 tablespoons extra-virgin olive oil

4 (6-ounce) white fish fillets (such as snapper)

1 teaspoon coarse sea salt

½ teaspoon ground black pepper

Juice of 1 lemon

1. Heat the olive oil in a large skillet over medium-high heat. Sprinkle both sides of the fish with the salt and pepper. Once the oil has thinned from the heat, sear the fish for 2 minutes per side, or until a light brown crust develops.

2. Sprinkle the cooked fish with the lemon juice. Let rest for 5 minutes before serving.

Lemon-Garlic Shrimp

Yield: 4 servings   Prep Time: 5 minutes   Cook Time: 8 minutes

1 tablespoon extra-virgin olive oil

1½ pounds large shrimp, peeled and deveined

½ teaspoon garlic powder

½ teaspoon coarse sea salt

Juice of 1 lemon

1. Heat the oil in a large skillet over high heat. Sprinkle the shrimp with the garlic powder and salt. Add the shrimp to the skillet and reduce the heat to medium. Cook for 3 minutes per side, or until pink.

2. Once cooked, add the lemon juice and stir to combine. Serve immediately.

Salmon Bake

Yield: 4 servings   Prep Time: 5 minutes   Cook Time: 15 minutes

1 (1½-pound) salmon fillet

¼ cup ranch dressing, store-bought or homemade (page 372)

1. Preheat the oven to 350°F. Line a rimmed baking sheet with parchment paper.

2. Place the fillet on the lined baking sheet, then spread the ranch dressing on top of the fish.

3. Bake for 15 minutes, or until flaky in the thickest portion of the fillet. Let rest for 5 minutes before serving.

Pan-Seared Salmon

Yield: 4 servings   **Prep Time:** 5 minutes   **Cook Time:** 6 minutes

1 tablespoon extra-virgin olive oil

4 (6-ounce) salmon fillets

1 teaspoon coarse sea salt

½ teaspoon ground black pepper

1. Heat the olive oil in a large skillet over medium heat. Sprinkle the salmon fillets with the salt and pepper.

2. Sear the salmon on each side for 3 minutes, or until the fish flakes at the thickest part. Let rest for 5 minutes before serving.

VEGGIES

Crispy Brussels Sprouts

Yield: 4 servings   Prep Time: 15 minutes   Cook Time: 45 minutes

12 ounces Brussels sprouts, trimmed and cut in half

Juice of 1 lemon

1 tablespoon extra-virgin olive oil

½ teaspoon coarse sea salt

¼ teaspoon ground black pepper

1. Preheat the oven to 375°F. Line a rimmed baking sheet with parchment paper.

2. In a medium-sized bowl, toss the Brussels sprouts in the lemon juice, olive oil, salt, and pepper. Spread them evenly on the lined baking sheet.

3. Bake for 45 minutes, or until the tops are crispy.

Sautéed Squash

Yield: 4 servings   Prep Time: 10 minutes   Cook Time: 5 minutes

2 teaspoons extra-virgin olive oil

4 zucchini or yellow squash, cut crosswise into ½-inch discs

½ teaspoon coarse sea salt

¼ teaspoon ground black pepper

1. Place a medium-sized skillet over medium heat. Add the olive oil, then the zucchini. Sprinkle with the salt and pepper.

2. Sauté for about 5 minutes, until the squash is wilted.

Simple Roasted Cauliflower

Yield: 4 servings   Prep Time: 10 minutes   Cook Time: 40 minutes

1 large head cauliflower (2½ to 3 pounds)

1 tablespoon extra-virgin olive oil

½ teaspoon garlic powder

½ teaspoon coarse sea salt

1. Preheat the oven to 375°F. Line a rimmed baking sheet with parchment paper.

2. Cut the florets from the head of cauliflower and separate or cut into bite-sized pieces. In a large bowl, toss the cauliflower in the olive oil, garlic powder, and salt. Spread evenly on the lined baking sheet.

3. Bake for 40 minutes, or until the tops are golden brown.

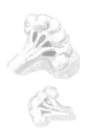

Roasted Broccoli

Yield: 4 servings   Prep Time: 10 minutes   Cook Time: 25 minutes

2 medium to large heads broccoli

1 tablespoon extra-virgin olive oil

½ teaspoon garlic powder

½ teaspoon coarse sea salt

1. Preheat the oven to 400°F. Line a rimmed baking sheet with parchment paper.

2. Cut the broccoli florets from the heads. Peel and slice the long stems and add to the florets.

3. In a large bowl, toss the broccoli in the olive oil, garlic powder, and salt. Spread evenly on the lined baking sheet.

4. Bake for 15 minutes, flip the broccoli over, and bake for an additional 10 minutes, or until the tops are browned.

Braised Collards

Yield: 4 servings   Prep Time: 10 minutes   Cook Time: 10 minutes

1 tablespoon extra-virgin olive oil

1 small bunch collard greens (about 1 pound), destemmed and coarsely chopped

Juice of ½ lemon

½ teaspoon coarse sea salt

1. In a large skillet that has a lid, heat the olive oil over medium heat. Add the collard greens, toss to coat in the oil, and cover to steam until tender, about 10 minutes.

2. Once the greens are wilted, add the lemon juice and salt and stir to combine.

Wilted Spinach

Yield: 4 servings   Prep Time: 10 minutes   Cook Time: 5 minutes

1 tablespoon extra-virgin olive oil

1 pound spinach

Juice of ½ lemon

½ teaspoon coarse sea salt

1. In a large skillet that has a lid, heat the olive oil over medium heat. Add the spinach, toss to coat in the oil, and cover to steam until wilted, about 5 minutes.

2. Once the spinach is wilted, add the lemon juice and salt and stir to combine.

Baked Okra

Yield: 4 servings   Prep Time: 10 minutes   Cook Time: 40 minutes

1 pound okra, cut crosswise into ½-inch-thick discs

2 teaspoons extra-virgin olive oil

1 teaspoon coarse sea salt

¼ teaspoon ground black pepper

1. Preheat the oven to 375°F. Line a rimmed baking sheet with parchment paper.

2. In a medium-sized bowl, toss the okra in the olive oil, salt, and pepper. Spread evenly on the lined baking sheet.

3. Bake for 40 minutes, or until the okra just begins to darken in color.

Lemony Kale

Yield: 4 servings   Prep Time: 10 minutes   Cook Time: 10 minutes

1 tablespoon extra-virgin olive oil

1 small bunch kale (about 1 pound), destemmed and coarsely chopped

Juice of ½ lemon

½ teaspoon coarse sea salt

1. In a large skillet that has a lid, heat the olive oil over medium heat. Add the kale, toss to coat in the oil, and cover to steam until soft and wilted, about 10 minutes.

2. Add the lemon juice and salt and stir to combine.

Roasted Asparagus

Yield: 4 servings   Prep Time: 10 minutes   Cook Time: 40 minutes

1 pound asparagus, tough bottoms removed

2 teaspoons extra-virgin olive oil

1 teaspoon coarse sea salt

¼ teaspoon ground black pepper

1. Preheat the oven to 375°F. Line a rimmed baking sheet with parchment paper.

2. In a medium-sized bowl, toss the asparagus in the olive oil, salt, and pepper. Spread evenly on the lined baking sheet.

3. Bake for 40 minutes, or until the asparagus just begins to darken in color.

Roasted Cherry Tomatoes

Yield: 4 servings   Prep Time: 5 minutes   Cook Time: 40 minutes

2 pints cherry tomatoes

2 teaspoons extra-virgin olive oil

1 teaspoon coarse sea salt

¼ teaspoon ground black pepper

1. Preheat the oven to 375°F. Line a rimmed baking sheet with parchment paper.

2. In a medium-sized bowl, toss the tomatoes in the olive oil, salt, and pepper. Spread evenly on the lined baking sheet.

3. Bake for 40 minutes, or until the tomatoes just begin to burst and darken in color.

Steamed Green Beans

Yield: 4 servings   Prep Time: 5 minutes   Cook Time: 12 minutes

1 pound green beans, trimmed

2 teaspoons extra-virgin olive oil

½ teaspoon coarse sea salt

¼ teaspoon ground black pepper

1. Place the green beans and about ½ cup of water in a medium-sized saucepan over medium heat. Cover and bring to a simmer. Continue to simmer for about 10 minutes, until the beans are bright green.

2. Drain the water, then toss the green beans with the olive oil, salt, and pepper.

Sautéed Bell Peppers

Yield: 4 servings   Prep Time: 10 minutes   Cook Time: 15 minutes

2 teaspoons extra-virgin olive oil

1 pound red bell peppers, seeded and sliced into strips

1 teaspoon coarse sea salt

¼ teaspoon ground black pepper

1. Place a large skillet over medium heat. Add the olive oil, then the bell pepper strips. Sprinkle with the salt and pepper.

2. Sauté for 10 to 15 minutes, until the peppers soften enough to be easily pierced with a fork.

Italian Side Salad

Yield: 4 servings   Prep Time: 10 minutes

6 cups chopped mixed lettuce, such as romaine or iceberg, and/or purple cabbage (about 8 ounces)

1 (6-ounce) jar marinated and quartered artichoke hearts, drained

2 ounces assorted pitted olives (about ½ cup)

2 tablespoons red wine vinegar

2 tablespoons extra-virgin olive oil

1 teaspoon fine sea salt

1 teaspoon ground black pepper

1. Place the lettuce in a large bowl and sprinkle the artichoke hearts and olives over the top.

2. In a small bowl, whisk together the vinegar, olive oil, salt, and pepper. Pour the dressing over the salad and enjoy!

note: *You can also add halved cherry tomatoes or roasted red bell peppers.*

Spinach Salad

Yield: 4 servings   Prep Time: 5 minutes

6 cups spinach (about 8 ounces)

½ pint fresh strawberries, quartered

½ cup raw pecans, coarsely chopped

2 tablespoons balsamic vinegar

2 tablespoons extra-virgin olive oil

1 teaspoon fine sea salt

1 teaspoon ground black pepper

1. Place the spinach in a large bowl and sprinkle the strawberries and pecans over the top.

2. In a small bowl, whisk together the vinegar, olive oil, and salt. Pour the dressing over the salad, sprinkle with the pepper, and enjoy.

Basic Cauliflower Rice

Yield: 4 servings   Prep Time: 5 minutes   Cook Time: 10 to 15 minutes, depending on method

1 large head cauliflower (about 3 pounds), or 18 ounces frozen riced cauliflower

1 tablespoon extra-virgin olive oil

½ teaspoon coarse sea salt

1. If using frozen riced cauliflower, skip ahead to Step 2. To "rice" cauliflower, cut the florets from the stem. Either grate it by hand using the largest holes on a box grater or affix the grating attachment to a food processor and pulse until a ricelike texture is achieved. One large head of cauliflower should give you about 4 cups of "rice."

2. Steam the cauliflower rice using one of these two methods:

- **Microwave Method** (Cook Time: 10 minutes)
  Place the riced cauliflower in a microwave-safe bowl with ¼ cup of water. Cover and microwave on high for 10 minutes, or until the cauliflower rice is tender. Let cool slightly, then drain. Add the olive oil and salt and toss to combine.

- **Stovetop Method** (Cook Time: 15 minutes)
  In a large skillet or sauté pan with a tight-fitting lid, heat the olive oil over medium heat, then add the riced cauliflower and salt. Stir to coat the rice in the oil, then cover, reduce the heat to medium-low, and steam for 12 to 15 minutes, until the cauliflower rice is tender.

STARCHES

Baked Acorn Squash

Yield: 4 servings   Prep Time: 10 minutes   Cook Time: 40 minutes

1 acorn squash, cut into quarters and seeded

2 teaspoons extra-virgin olive oil

½ teaspoon coarse sea salt

¼ teaspoon ground black pepper

1. Preheat the oven to 375°F.

2. Rub the cut sides of the squash with the olive oil and sprinkle with the salt and pepper. Place the squash wedges cut side up in a baking dish.

3. Bake for 40 minutes, or until fork-tender.

Roasted Carrots

Yield: 4 servings   Prep Time: 10 minutes   Cook Time: 45 minutes

2 bunches slender carrots (about 1 pound), peeled

1 tablespoon fresh lemon juice

2 teaspoons extra-virgin olive oil

½ teaspoon coarse sea salt

¼ teaspoon ground black pepper

1. Preheat the oven to 375°F. Line a rimmed baking sheet with parchment paper.

2. In a large bowl, toss the carrots in the lemon juice, olive oil, salt, and pepper. Spread in an even layer on the lined baking sheet.

3. Bake for 45 minutes, or until the tops start to brown.

Perfect Parsnips

Yield: 4 servings   Prep Time: 10 minutes   Cook Time: 35 minutes

2 pounds parsnips, peeled and cut crosswise into ½-inch discs

1 tablespoon extra-virgin olive oil

½ teaspoon coarse sea salt

¼ teaspoon ground black pepper

1. Preheat the oven to 375°F. Line a rimmed baking sheet with parchment paper.

2. In a large bowl, toss the parsnips in the olive oil, salt, and pepper. Spread in an even layer on the lined baking sheet.

3. Bake for 35 minutes, or until the tops start to brown.

Baked Sweet Potatoes

Yield: 4 servings   Prep Time: 5 minutes   Cook Time: 40 minutes

4 small to medium sweet potatoes (about 1 pound)

1. Preheat the oven to 425°F.

2. Wash each potato and poke with a fork four or five times. Place the potatoes in the oven and bake until soft to the touch, about 40 minutes.

Baked Russet Potatoes

Yield: 4 servings   Prep Time: 5 minutes   Cook Time: 40 minutes

4 small to medium russet potatoes (about 1 pound)

1. Preheat the oven to 425°F.

2. Wash each potato and poke with a fork four or five times. Place the potatoes in the oven and bake until soft to the touch, about 40 minutes.

Roasted Butternut Squash Cubes

Yield: 4 servings   Prep Time: 15 minutes   Cook Time: 40 minutes

1 medium butternut squash (about 2 pounds)

1 tablespoon extra-virgin olive oil

1 teaspoon coarse sea salt

¼ teaspoon ground black pepper

1. Preheat the oven to 375°F. Line a rimmed baking sheet with parchment paper.

2. Peel the squash, cut it in half lengthwise, and remove the seeds, then cut the squash into ½-inch cubes.

3. In a medium-sized bowl, toss the squash cubes in the olive oil, salt, and pepper. Spread evenly on the lined baking sheet.

4. Bake for 40 minutes, or until the tops start to brown.

Easy Baked Beets

Yield: 4 servings   Prep Time: 5 minutes   Cook Time: 1 hour

3 or 4 large beets, trimmed

2 teaspoons extra-virgin olive oil

1 teaspoon dried thyme leaves

½ teaspoon coarse sea salt

1. Preheat the oven to 400°F.

2. Wrap each beet in aluminum foil. Bake for 45 minutes to 1 hour, until the beets give when squeezed.

3. Let the beets cool to room temperature, then rub the skins off. Cut the beets into wedges, place in a bowl, and toss with the olive oil, thyme, and salt. Serve at room temperature or chilled.

Green Peas

Yield: 4 servings   Prep Time: 10 minutes   Cook Time: 5 minutes

1 tablespoon extra-virgin olive oil

1 (10-ounce) package frozen green peas

2 tablespoons fresh lemon juice (about 1 small lemon)

1 teaspoon dried dill weed

½ teaspoon coarse sea salt

1. Heat the olive oil in a medium-sized saucepan over medium heat. Add the peas and stir to coat. Cover and steam for 5 minutes.

2. Add the lemon juice, dill, and salt and stir to combine.

Pan-Fried Plantains

Yield: 4 servings   Prep Time: 10 minutes   Cook Time: 10 minutes

2 tablespoons extra-virgin olive oil

2 large yellow plantains (about 1 pound), peeled and cut crosswise into ½-inch-thick discs

½ teaspoon coarse sea salt

1. Heat the olive oil in a medium-sized skillet over medium heat. Add the plantains one layer at a time. Fry for 3 to 4 minutes, until golden brown on one side. Flip over and repeat on the other side.

2. Transfer the plantains to a plate lined with paper towels and sprinkle with the salt.

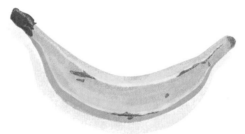

Basic White Rice

Yield: 4 servings   Prep Time: 2 minutes   Cook Time: 25 minutes

2 cups water

1 tablespoon extra-virgin olive oil

1 teaspoon coarse sea salt

1 cup white rice

1. Bring the water, olive oil, and salt to a boil in a medium-sized saucepan, covered, over medium heat. Once boiling, add the rice and stir.

2. Reduce the heat to low and simmer, covered, for 20 minutes, until all of the water is absorbed.

3. Remove from the heat, fluff with a fork, and serve.

pro tip: *Use basmati rice for the most aromatic and best-tasting rice.*

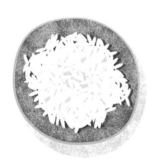

Basic Quinoa

Yield: 4 servings   Prep Time: 2 minutes   Cook Time: 25 minutes

1 cup quinoa

2 cups water

1 tablespoon extra-virgin olive oil

1 teaspoon coarse sea salt

1. Bring the quinoa, water, olive oil, and salt to a boil in a medium-sized saucepan over medium heat. Once boiling, stir and cover.

2. Reduce the heat to low and simmer, covered, for 15 to 20 minutes, until all of the water is absorbed.

3. Remove from the heat, fluff with a fork, and serve.

Basic Polenta

Yield: 4 servings   Prep Time: 2 minutes   Cook Time: 30 minutes

2½ cups chicken broth

½ to 1 teaspoon coarse sea salt, divided

¾ cup polenta meal or corn grits

2 tablespoons extra-virgin olive oil

¼ teaspoon ground black pepper

1. In a large saucepan, bring the broth and ½ teaspoon of salt to a boil over high heat.

2. Reduce the heat to low, then whisk in the polenta meal and bring back up to a boil.

3. Cover and cook for 10 minutes, then whisk the polenta again, making sure to scrape everything up from the bottom of the pan. Place the lid back on the pan and cook for 15 more minutes.

4. Stir in the oil and pepper, then taste for seasoning and add up to ½ teaspoon more salt, if desired.

SAUCES AND SPICE BLENDS

Avocado Oil Mayonnaise

Yield: 2 cups (2 tablespoons per serving)   Prep Time: 5 minutes

1 large egg, room temperature

2 tablespoons fresh lemon juice (about 1 small lemon)

½ teaspoon coarse sea salt

1½ cups avocado oil

1. Place the egg, lemon juice, and salt in a food processor or blender. Blend for about 30 seconds, until smooth and frothy.

2. With the machine running, drizzle in the avocado oil as slowly as possible. It should take at least 2 minutes to add all of the oil. After adding the oil, stop the machine to check that the mayo has emulsified. It should be thick enough to form a peak on your finger. If it isn't, with the machine running, slowly drizzle in more oil, 1 tablespoon at a time, until you reach a desired consistency.

3. Use right away or transfer to a jar for storage. It will keep in the refrigerator for up to 2 weeks.

3-Ingredient Ranch Dressing

Yield: 2 cups (1 tablespoon per serving)   Prep Time: 5 minutes

If you own a copy of my first book, Fed + Fit, *this recipe will look familiar to you! I'm including it here, too, because it's just that great of a kitchen staple. And if you don't own a copy of* Fed + Fit, *I don't want you to miss out!*

¼ cup fresh lemon juice (about 2 small lemons)

1 tablespoon dried dill weed

2 cups avocado-oil mayonnaise, store-bought or homemade (above)

1. Whisk the lemon juice and dill into the mayo until well combined.

2. Enjoy right away or transfer to a jar for storage. If using homemade mayonnaise, it will keep in the refrigerator for up to 2 weeks; if using store-bought mayonnaise, it will keep for about 1 month.

BBQ Sauce

Yield: 1½ cups (2 tablespoons per serving)   Prep Time: 10 minutes

1 (6-ounce) can tomato paste
¼ cup apple cider vinegar
¼ cup molasses
¼ cup water
1 teaspoon chili powder
½ teaspoon coarse sea salt
¼ teaspoon ground black pepper

1. Place all of the ingredients in a medium-sized saucepan and whisk until smooth. Bring to a simmer over medium heat, then continue to simmer for 5 minutes, whisking often, until the sauce has darkened slightly in color.

2. Remove from the heat and let cool for at least 5 minutes.

3. Use right away or transfer to a jar for storage. It will keep in the refrigerator for up to 2 weeks.

Teriyaki Sauce

Yield: ¼ cup (1 tablespoon per serving)   Prep Time: 5 minutes   Cook Time: 15 minutes

1 (8-ounce) bottle coconut aminos
1 tablespoon unseasoned rice wine vinegar
2 teaspoons toasted sesame oil
½ teaspoon garlic powder
½ teaspoon ginger powder
¼ teaspoon fish sauce

1. Place the coconut aminos in a large skillet over medium heat. Simmer for 10 to 15 minutes, until it thickens enough to coat the back of a spoon. Scrape the thickened aminos into a bowl and stir in the vinegar, sesame oil, garlic powder, ginger powder, and fish sauce.

2. Store in the refrigerator for up to 2 weeks. The sauce will thicken in the fridge but will thin out again when reheated.

Low-Carb Teriyaki Sauce

Yield: ¼ cup (1 tablespoon per serving)   Prep Time: 5 minutes   Cook Time: 3 minutes

2 tablespoons chicken broth
1 tablespoon tamari
1 tablespoon coconut aminos
½ teaspoon apple cider vinegar
¼ teaspoon toasted sesame oil
¼ teaspoon fish sauce
⅛ teaspoon garlic powder
⅛ teaspoon ginger powder

1. Place all of the ingredients in a small pot over medium heat. Bring to a simmer, whisk, and take off heat.

2. Store in the refrigerator for up to 2 weeks.

note: *This lower-carb teriyaki sauce tastes like the real thing, but it will not be as sticky or thick. I suggest you use Coconut Secret brand coconut aminos for both teriyaki sauce recipes. In my extensive recipe testing, this brand yielded the most reliable teriyaki sauce.*

BBQ Spice Rub

Yield: about ½ cup   Prep Time: 5 minutes

¼ cup paprika

2 tablespoons coconut sugar

1 tablespoon plus 1 teaspoon coarse sea salt

2 teaspoons ancho chili powder

2 teaspoons dried oregano leaves

2 teaspoons cracked black pepper

1. Place all of the ingredients in a bowl and whisk until fully combined.

2. Store in an airtight container in the pantry for later use. Spice blend will be good for up to 4 months if stored in a cool, dark space.

Texas Chili Spice Blend

Yield: about ¾ cup   Prep Time: 5 minutes

½ cup chili powder

¼ cup ground cumin

2 teaspoons coarse sea salt

1 teaspoon ground black pepper

1. Place all of the ingredients in a bowl and whisk until fully combined.

2. Store in an airtight container in the pantry for later use. Spice blend will be good for up to 4 months if stored in a cool, dark space.

Texas Grill Rub

Yield: about ¾ cup   Prep Time: 5 minutes

1½ tablespoons dried minced garlic

1½ tablespoons dried minced onions

1 tablespoon coarse sea salt

1 tablespoon cracked black pepper

2½ teaspoons mustard seeds

2½ teaspoons dill seeds

1½ teaspoons coriander seeds

1½ teaspoons red pepper flakes

1. Place all of the ingredients in a bowl and whisk until fully combined.

2. Store in an airtight container in the pantry for later use. Spice blend will be good for up to 4 months if stored in a cool, dark space.

Jerk Seasoning

Yield: about ½ cup   Prep Time: 5 minutes

2 tablespoons coarse sea salt

2 tablespoons coconut sugar

1 tablespoon plus 1 teaspoon ground allspice

1 tablespoon plus 1 teaspoon dried thyme leaves

1 tablespoon plus 1 teaspoon ginger powder

2 teaspoons garlic powder

2 teaspoons ground black pepper

1 teaspoon ground cinnamon

½ to 1 teaspoon cayenne pepper, to taste

½ teaspoon ground cloves

½ teaspoon ground nutmeg

1. Place all of the ingredients in a bowl and whisk until fully combined.

2. Store in an airtight container in the pantry for later use. Spice blend will be good for up to 4 months if stored in a cool, dark space.

Tex-Mex Seasoning

Yield: about ½ cup   Prep Time: 5 minutes

2 tablespoons ancho chili powder

2 tablespoons dried oregano leaves

2 tablespoons ground cumin

2 teaspoons garlic powder

2 teaspoons onion powder

2 teaspoons coarse sea salt

1 teaspoon ground black pepper

1. Place all of the ingredients in a bowl and whisk until fully combined.

2. Store in an airtight container in the pantry for later use. Spice blend will be good for up to 4 months if stored in a cool, dark space.

ACKNOWLEDGMENTS

Fed + Fit Readers

Do your ears burn from time to time? They should. I talk about you A LOT. Whenever the topic turns to business, I can't help but sing your praises. The first words that rattle out of my mouth are, "Our readers are THE MOST amazing humans." You really are! You're friendly, positive, uplifting, encouraging, and just dang nice. You're curious about nutrition, you love spending quality time with family/friends, you are open to new avenues of personal growth, and you also like to eat. We're birds of a feather, and it is an absolute pleasure writing for and working with you.

The Cook Once, Eat All Week concept, which got a trial run in January 2018 as a mini blog series, was born from our desire to solve the meal prep riddle. Because YOU liked it so much, we buckled down and solved the riddle further. It's because you found this meal prep concept helpful, because it gave you time back in your week, and because it helped you save money that we expanded the concept into a book. We created it for you, as a love letter of sorts, as a way to say "thank you," and as a way to continue to serve you well.

Thank you for your support. Thank you for comprising the most incredible community of human beings. Thank you for your kind words, for trusting us with your grocery budget, for trusting us with dinner, and for sharing your wishes with us. We hold them very sacred and will always keep our heads down on how we can continue to support, wow, and empower you.

Amber Goulden

Amber Goulden and I met in late 2016. She applied for a position I'd sneaked into the bottom of a *Fed + Fit* newsletter, and even during the interview process, I could tell there was something really special about her. Over the years of working together, I've been constantly impressed by Amber's intelligence, curiosity, dedication to continued education, good humor, wit, grace, and balanced perspective. She's become an invaluable member of the Fed + Fit team. I now see her as more of a partner than a contributor, and I feel so lucky that she chose us. She takes great pride and ownership in the quality of content we publish (like her tireless efforts to perfect gluten-free baked goods for the website), the resources we develop (those fabulous free mini e-courses? Those are all Amber), and the impact we're leaving on the world (positivity, self-care, and true self-acceptance).

Without Amber's continued support and dedication to this project (born from a dedication to our readers), this book never would have made it to print. All of the credit for *Cook Once, Eat All Week* goes to Amber.

She truly embodies our shared vision for the future of this business we'll continue to grow together. I look forward to many more years of working with this amazing human.

My Amazing, Amazing Family and Friends

Some of us are related by blood, some by marriage, and some simply by friendship. You know who you are, and you know that your unwavering encouragement, support, and perspective mean the world to me. Thank you for supporting our family, our dreams, and our hearts for blazing new trails.

Recipe Testers

Thank you to each and every *Cook Once, Eat All Week* recipe tester! Your notes, feedback, and excitement for this project were vital in helping to form it into its now polished, final form. I'll be forever grateful for your eager and enthusiastic collaborative support!

Jaime Andreason	Teresa Hansen	Veronica Smith
Ashley Bailey	Lindsey Harris	Amy Spzindor
Whitney Bassett	Angelica Hiney	Taylor Thompson
Jenna Bell	Misty Hinkle	Virginia Thornton
Rhonda Bonnabeau	Justine Jahn	Samantha Thorson
Erika Brown	Khrystyne Jamerson	Pamela Tognoli
Kelsey Burns	Susan Jessup	Amanda Treiber
Mandy Carter	Nicole Johnston	Nicole Valenzuela
Chelsea Churchill	Ruby Kline	Taylor Walker
Theresia Cooper	Lauren Mastracco	Cindi Wall
Heather Crawley	Jennifer McCormack	Michelle Warth
Theresa Diulus	Janna Medina	Allison Weibel
Lauren Ferriter	Sherry Patterson	Andrea Westfall
Belinda Galvanin	Brooke Perlman	Laiken Williams
Jan Garner	Katherine Schneider	Chelsea Wuth
Maddie Gillette	Tiffany Schneider	

RECOMMENDED SOURCES

Tools

Appliances

BLENDER—your blender is not a tool on which to skimp. Look for a high-powered blender. Vitamix is my personal favorite.

FOOD PROCESSOR—any brand with a 10-cup (or larger) container! Cuisinart is a quality, affordable brand.

IMMERSION BLENDER—I suggest looking for an immersion blender with a blade that detaches from the electronic mechanism. This makes for much easier cleaning. Cuisinart is a great option.

INSTANT POT—if you're limited on space, this is the most multi-use appliance out there. It will sear, slow cook, pressure cook, and much more. I use mine weekly.

SLOW COOKER—look for a slow cooker that allows you to place the insert directly on the stovetop. This makes searing ingredients much easier as you only need to dirty one pan. All-Clad is my favorite brand.

STAND MIXER—you'll use your stand mixer for more than baking, I promise. It's the easiest and fastest way to shred protein! KitchenAid is my preferred brand.

Cookware

CAST-IRON SKILLET—these pans are affordable and durable. Lodge is my preferred brand.

CERAMIC SKILLETS—these pans are ideal for anything that may stick (think: eggs), and are a nice option if you prefer to avoid Teflon-coated pans. GreenLife Ceramic is my favorite.

STAINLESS-STEEL SKILLETS—these pans are timeless and versatile. I use them for making sauces, sautéing, searing, and baking. All-Clad is my preferred brand.

Ingredients

AVOCADO OIL
Primal Kitchen Foods

Sir Kensington's

BBQ SAUCE
Primal Kitchen Foods

BROTH, CHICKEN AND BEEF
Pacific Foods

Bonafide Provisions

Osso Good Co.

BUTTER
Kerrygold—*Butter made from grass-fed cow's milk contains more micronutrients!*

COCONUT AMINOS
Coconut Secret

COCONUT MILK
Native Forest

COCONUT OIL
365 Everyday Organic Brand

COCONUT SUGAR
Navitas Natural

DAIRY-FREE CREAM CHEESE–STYLE SPREAD
Kite Hill

FISH SAUCE
Red Boat Fish Sauce

GELATIN
Primal Kitchen Foods

Vital Proteins

GHEE
Fourth and Heart—*Ghee made from grass-fed cow's milk contains more micronutrients! This brand is my favorite for its nutritional value, flavor, and consistent cooking results.*

GREEK-STYLE YOGURT
Maple Hill Creamery

Stonyfield

HONEY
Beeotic

HOT SAUCE
Frank's RedHot

MAPLE SYRUP
365 Everyday Value (Whole Foods)

MAYONNAISE
Primal Kitchen Foods

Sir Kensington's

OLIVE OIL
Kasandrinos—*True and pure olive oil is unparalleled in flavor and nutritional value. Unfortunately, it's hard to come by. Kasandrinos is my personal favorite and is easy to order online.*

RANCH DRESSING
Primal Kitchen Foods

Sir Kensington's

RICE WINE VINEGAR
Trader Joe's

SPICE BLENDS
Balanced Bites

Primal Palate

TOASTED SESAME OIL
La Tourangelle

TOMATO SAUCE
Thrive Market Organic Tomato Basil

TORTILLAS
Siete Grain-Free Tortillas

VEGAN MAYO
Sir Kensington's

VEGAN RANCH DRESSING
Primal Kitchen Foods

Nutritional Information

	RECIPE	Page	Servings	Calories	Fat	Saturated Fat	Total Carbo-hydrate	Dietary Fiber	Total Sugars	Protein
WEEK 01	BBQ Chicken and Rice Casserole (white rice)	34	6	544	14 g	4 g	60.8 g	4.8 g	13.1 g	42.8 g
	BBQ Chicken and Rice Casserole (cauli rice)	34	6	379	10.5 g	4 g	33.7 g	8.2 g	20.2 g	40.5 g
	BBQ Chicken and Rice Casserole (cauli rice and low-carb BBQ sauce)	34	6	374	17.3 g	5.9 g	22.5 g	8.1 g	9.4 g	40.4 g
	White Chicken Chili	36	4	589	26.5 g	8 g	33.2 g	6.2 g	5.3 g	55.2 g
	White Chicken Chili (low-carb/Paleo)	36	4	482	25.5 g	8 g	12.7 g	1.5 g	3.3 g	40.5 g
	Chicken and Broccoli Fried Rice (white rice)	38	4	651	19.7 g	3.5 g	71.8 g	2.5 g	6.6 g	42.7 g
	Chicken and Broccoli Fried Rice (cauli rice)	38	4	403	19.5 g	3.5 g	16.5 g	4.9 g	8.8 g	39.9 g
WEEK 02	Spinach Artichoke Meatza	46	4	439	18.4 g	7.1 g	31 g	16.3 g	5.1 g	46.7 g
	Enchilada-Stuffed Zucchini Boats	48	4	267	10.7 g	4.1 g	11.1 g	4.2 g	5.2 g	32.6 g
	Ground Beef Stroganoff	50	4	438	21.1 g	9.3 g	11.6 g	1.6 g	4.3 g	49.7 g
WEEK 03	Loaded Cauliflower Casserole	58	6	512	32.7 g	13.4 g	14.4 g	4.6 g	5 g	40.5 g
	Balsamic Chicken Sheet Pan Dinner	60	4	503	41.2 g	8.1 g	5.7 g	1.5 g	3.9 g	25.6 g
	Buffalo Chicken–Stuffed Avocados	62	4	507	34.4 g	5 g	11.9 g	9.3 g	0.5 g	40.9 g
WEEK 04	Bacon Burgers with Broccoli and Twice-Baked Fries	70	4	606	34.6 g	12.3 g	29.6 g	6.7 g	4.6 g	45.9 g
	Picadillo Tacos	72	4	654	19.3 g	8.3 g	52.4 g	8 g	4.9 g	38.3 g
	Cottage Pie	74	6	487	14.3 g	8.3 g	46.9 g	9.1 g	6.6 g	36.9 g
WEEK 05	Green Chili Chicken Casserole (white rice)	82	6	461	15.9 g	7.8 g	38.7 g	0.9 g	1.8 g	39.4 g
	Green Chili Chicken Casserole (cauli rice)	82	6	287	12.2 g	5.7 g	10.5 g	2.4 g	2.8 g	33.5 g
	Chicken Parmesan Bake (GF noodles)	84	5	479	12.3 g	3.8 g	46 g	2.8 g	4.8 g	46.2 g
	Chicken Parmesan Bake (zucchini noodles)	84	5	293	11.6 g	3.7 g	8.3 g	1.4 g	3.4 g	40 g
	Cajun Chicken and Rice Skillet (white rice)	86	4	454	19.5 g	8.3 g	32.8 g	1.6 g	2.7 g	35.6 g
	Cajun Chicken and Rice Skillet (cauli rice)	86	4	361	19.6 g	8.4 g	10.6 g	3.8 g	4.9 g	35.6 g
WEEK 06	Curried Chicken Lettuce Cups	94	4	461	15.9 g	7.8 g	38.7 g	0.9 g	1.8 g	39.4 g
	Firecracker Meatballs (white rice)	96	4	584	19.8 g	7.4 g	64.4 g	0.6 g	22 g	37 g
	Firecracker Meatballs (cauli rice)	96	4	421	19.7 g	7.4 g	27.5 g	2.1 g	23.5 g	35.2 g
	Chicken Burrito Bowls (white rice)	98	5	549	24.1 g	5.3 g	42.7 g	5.0 g	3.6 g	40.7 g
	Chicken Burrito Bowls (cauli rice)	98	5	404	23.9 g	5.3 g	10.8 g	5 g	3.6 g	38 g
WEEK 07	Roasted Tomato Soup and Grilled Turkey and Cheese Sandwiches	106	4	634	41.9 g	19.9 g	30.8 g	3.7 g	8.5 g	37.6 g
	Buffalo Turkey Casserole	108	6	462	27.5 g	10.1 g	24.1 g	3.6 g	2 g	31 g
	Turkey Pizza Sheet Pan Dinner	110	4	443	25 g	8.2 g	22.4 g	3.7 g	3.8 g	33.3 g
WEEK 08	BBQ Mini Meatloaves with Carrot Fries	118	4	561	32.3 g	10.9 g	17.5 g	3.5 g	9.1 g	47.2 g
	Taco Casserole (white rice)	120	6	452	9 g	2.7 g	52.6 g	5 g	4.1 g	35.1 g
	Taco Casserole (cauli rice)	120	6	290	9 g	2.7 g	20.2 g	5.5 g	5.2 g	33.3 g
	Korean Beef Bowls (white rice)	122	5	675	29.2 g	6.5 g	64.9 g	1.3 g	4 g	43.3 g
	Korean Beef Bowls (cauli rice)	122	5	480	29.1 g	6.5 g	20.7 g	3.1 g	5.8 g	41.2 g

	RECIPE	Page	Servings	Calories	Fat	Saturated Fat	Total Carbo-hydrate	Dietary Fiber	Total Sugars	Protein
WEEK 09	Confetti Chicken Casserole	130	6	523	35.3 g	8.5 g	15.5 g	2.5 g	6.3 g	38 g
	Mexican Chicken and Corn Street Tacos	132	4	516	25.8 g	7.6 g	36 g	4 g	3.7 g	38.4 g
	Green Goddess Salad	134	4	553	40 g	8.4 g	13.1 g	3.7 g	3.2 g	38.8 g
WEEK 10	Philly Cheesesteak Loaded Fries	142	5	569	25.2 g	9.6 g	38.6 g	3.7 g	3.4 g	46.8 g
	Pepper Steak Stir-Fry (white rice)	144	5	547	16.6 g	4.5 g	59.4 g	1.6 g	8.3 g	36.2 g
	Pepper Steak Stir-Fry (cauli rice)	144	5	352	16.6 g	4.5 g	15.2 g	3.4 g	10.1 g	34.1 g
	Gyro Salad with Garlic Potato Wedges	146	4	661	38.7 g	9.6 g	32.6 g	7.4 g	9.1 g	48.6 g
WEEK 11	Chicken Bacon Ranch Casserole	154	6	777	65.1 g	19.4 g	15.1 g	1.9 g	2.1 g	37.4 g
	Lemon Ginger Chicken Stir-Fry	156	4	328	12.1 g	12.1 g	10.8 g	1.6 g	6.2 g	42.9 g
	Chicken Vesuvio	158	4	482	19.9 g	7.8 g	38.2 g	7.8 g	4.9 g	34.3 g
WEEK 12	Rustic Beef–Stuffed Acorn Squash	166	4	750	49.3 g	15.9 g	31.3 g	5.6 g	1.2 g	47.1 g
	Italian Beef Rolls with Vodka Sauce	168	4	601	35.8 g	18.2 g	16.3 g	4.2 g	9.7 g	39.9 g
	Red Curry Acorn Squash Soup with Crispy Beef	170	4	636	41.1 g	21.2 g	32.5 g	5.3 g	3.3 g	35 g
WEEK 13	Sweet-and-Sour Chicken Chow Mein	178	4	444	10 g	1.7 g	50 g	5 g	37.4 g	34.7 g
	Chicken Souvlaki Bowls (white rice)	180	5	585	24.4 g	4.5 g	47.5 g	6.1 g	8.4 g	43.6 g
	Chicken Souvlaki Bowls (cauli rice)	180	5	440	24.2 g	4.5 g	15.6 g	6.1 g	8.4 g	41 g
	Chicken Tetrazzini	182	6	385	17.8 g	8.2 g	21.1 g	5.2 g	6.5 g	36 g
WEEK 14	Rustic Polenta and Beef Casserole	192	5	668	37.2 g	15.4 g	28.8 g	10.9 g	1.2 g	39.6 g
	Barbacoa-Stuffed Poblanos	194	6	479	26.8 g	11.5 g	20.7 g	7.7 g	0.2 g	33 g
	Beef Ragu	196	5	459	28 g	11.2 g	15.1 g	4 g	7.3 g	38.3 g
WEEK 15	Bolognese Casserole	204	5	398	20.6 g	6.9 g	21.2 g	4.9 g	10.6 g	35.5 g
	Mediterranean Skillet	206	5	428	25.7 g	8.5 g	14.2 g	5.2 g	3.8 g	37 g
	Spinach Pesto Spaghetti Squash Boats	208	4	793	53.4 g	13.7 g	32.1 g	15.2 g	6.3 g	60.3 g
WEEK 16	Al Pastor Pizzas	216	4	871	58.4 g	25.2 g	63 g	4.3 g	30.6 g	25 g
	Green Pork Chili	218	5	465	29.2 g	11 g	7.7 g	0.5 g	0.9 g	38.5 g
	Caribbean Plantain Bowls	220	4	741	53.2 g	11.8 g	31.3 g	2.7 g	14 g	34.6 g
WEEK 17	Mashed Potato and Parsnip–Crusted Chicken Pot Pie	228	6	424	20.3 g	10.8 g	34.4 g	6.6 g	6.2 g	27 g
	Buffalo Chicken Sheet Pan Dinner	230	4	617	40.3 g	15.6 g	34.6 g	10.6 g	9.8 g	29.9 g
	Cashew Chicken (white rice)	232	4	509	12.8 g	2.2 g	56 g	3.7 g	10.8 g	38.7 g
	Cashew Chicken (cauli rice)	232	4	356	12.8 g	2.2 g	20.6 g	6 g	13 g	37.7 g
WEEK 18	Twice-Baked Loaded Butternut Squash	240	4	392	17.5 g	6.4 g	18.2 g	2.8 g	4.9 g	43.6 g
	Tuscan Turkey Kale Soup	242	4	234	2.9 g	0.9 g	16.3 g	3.8 g	8.7 g	39.1 g
	Harvest Casserole	244	5	421	25.2 g	7.7 g	23.7 g	5.3 g	9.4 g	31.5 g
WEEK 19	Smashed Sweet Potato and Pork Bowls	252	5	707	47.7 g	12 g	32 g	5.8 g	6.8 g	35.6 g
	Harvest Sheet Pan Dinner	254	4	499	33 g	9 g	14 g	3.5 g	7 g	34.8 g
	Southwestern Stuffed Sweet Potatoes	256	4	593	25.7 g	9.3 g	46.6 g	6.8 g	10.1 g	40.4 g

Nutritional Information

(per serving)

	RECIPE	Page	Servings	Calories	Fat	Saturated Fat	Total Carbo-hydrate	Dietary Fiber	Total Sugars	Protein
WEEK 20	Chipotle Chicken Casserole	264	4	488	25.4 g	3.9 g	29 g	4.4 g	6.5 g	35.4 g
	Buffalo Chicken–Stuffed Sweet Potatoes	266	4	469	16.4 g	8.2 g	34.2 g	5.1 g	7.1 g	44.2 g
	Chicken Florentine Lasagna	268	6	423	12.9 g	4.6 g	35.9 g	4.2 g	7.6 g	41.5 g
WEEK 21	Italian Wedding Soup	276	6	581	34.8 g	11.1 g	18.1 g	4.7 g	8.5 g	49.5 g
	Texas Beef Chili (white rice)	278	4	517	10.9 g	5.7 g	57.6 g	2.5 g	5.8 g	44.6 g
	Texas Beef Chili (cauli rice)	278	4	420	23.8 g	10 g	14.5 g	4.3 g	7.5 g	39.2 g
	Asian Beef Lettuce Cups (white rice)	280	4	711	25.8 g	8.3 g	73.9 g	1.9 g	13.7 g	42.3 g
	Asian Beef Lettuce Cups (cauli rice)	280	4	494	25.7 g	25.7 g	24.7 g	3.9 g	15.7 g	39.8 g
WEEK 22	Jerk Pork–Stuffed Sweet Potatoes with Mango Kale Slaw	288	4	594	29.9 g	7.3 g	54.7 g	8.7 g	16.4 g	27.2 g
	Honey Garlic Pork Skillet (white rice)	290	5	684	27.6 g	9.7 g	64.6 g	0.1 g	15.8 g	39 g
	Honey Garlic Pork Skillet (cauli rice)	290	5	489	27.5 g	9.7 g	20.3 g	1.9 g	17.6 g	36.8 g
	Sweet Potato Tamale Pie	292	5	596	32.5 g	12.2 g	44 g	7.5 g	11.8 g	39.6 g
WEEK 23	Chorizo and Potato Tacos with Cilantro-Lime Slaw	300	5	709	41.9 g	11.8 g	42.1 g	5.6 g	4.6 g	40.1 g
	Egg Roll in a Bowl	302	4	491	24.2 g	6.8 g	22.1 g	4 g	13.6 g	42.8 g
	Swedish Meatballs Over Mashed Potatoes	304	4	734	45.1 g	23 g	40.4 g	4 g	4.4 g	41 g
WEEK 24	Chicken Marsala Casserole	312	6	329	17.9 g	5.5 g	10.8 g	1.9 g	3.9 g	29.9 g
	Spaghetti Squash Chicken Chow Mein	314	4	436	14.7 g	2.4 g	28.6 g	3.9 g	18.7 g	43.7 g
	Creamy Chicken and Mushroom Soup	316	4	436	23 g	11.7 g	8.7 g	0.7 g	2.8 g	45.6 g
WEEK 25	BBQ Brisket Bowls (white rice)	324	5	515	18 g	4.8 g	49.3 g	3.4 g	6.7 g	37.8 g
	BBQ Brisket Bowls (cauli rice)	324	5	351	17.8 g	4.8 g	13.1 g	3.8 g	7.2 g	34.9 g
	Chipotle Brisket Tacos with Green Apple Slaw	326	4	609	32.4 g	7 g	38.2 g	5.6 g	10.7 g	43.4 g
	Brisket Fried Rice (white rice)	328	5	619	23.9 g	5.7 g	58.6 g	4.9 g	7.7 g	41.1 g
	Brisket Fried Rice (cauli rice)	328	5	426	23.6 g	5.6 g	16 g	4.9 g	7.7 g	37.5 g
WEEK 26	Honey Mustard Sheet Pan Dinner	336	5	329	17.9 g	5.5 g	10.8 g	1.9 g	3.9 g	29.9 g
	Enchilada Verde Casserole with Avocado Slaw	338	6	485	29.2 g	9.1 g	25 g	4.5 g	3.6 g	29.2 g
	Mini Sloppy Joe–Stuffed Potatoes	340	4	638	23.9 g	7.6 g	66 g	5.4 g	21.2 g	38.7 g
PROTEINS	Seared Chicken Breasts	346	4	234	8 g	1.5 g	0 g	0 g	0 g	38.3 g
	Lemon Pepper Chicken Breasts	347	4	237	8 g	1.5 g	0.8 g	0.1 g	0.2 g	38.3 g
	Paprika Lime Chicken Breasts	347	4	242	8.2 g	1.5 g	1.8 g	0.7 g	0.3 g	38.6 g
	Crispy Curried Chicken Thighs	348	4	282	9.6 g	2.5 g	1.7 g	1 g	0.2 g	44.9 g
	Balsamic Chicken Thighs	348	4	218	6.8 g	1.5 g	1.6 g	0.1 g	1.2 g	33.1 g
	Ranch Chicken Thighs	349	4	312	17.8 g	3 g	0.5 g	0.1 g	0.1 g	33.1 g
	Simple Seared Pork Chops	349	4	241	9.5 g	2.8 g	0.3 g	0 g	0 g	37.6 g
	Southwestern Pork Chops	350	4	247	9.8 g	2.8 g	1.2 g	0.8 g	0.1 g	37.8 g
	Basic Pork Tenderloin	350	4	183	6.6 g	1.8 g	2 g	0.2 g	0 g	30.1 g
	Honey Mustard Pork Tenderloin	351	4	213	7.8 g	1.8 g	6.7 g	0.5 g	4.5 g	30.9 g
	Jerk Pork Tenderloin	351	4	186	6.9 g	1.8 g	2.4 g	0.9 g	0 g	30.3 g
	Pan-Seared Steak	352	4	403	28.6 g	10 g	0 g	0 g	0 g	36 g

	RECIPE	Page	Servings	Calories	Fat	Saturated Fat	Total Carbo-hydrate	Dietary Fiber	Total Sugars	Protein
PROTEINS	Mocha Coffee Steak	352	4	405	28.7 g	10 g	0.7 g	0.2 g	0 g	36.2 g
	Easy Tuna Steak	353	4	242	7.8 g	1 g	0.2 g	0.1 g	0 g	40.7 g
	Pan-Seared White Fish	353	4	233	9.3 g	1.5 g	0.8 g	0.1 g	0.2 g	34.9 g
	Lemon-Garlic Shrimp	354	4	178	4.4 g	0.7 g	1 g	0.1 g	0.2 g	34.3 g
	Salmon Bake	354	4	325	19 g	2.9 g	0.6 g	0.1 g	0.2 g	37.9 g
	Pan-Seared Salmon	355	4	384	25.5 g	5.7 g	0 g	0 g	0 g	34 g
VEGETABLES	Crispy Brussels Sprouts	356	4	68	3.8 g	0.6 g	8.1 g	3.3 g	2.1 g	2.9 g
	Sautéed Squash	356	4	24	2.4 g	0.3 g	0.6 g	0.2 g	0 g	0.5 g
	Simple Roasted Cauliflower	357	4	84	4.1 g	0.8 g	10.8	4.3 g	4 g	4.1 g
	Roasted Broccoli	357	4	83	4.1 g	0.6 g	10.5 g	4 g	2.6 g	4.4 g
	Braised Collards	358	4	43	3.7 g	0.5 g	2.3 g	1.5 g	0.3 g	1.1 g
	Wilted Spinach	358	4	57	4 g	0.6 g	4.4 g	2.5 g	0.6 g	3.3 g
	Baked Okra	359	4	57	4 g	0.6 g	4.5 g	2.5 g	0.6 g	3.3 g
	Lemony Kale	359	4	39	3.7 g	0.5 g	1.8 g	0.6 g	0.5 g	0.7 g
	Roasted Asparagus	360	4	60	4.2 g	0.8 g	5.1 g	0.3 g	0 g	1.1 g
	Roasted Cherry Tomatoes	360	4	41	2.6 g	0.4 g	4.5 g	1.4 g	2.9 g	1 g
	Steamed Green Beans	361	4	98	2.8 g	0.4 g	16.3 g	6.6 g	6.4 g	3.7 g
	Sautéed Bell Peppers	361	4	54	2.7 g	0.4 g	6.7 g	2.3 g	4.6 g	1.1 g
	Italian Side Salad	362	4	115	9.5 g	1.3 g	6.8 g	3.7 g	1.2 g	2.1 g
	Spinach Salad	362	4	181	16.3 g	1.8 g	9.1 g	3.3 g	4.6 g	2.8 g
	Basic Cauliflower Rice	363	4	83	4.1 g	0.8 g	10.4 g	4.2 g	4 g	4 g
STARCHES	Baked Acorn Squash	364	4	63	2.4 g	0.4 g	11.2 g	1.6 g	0 g	0.9 g
	Roasted Carrots	364	4	67	2.6 g	0.4 g	11.1 g	3.2 g	5.5 g	1.1 g
	Perfect Parsnips	365	4	200	4.2 g	0.6 g	40.8 g	11.1 g	10.9 g	2.7 g
	Baked Sweet Potatoes	365	4	98	0.1 g	0 g	22.8 g	3.4 g	4.7 g	1.8 g
	Baked Russet Potatoes	366	4	90	0.1 g	0 g	20.5 g	1.5 g	0.7 g	2.4 g
	Roasted Butternut Squash Cubes	366	4	132	3.7 g	0.5 g	26.5 g	4.5 g	5 g	2.3 g
	Easy Baked Beets	367	4	55	2.5 g	0.4 g	7.8 g	2.3 g	5.5 g	1.3 g
	Green Peas	367	4	90	3.8 g	0.6 g	10.9 g	4.1 g	4.2 g	3.9 g
	Pan-Fried Plantains	368	4	169	7.3 g	1.1 g	28.5 g	2.1 g	13.4 g	1.2 g
	Basic White Rice	368	4	206	3.8 g	0.6 g	38.7 g	0 g	0 g	3.2 g
	Basic Quinoa	369	4	186	6.1 g	0.8 g	27.3 g	3 g	0 g	6 g
	Basic Polenta	369	4	208	7.9 g	1.1 g	30.5 g	0.9 g	0.6 g	4.2 g
SAUCES	Avocado Oil Mayonnaise	372	16	150	16.8 g	2.3 g	0.2 g	0 g	0.1 g	0.4 g
	3-Ingredient Ranch Dressing	372	32	134	2 g	0 g	0.2 g	0 g	0.1 g	0 g
	BBQ Sauce	373	12	32	0 g	0 g	7.9 g	0.9 g	7 g	0.4 g
	Teriyaki Sauce	373	4	83	2.3 g	0.3 g	12.5 g	0.1 g	12 g	0.1 g
	Low-Carb Teriyaki Sauce	373	4	12	0.3 g	0 g	1.6 g	0.1 g	0.9 g	0.7 g

Allergen Chart

	LOW-CARB	PALEO	GRAIN-FREE	DAIRY-FREE	EGG-FREE	NUT-FREE	KID-FRIENDLY
Week 1: Shredded Chicken, Broccoli, and Rice	X	X	X	X	X	X	X
Week 2: Ground Beef, Zucchini, and Mushrooms	X	X	X	X	X	X	X
Week 3: Roasted Chicken and Cauliflower	X	X	X	X	X	X	
Week 4: Ground Beef, Broccoli, and Yukon Gold Potatoes		X	X	X	X	X	X
Week 5: Baked Chicken Breast, Tomatoes, and Rice	X	X	X	X	X	X	X
Week 6: Ground Chicken, Bell Peppers, and Rice		X	X	X	X	X	X
Week 7: Turkey Breast Tenderloins, Cherry Tomatoes, and Yukon Gold Potatoes					X	X	X
Week 8: Ground Beef, Carrots, and Rice	X	X	X	X	X	X	
Week 9: Baked Chicken Breast, Kale, and Corn				X		X	X
Week 10: Brisket, Bell Peppers, and Russet Potatoes		X	X	X	X	X	X
Week 11: Roasted Chicken, Green Beans, and Yukon Gold Potatoes		X	X	X	X	X	
Week 12: Shredded Beef, Collard Greens, and Acorn Squash		X	X	X	X	X	
Week 13: Baked Chicken Breast, Bell Peppers, and Spaghetti Squash		X	X	X	X	X	
Week 14: Shredded Beef, Kale, and Polenta				X	X	X	
Week 15: Ground Beef, Spinach, and Spaghetti Squash	X	X	X	X	X		
Week 16: Shredded Pork, Kale, and Plantains		X	X	X	X	X	X
Week 17: Roasted Chicken, Brussels Sprouts, and Parsnips		X	X	X	X	X	
Week 18: Baked Turkey Breast, Kale, and Butternut Squash		X	X	X	X	X	
Week 19: Pork Shoulder, Brussels Sprouts, and Sweet Potatoes		X	X	X	X	X	X
Week 20: Baked Chicken Breast, Collard Greens, and Sweet Potatoes				X	X	X	
Week 21: Ground Beef, Cabbage, and Carrots	X	X	X	X	X	X	
Week 22: Shredded Pork, Kale, and Sweet Potatoes		X	X	X	X	X	
Week 23: Ground Pork, Cabbage, and Red Potatoes		X	X	X	X	X	X
Week 24: Roasted Chicken, Mushrooms, and Spaghetti Squash	X	X	X	X	X	X	
Week 25: Brisket, Brussels Sprouts, and Rice	X	X	X	X	X	X	
Week 26: Shredded Pork, Cabbage, and Red Potatoes		X	X	X	X	X	

Index